CONTENTS

Chapter 1 – Before the Tomcat — 6

Chapter 2 – First Decade — 8

Chapter 3 – The Big Stick — 40

Chapter 4 – TARPS — 48

Chapter 5 – Second Decade — 56

Chapter 6 – The Bombcat — 76

Chapter 7 – Third Decade — 84

Chapter 8 – TOPGUN and the Tomcat — 102

Chapter 9 – Last Decade — 114

Published in Great Britain by Tempest Books an imprint of Mortons Books Ltd.
Media Centre Morton Way
Horncastle LN9 6JR
www.mortonsbooks.co.uk

Copyright © Tempest Books, 2024
All rights reserved. No part of this publication may be reproduced or transmitted in any form or by any means, electronic or mechanical including photocopying, recording, or any information storage retrieval system without prior permission in writing from the publisher.

ISBN 978-1-911703-65-5

The right of David Parsons and Mads Bangsø to be identified as the authors of this work has been asserted in accordance with the Copyright, Designs and Patents Act 1988.

All artworks by Mads Bangsø.

The appearance of US Department of Defense (DoD) visual information does not imply or constitute DoD endorsement.

Acknowledgements – David

This book was greatly enhanced by collaboration with number of key individuals who directly or indirectly contributed their recollections, expertise, research and passion for the Tomcat. Krista Hoerner Spalding was a continual source of support when other demands for my time were overwhelming. Her father, Fred Hoerner, a test pilot and expert in HUD technology was a card-carrying member of the F-14D Control and Display Working Group.
Phil Edwards of the National Air and Space Museum Library has been a long-time confidante and contributor of all my writing projects and particularly in matters related to BuNo 159610, which is part of the Udvar-Hazy modern era jet collection.
David F Brown (aka Mr Tomcat) has been a mutual collaborator for decades and was instrumental in saving 159610 from the shredder and rescuing the historic airframe from the SARDIP salvage line as well as reconstructing it for Udvar-Hazy.
Rob Todd, whose enthusiasm for the Tomcat is unmatched. His efforts to save a forlorn Tomcat and revive the F-14 Reunion as well as contribute to this book are greatly appreciated.
'Hot Dog' Brown, who flew the F-8 and F-4, and commanded the F-14 Det at Estefan, Iran, was a continual source of information and colourful history.
Thanks also to Peter Chilleli, Tony Holmes and Barrett Tillman.

Acknowledgements – Mads

Jim Sullivan, Craig Kaston, Mathew Lawson, Robert Lawson, Phil Edwards, Michael Andersen, Erik Holm, Jan Nielsen, Mark Aldrich, Rich Renthorp, The Scanmasters Group, Paul Minert, Michael Grove, Don Linn, Peter Mancus, Jan Jacobs, David 'Bio' Baranek, Don Jay, Scott Brown, Antonis Karidis, Chris Sandham-Bailey and Rachid Abudulla.

INTRODUCTION

TOMCAT: HAIL AND FAREWELL

I've written a bunch of books and articles about fighters (and other birds) with tailhooks on 'em. So here's my offering with an eye toward the Tom's place in history.

When VF-1 and -2 stood up, those of us in the history community realised that we were witnessing something extraordinary. The F-14 obviously was going to be around for a long time, and we would see its rise and inevitable decline in much the same way as the Crusader and Phantom. The Tomcat was a cult machine from the start.

Let's begin with the name. How many people realised that it wasn't simply the continuation of Grumman's decades-long feline family? As last kitten in the litter, the '14 certainly enjoyed a solid pedigree tracing back to the Wildcat and the successor VF types: ace-maker Hellcats; sports-car Bearcats; pioneering Panther and Cougar jets; and (to me, anyway) the classic Blues bird, the elegant little Tiger.

But there were two stories about the origin of the name. The one that received most publicity said that an alley-fighting tomcat was the meanest scrapper on the street – and knew how to enjoy himself.

More to the point though, in 1967 Vice Admiral Thomas F Connolly, OP-05, had testified in Congress about the Navy's opinion of the F-111B (aka Flying Edsel, in reference to SecDef Robert Strange McNamara's background with Ford Motor Company). Connolly, a well-regarded test pilot in his younger days, had done something remarkable: he spoke his mind rather than parroting what RSM wanted him to say. Asked about the Naval 'vark's performance, he said, "Gentlemen, there isn't enough thrust in Christendom to make that airplane into a fighter." That killed the -111B and Connolly's career.

As expected, McNamara got his revenge – he was nothing if not vindictive – and assured that Tom Connolly never wore a fourth star. In turn, the Navy got its revenge about five years later by naming the F-14 the Tomcat!

The VF-31 Tomcatters flightline at Tomcat Sunset at NAS Oceana, in September 2006 (Don Jay)

HALF CENTURY, BABY! FIFTY YEARS OF THE GRUMMAN F-14 TOMCAT

164603 taxing after its final performance at the Tomcat Sunset ceremony. (Don Jay)

When USS *Theodore Roosevelt* (CVN-71) returned to CONUS on March 11, 2006, the two fighter squadrons of CVW-8 flew to their homebase NAS Oceana. This photo was taken as a formation of VF-31 and VF-213 F-14Ds flew over the base, on their homecoming from the last ever deployment with the F-14 Tomcat (Don Jay)

I remember seeing my first Tom, parked on the ramp during a drizzly Oregon afternoon at the Rose Festival airshow. The weather kept people away in droves, and it was possible to get up close without fighting the usual crowd. My first impression was, "My lord, it's big!" Yet sitting there in its two-tone grey paint with wings swept back, it reminded me of nothing so much as a pouter pigeon shrugging off inclement weather, awaiting clearing skies and following winds.

A couple of other devotees were present, and I overheard one of them ask, "Is this a Tomcat or an Eagle?" Both fighters were brand new at the time, and I suppose the twin tail configuration was enough to cause confusion. Or maybe the spectators were erstwhile attack pukes who subscribed to the notion that anything beginning with 'F' is just support (at least that's what the poster at Strike U always said).

Now, being historically inclined I'm bound to admit that the Tom had its faults. Everybody knows the story: the A models were underpowered, and the Phoenix certainly had problems. One early Turkey driver, whose call sign was 'Turkey', by the way, opined: "The best way to kill somebody with an AIM-54 is to drop it on him."

Yet the flaws never overshadowed the '14's aura, its public image as a big, glamorous incarnation of carrier airpower. Lest anyone doubt it, I recall in 1986 when Top Gun was all the rage, bringing the Tom to the public's attention. Yes, the movie was a live-action cartoon with cutout characters and a skinny plot, but that didn't matter. I didn't realise just how influential the big Grumman had become until I heard of Air Force recruiters setting up shop in the lobbies of movie theatres! Forget Tom Cruise: the star was the Tomcat, Hollywood's big-screen glamour puss.

As with any machine that acquires cult status, the hardware is just an extension of the people who make it go. That certainly was true of the Tom. I recall interviewing VF-41's crew of Larry 'Music' Muczinsky and Jim 'Amos' Anderson at Tailhook '81. They had been partying hearty the night before, but you couldn't tell it to look at Music. Amos, on the other hand, was still spooling up. He recovered in fine style, however, when the Black Aces crew was introduced to a few thousand Tailhookers later that day: folks who appreciated what the squadron had done on the far side of Colonel Qadhafi's 'Line of Death', downing two Su-22 Fitters handily after being fired on by the Libyan pilots.

What a shock to learn a few years later that Amos had been killed in a skiing accident. Skipper Hank Kleeman had already died in a Hornet. The Gulf of Sidra incident was, of course, the first time the Tomcat drew blood (remember all the buttons and bumper stickers? "Navy 2, Libya 0"?). And that raises a point about the '14's mystique. No other fighter has garnered such a following while carving so few notches: only five in US service, but perhaps 130 or more by Iran against Iraq.

As with the performance faults, it didn't matter. The pilots, RIOs, and maintainers believed in their machine and constantly looked for new ways to get the most out of it. One of my all-time favourite VF guys remains Capt Monroe 'Hawk' Smith (ret), whose career stands as a timeless beacon to JOs everywhere. He likes to say, "I proved that you can survive seven JAG investigations and still make O-6."

Hawk was irrepressible. When the Bears came out to play, Toms were always on hand to intercept and escort them away from the carrier, but sometimes diplomatic niceties got in the way: the commies complained about aggressive Yankee Air Pirates. Not to worry. Monroe and VF-213 took themselves to the local sporting goods store and purchased some variable-power rifle scopes. The Black Lions' metalsmiths built mounts over the instrument panel, permitting the optics to be affixed and removed as needed for better long-range VID. That invention went into history as the Tomcat Integrated Telescope System, and if there were a more un-PC acronym, I don't know what it was.

During the Carter era, readiness reached keel level and sulked there until Ronald Reagan was elected. Hey, I'm sorry, but the perennially simpering peanut farmer was a product of Canoe U. In that dismal era, Hawk Smith was one of a handful of active-duty officers who would face a TV camera and, like Tom Connolly, speak the truth. For one memorable interview he positioned himself at the stern of a '213 airplane with a notably empty engine bay. Then he looked into the lens and said, "When I was a boy growing up in Carolina I wanted to do two things. I wanted to command a Navy fighter squadron and run a junkyard, and now I'm doing both."

Things did get better, of course. Eventually Ronald Reagan replaced the Georgia pacifist and wow – it was Morning In America Again. One of the most 'funs' we had at *The Hook* magazine in the late 80s again involved the Black Lions. In those days VF-114 was the San Francisco 49ers of Naval Aviation – everybody wanted to go there, but 213 found a way to shine. When Joltin' Joe DiMaggio visited Miramar, he was greeted with all the deference due a major league slugger and TV pitch man. When he looked in the cockpit of a squadron Tomcat, he found a Mr Coffee machine amid the dials and scopes!

Now the Tomcat is gone, and with it the end of a long, long era. Not merely the F-14, but the dedicated fighter has gone the way of the dedicated attack aircraft. Now we fly 'F and A' airplanes with more on the horizon. In one of the biggest ironies in aviation history, the F-14 continues flying in the hands of one of America's bitterest opponents, and who can say where that situation will lead? It's possible that eventually the Tomcat will finish its days fighting Hornets and Eagles, but maybe that's not entirely bad. The F-14 was born and bred a warrior; better to die in harness than submit to the cutter's torch or to become fish habitat.

As the Romans used to say at such times, In perpetuum, frater: ave atque valle.

**Barrett 'Shooter' Tillman
Dean of Naval Aviation Historians**

BEFORE THE TOMCAT

The Tomcat was born in controversy. The Navy was forced in a shotgun marriage to develop a fleet air defence version of the General Dynamics F-111 fighter-bomber as part of the joint Tactical Fighter Experimental (TFX) programme. The proposed F-111B variant was integrated with the Hughes AWG-9 weapons system which included the AIM-54 Phoenix.

Grumman, with its long history of designing carrier aircraft, was responsible for making the F-111B design carrier-capable – a process which gave the company valuable insights into what its mission entailed. When flight testing ensued and an ever-growing list of issues arose, Grumman then gained a clear understanding of where the aircraft's original design had underperformed.

When the matter went before Congress, Navy representative Vice Admiral Connolly told the hearing: "I think the F-111B has gotten too heavy to ever be a good performing airplane. There is not enough thrust in all Christendom to put that airplane back in business really. It has gotten awfully expensive. It has gone way up in cost, and I think we ought to consider very carefully using the Navy money and the country's money in a better way."

This ended the F-111B in May 1968 alongside Connolly's career – since the Secretary of Defense Robert S McNamara, Secretary of Navy Paul Ignatius and Chief of Naval Operations Admiral Tom Moorer had all been pressuring him to advocate for the F-111B, not condemn it.

Grumman, having had an inkling of what was coming, had already prepared an unsolicited design that answered

NAVY FIGHTERS FROM 1950

Although the Tomcat was revolutionary in so many aspects and had staying power that lasted decades, it came into being at the end of an era of many different fighter and interceptor designs that ushered in a revolution on the carrier flight deck.

It all started in 1950 with the first jets arriving in time for the Korean War; Grumman F9F Panthers were operated alongside the venerable Vought F4U Corsair. At the same time, the night fighter versions of existing aircraft introduced during the Second World War had given way to specialised night fighter interceptors such as Douglas's F3D Skyknight. These aircraft carried large radars and were not considered dogfighters at all. The sleeker McDonnell F3H Demon looked fast and more like a fighter but it was underpowered and relegated to an intercept role.

Two different communities coalesced – the 'dayfighter' community and the 'interceptor' community. By the end of the decade, two fighters emerged that epitomised the best of each; Vought's F-8 Crusader was the ultimate dayfighter, equipped with 20mm and the AIM-9 Sidewinder, while the ultimate interceptor was McDonnell's F-4 Phantom equipped with medium-range radar-guided Sparrow missiles and heat-seeking short-range Sidewinders but no gun. With the F-14, these two communities were finally brought together.

An F-8J Crusader (150317) of VF-53 Iron Angels is about to launch from the deck of USS *Bon Homme Richard* (CVA-31) in the summer of 1970. VF-53 was disestablished just a few years short of the fleet introduction of the F-14 Tomcat, but several aviators would fly both this late version of the 'sader and the Tomcat. (Paul Minert Collection)

HALF CENTURY, BABY! FIFTY YEARS OF THE GRUMMAN F-14 TOMCAT

F-111B prototype in July 1968.

the Navy desire for a fighter/interceptor integrated with the AWG-9 and AIM-54 long-range missile. It would also have air-to-ground capability, desired for the Marine Corps to replace their venerable F-4 Phantoms. The Navy was solely interested in fleet air defence but also wanted the aircraft to have superior air combat manoeuvring ability. NAVAIR subsequently issued a request for proposal for a new Naval Fighter Experimental (VFX).

Instead of the side by side seating of TFX, VFX called for a tandem cockpit, dash speed of Mach 2.2, an internal 20mm cannon, integration of the AWG-9 weapon system and AIM-54 missiles as well as AIM-7 Sparrow medium range and AIM-9 Sidewinder short range missiles, with a secondary air-to-ground capability. Grumman had to compete with Ling-Temco-Vought, McDonnell Douglas and North American Rockwell. But they had an edge from their experience with TFX.

The Navy selected McDonnell Douglas and Grumman as finalists in December 1968 and in January 1969 it was announced that Grumman's design had been chosen. The company subsequently elected to enter an aggressive full-scale development (FSD) of the F-14 Tomcat, committing to a first flight by the end of 1970. Unfortunately, the desired high thrust Pratt & Whitney F401-400 engine in development was not ready so the lower thrust Pratt & Whitney TF30 engine used in the TFX programme was selected as an interim solution until the F401 was available. The F-14 Tomcat first took to the air on December 21, 1970 – just 22 months after contract award.

VF-31 Tomcatters would eventually become the last squadron to fly the F-14, but before the squadron received the F-14, they operated the F-4 Phantom (the 'Tomcatters' name pre-dates the F-14 by several decades). This F-4J Phantom (155840) is parked at NAS Oceana on May 12, 1977. In these days the Phantom was slowly but surely being phased out of frontline service. Less than ten years later it was entirely gone from US Navy frontline service. (Jim Sullivan)

F-8J Crusader of VF-211 Checkertails in 1972.

F-4B Phantom of VF-51 Screaming Eagles in 1972.

FIRST DECADE

A rare shot of the first prototype (157980) F-14A-1-GR Tomcat in flight. (Tailhook Collection)

Grumman pulled out all the stops in 1970 in an effort to get airborne with the first prototype by year's end in time to let the employees enjoy their Christmas holiday. By December BuNo 157980, which was the first FSD example, was transferred from the assembly plant at Grumman's Bethpage facility to the Calverton Flight Test Center, both on Long Island, NY.

Various ground tests with engines turning were conducted to determine any vibration or fuel function issues. By December 14, 1970, the test team were ready for taxi trials which had concluded by December 21. Despite poor weather at the field and sunset approaching, Grumman chief test pilot Bob Smyth elected to try and get in the air for a few circuits of the field with gear extended and wings locked forward. With project test pilot Bob Miller in the rear cockpit, he took to the air just after 4 o'clock and flew two circuits of the field, reaching 3,000ft, before landing as the sun began setting.

A crowd of Grumman employees cheered as the Tomcat returned safely, thereby completing the contracting line item requirement a month ahead of schedule and enabling Grumman to receive a critical progress payment. Broken up for Christmas, the team reassembled after the holiday to resume flight testing.

Smyth and Miller swapped seats and took to the air for the second flight on December 30. On this flight, they left the airport proper and proceeded to the flight test area. Once in the assigned space, Miller conducted stability and flight control checks before retracting the landing gear and accelerating to 180 knots. Twenty-five minutes into the flight, the chase aircraft reported a thin trail of smoke coming from the Tomcat. Miller then noticed his primary flight hydraulic system had failed.

Turning the aircraft back towards Calverton, he bypassed a nearby airfield that did not have adequate emergency equipment, opting to return to the longer runway with arresting gear at Calverton. This was an unfortunate decision as it turned out, as recalled by Smyth afterwards. Four miles from the field at Calverton, Miller blew down the gear which was followed by failure of the combined hydraulic system. They were now flying on the backup module, which had limited control authority for emergencies just like this one. That also failed on short final, giving the aircrew no choice but to eject when the aircraft stopped responding to control inputs. Smyth initiated command ejection just 25ft over the trees, saving both pilots who escaped with only minor injuries. It was a gallant effort to prevent the valuable prototype's destruction but such are the risks with flight testing.

It was an inauspicious start to a bold venture and a demanding timeline. The initial compromise to install the TF30 engine in the first 66 aircraft was based on the unavailability of the F401 engine, which was experiencing delays and challenges. Grumman conducted an investigation into the causes of the hydraulic failures and made urgent changes to the subsequent prototypes.

By 1971, the Tomcat was ready for Navy aircrews to begin their flight testing and conduct a Navy Preliminary Evaluation (NPE1) followed by NPE2 and the Bureau of Inspection and Survey (BIS) trials before moving forward. It was no surprise that the NPE events were delayed by upwards of eight months from the original schedule, but VF-124 began receiving their first Tomcats in fall of 1972 with Secretary of the Navy John Warner participating in the delivery by flying in the back seat of one of the first Tomcats to be delivered to Miramar. The Tomcat era was officially underway.

The Marines were full partners in the Tomcat programme in 1971 and were selecting aircrew to participate in the all-important NPE rounds. Major Bill Bauer was part of the NPE contingent that gathered at NAS Patuxent to evaluate the F-14A Tomcat.

THE F-14 AND THE MARINES
I was the first Marine to fly the F-14 as part of NPE1. I had flown the F-8 Crusader and the F-4 Phantom in the fleet before attending Flight School (Class 56) in 1970. After graduation, I reported to the Flying Qualities and Assurance Branch of the Naval Air Test Center (NATC) at Patuxent River, MD. This positioned me to be ready, willing and able to fly the Tomcat when it arrived

F-14A-1-GR Tomcat (157980). The first prototype of the F-14 Tomcat as it appeared on its maiden flight on December 21, 1970. The aircraft took off from Grumman's Flight Test facility, in Calverton, NY, with Robert Smyth and William Miller in the cockpit. The aircraft suffered a hydraulics failure on its second flight on December 30, 1970, crashing on approach to Calverton. It was destroyed but both crew members ejected successfully.

The first prototype F-14A-1-GR Tomcat (157980) in flight on December 30, 1970. Soon after this photo was taken the aircraft would suffer a hydraulics failure and crash. (US Navy via Craig Kaston)

An F-14A-60-GR Tomcat (158618) of VX-4 Evaluators on May 19, 1973. (Paul Minert Collection)

FIRST DECADE

The fifth prototype (157984) here seen parked at NAS Patuxent River in November 1971. (Paul Minert Collection)

The fifth prototype (157984) F-14A-20-GR Tomcat circa 1972. This prototype's main objective was to demonstrate systems compatibility. Today the aircraft is on display at the National Museum of Naval Aviation, FL. (Tailhook Collection)

for NPE1 in November of 1971 and also NPE2 the following spring.

On NPE1 we had two Tomcats, one of which was marked as #1 but was not the actual number prototype. The original #1 crashed after a total hydraulic failure with Bill Miller (Grumman test pilot) flying and Bob Smyth (Grumman chief test pilot) in the back seat. They ejected at the last second trying to save it but, having lost control, they had run out of time. Bob was carried up and out of the fireball due to the heat. So we had the redesignated Tomcat #1 (actually number #3) and #2. I made my first flight in December 1971 in #1, which had variable-sweep wings.

NPE1 was conducted at the NATC and was flown by an assemblage of amazing talent (Rick Hauck and Dave Walker went on to be astronauts. Rick was mission commander and Dave was the pilot on one of the Shuttle missions). There were three flights on the very first day of NPE1. George White and Gene Tucker made the first two flights in #8, which was the Carrier Suitability Aircraft and which had the wings fixed in the landing configuration.

I got orders to 1st MAW in 1973 where I was staff secretary to General Lang. From there I got orders to Yuma with the expectation that I was to be in the first Marine F-14 squadron. On a different track, Don Keast was forming the first Tomcat squadron at Miramar at VF-124. He was assembling some great talent there, including Howard DeCastro and Dave Vest, both Marine Aviator of the Year recipients. I don't know if I would have made it into the squadron, but when the F-14 was cancelled [for the Marines] I was fortunate to become the CO of VMFAT-101 (the F-4 RAG) in Yuma. That was a great assignment.
Col Bill 'Bullet' Bauer, USMC

Cdr Emory Brown was also assigned to the NPE:

I was the first Naval aviator to land the Tomcat on a carrier, with Commander

HALF CENTURY, BABY! FIFTY YEARS OF THE GRUMMAN F-14 TOMCAT

F-14A-5-GR (157981). The second prototype was used for low speed handling tests. This aircraft was lost on May 13, 1974 due to an inflight hydrazine fire; the aircraft landed despite the fire but was written off due to the extensive damage caused. Following the early loss of the first prototype, 157981 was marked with the number 1 on the vertical stabilizers for a time. The aircraft with these markings might have been the third prototype (157982), which is the oldest surviving F-14 Tomcat currently on display at the Cradle of Aviation Museum, NY.

F-14A-70-GR Tomcat (158979) of VF-1 Wolfpack in 1974. The first squadrons to receive the F-14A Tomcat for front line service were VF-1 Wolfpack and VF-2 Bounty Hunters, both a part of CVW-14 which at the time was deployed aboard USS Enterprise (CVAN-65). The first deployment lasted from September 17, 1974 to May 20, 1975, and took the airwing to Westpac. CVW-14 flew missions over Vietnam and over the Tonkin Gulf as a part of Operation Frequent Wind, the objective of which was to evacuate Americans and at-risk Vietnamese citizens ahead of the imminent takeover of Saigon by the North Vietnamese Army. This aircraft served until August 30, 1990 when it was put in storage at AMARC.

An F-14A-65-GR Tomcat (158629) of VF-2 Bounty Hunters in 1973. This photo was taken before the squadron was fully operational with the Tomcat. (Tailhook Collection)

George White, the first Naval aviator to fly the Tomcat, riding in back. We had throttles that would stick, and sometimes require a substantial amount of force to unstick. Grumman was under a lot of pressure to meet the Navy specifications on the airplane, and with Direct Lift Control (DLC) engaged in the landing configuration, the F-14 was roughly 4-6 knots faster than 'spec'. Grumman was afraid they would be penalised for this breach, and they proposed first eliminating DLC, then changing the Tomcat's approach angle of attack (AOA) from 15 to 17 units to meet the approach speed spec. This would have resulted in a higher pitch attitude and reduced visibility coming aboard the carrier. The airplane simply handled better at 15 than it did at 17 units AOA. We made a film showing landings and successful recovery rates with and without DLC engaged. With DLC it was something on the order of 96 per cent, without it, it was in the 60s. After

FIRST DECADE

An F-14A-80-GR Tomcat (159439) of VF-142 Ghostriders in March 1973. This photo was taken at NAS Oceana, shortly before the squadron left for a deployment aboard USS America (CV-66) that lasted from April 15 to October 25, 1976. (Tailhook Collection)

An F-14A Tomcat (158986) of VF-2 Bounty Hunters in 1974. Alongside VF-1 Wolfpack, VF-2 Bounty Hunters were the first to fly the Tomcat operationally. VF-2 was established on October 14, 1972 and was fully operational in the spring of 1974 in time for deployment aboard USS *Enterprise* with the rest of CVW-14. This aircraft was put in storage at AMARC on July 19, 1991.

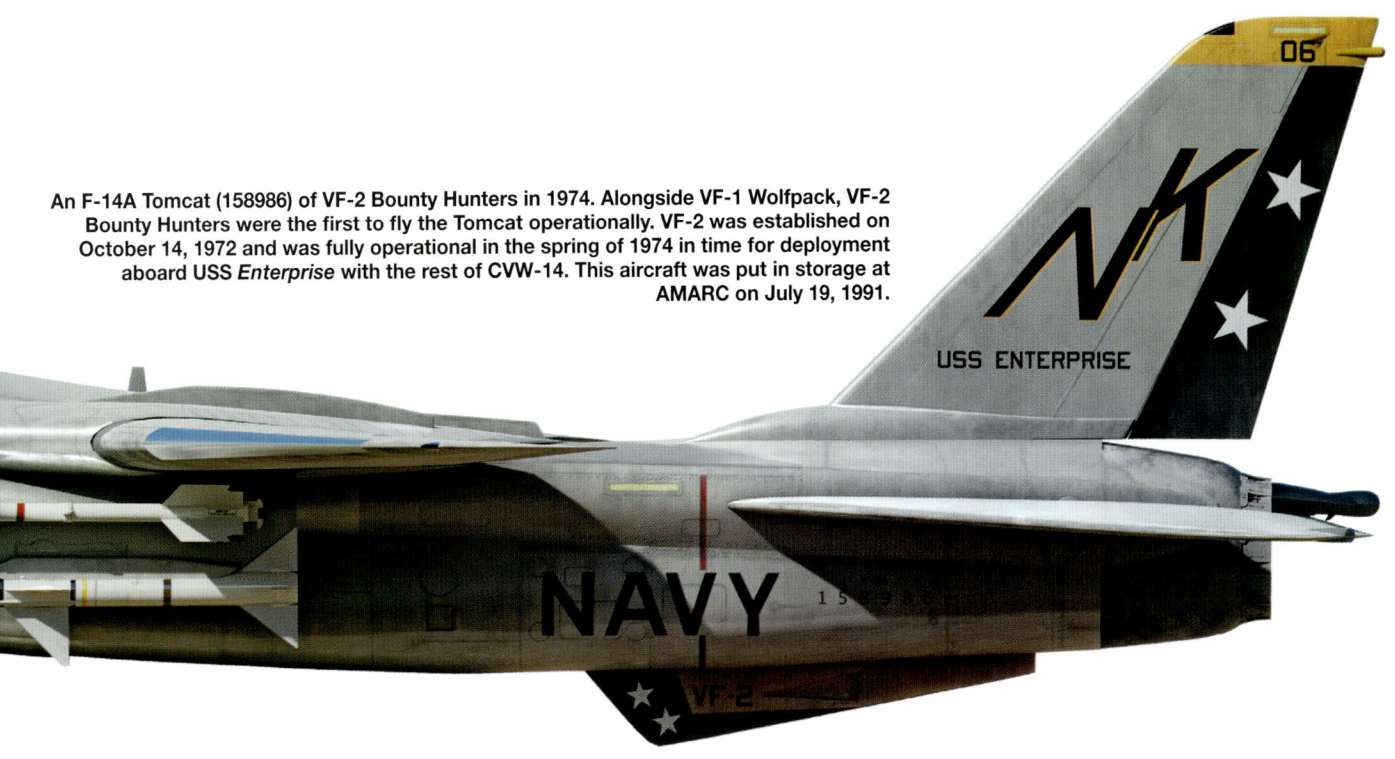

VF-124 Gunfighters were the first squadron to receive the F-14 Tomcat. This aircraft (158620) F-14A-65-GR Tomcat is here seen flying above the coast of SoCal in 1973. (Tailhook Collection)

FIRST DECADE

The same F-14A-65-GT Tomcat (158620) as pictured on page 13. (Tailhook Collection)

HALF CENTURY, BABY! FIFTY YEARS OF THE GRUMMAN F-14 TOMCAT

F-14B-30-GR Tomcat (157986). The story of the F-14B Tomcat begins as early as 1973, when the seventh Tomcat produced had its TF30 engines replaced with Pratt & Whitney F401-P400 engines. The aircraft flew for the first time in this configuration on September 12, 1973. At that time the aircraft was sporting the paint scheme seen here. The test proved unsatisfactory and the aircraft was placed in storage until 1981 when it was fitted with General Electric F101DFE engines. Those engines gave the aircraft a significant performance boost. However, the aircraft went into storage yet again in late 1981, much to the dismay of the pilots who flew it. In July 1984 the aircraft was again pulled out of storage to test a new engine: the General Electric F110-GE-400. This led to the F-14A+ programme, which eventually was redesignated to F-14B Tomcat. The aircraft is on display at the USS Intrepid Museum in New York.

seeing the films, the Navy had no choice but to back us on this.

The Tomcat passed NPE and entered BIS as the standup of VF-124 at Miramar approached. Disaster struck at NAS Patuxent River on June 30, 1972, with the loss of another F-14. Test pilot Miller was flying Tomcat #10 without a RIO on a practice flight for a scheduled airshow. It was determined that he experienced several distractions in the cockpit after takeoff and impacted the Chesapeake Bay doing 350 knots while addressing the issue(s). **Brown** again:

Bill Miller was a class act, a first-class test pilot, and a real stand-up guy. The Navy had him fly an airshow to demonstrate the Tomcat and unfortunately they chose our specially instrumented carrier suitability aircraft. Bill was flying an airshow routine solo, in low ceilings of only approximately 2,000ft. I had my suspicions of what happened right away, and sure enough, when we recovered him and the airplane, we found evidence on his flight helmet consistent with his head being down to reset the wing sweep angle and flaps. Sometimes the wings would stick as well. It could be cured by going head down and reaching for the flap handle and wing sweep handle while flying the airplane's stick between one's knees. My theory then was that this was certainly something that contributed to Bill's crash.

Aircrews that would become the first two squadrons began reporting to VF-124 without being assigned to either squadron in October 1972. The aircrews were senior to a typical squadron and represented the best of the Phantom and Crusader aircrew community. Eventually the two prospective commanding officers got together and picked which aircrews

FIRST DECADE

F-14A-65-GR Tomcat (158629) of VF-2 Bounty Hunters parked at NAS Miramar in December 1973. (Paul Minert Collection)

F-14A-70-GR Tomcat (158993) of VF-1 Wolfpack overflying Catalina Island in January 1974. (Bob Lawson)

would comprise VF-A or VF-B, which would become VF-1 and VF-2, splitting the expertise without knowing which squadron they would command. While the official date for establishing both squadrons is given as October 14, 1972, they were squadrons on paper only.

Once training had been completed at VF-124 with adequate aircrews and maintainers ready to conduct flight operations, they received their first Tomcats on July 1, 1973. The first cadre of Marines arrived at VF-124 in 1973 in advance of the standup of the first Marine F-14 Squadron, VMFA-122.

FIRST FLEET SQUADRONS
Cdr Sam Leeds and I got orders to Miramar as the PCOs (prospective COs) of the first two F-14 squadrons. When we arrived the hangar just beyond the ops/tower building was new and yet unused. One day we sat on chairs in an empty ready room and talked over how we could take a low-risk approach to establishing the new squadrons like current squadrons, or push the envelope to maximise the performance of the squadrons and fully exploit the quantum jump in fighter capabilities that the F-14 possessed. We took the high road and looking at the F-14 track record over the years, I would like to think that the foundations were well laid and worth the effort by the hand-picked officers and maintenance personnel who got things started right.

We became the core of VF-124's F-14 people as it transitioned as the new F-14 RAG squadron, and we were back-filled with new people ordered to VF-124 as VF-1 and VF-2 stood up as fleet squadrons. To ensure equal distribution of talent, Sam and I took turns picking who would go to both squadrons designated VF-A and B, not knowing which squadron we would get after the selections were

F-14A-80-GR Tomcat (159449) of VF-142 Ghostriders in 1976. Like VF-143, VF-142 transitioned from CVW-8 to CVW-6 – replacing VF-84 and VF-41. VF-143 and VF-142 became the first squadrons to transfer from F-4J Phantoms to F-14A Tomcats in the process. Like those of CVW-1, CVW-6's fighter squadrons were trained by VF-124 at NAS Miramar, as the training squadron at NAS Oceana had yet to receive their Tomcats by April 1, 1975 when the transition took place. This aircraft was sent into storage at AMARC on May 12, 1992.

Two F-14A-75-GR Tomcats (AB-100/159007 and AB101/159019) over NAS Oceana in late 1974/early 1975. (Tailhook Collection)

FIRST DECADE

An F-14A-80-GR Tomcat (159430) from VF-143 Pukin' Dogs captured at NAS Oceana on April 14, 1975. Although obscured from this angle, the tailcode of this aircraft was AJ, indicating affiliation with CVW-8. Pukin' Dogs Tomcats would only carry this tailcode for a very short time. (Jim Sullivan)

HALF CENTURY, BABY! FIFTY YEARS OF THE GRUMMAN F-14 TOMCAT

F-14A-75-GR Tomcat (159011) of VF-14 Tophatters in 1975. CVW-1 became the first Atlantic fleet wing to deploy the F-14 Tomcat aboard an aircraft carrier, and VF-14 and VF-32 became the first frontline fighter squadrons to transfer from the F-4 Phantom to the F-14 Tomcat. CVW-1 was embarked aboard USS *John F. Kennedy* (CV-67) from April 7, 1975 to May 12, 1975 after USS *John F. Kennedy* spent a large part of 1974 in dry dock. Following the short shakedown deployment, CVW-1 went on a full length deployment from June 28, 1975, to January 27, 1976, in the Mediterranean Sea. 159011 would crash into the Red Sea on February 6, 1982, while conducting an ACM exercise.

made. All the aircrew were highly experienced aviators with over a dozen lieutenant commanders available for each squadron. Competition to join the first cadre was intense. After we fleshed out two squadrons, we flipped a coin to see who would get which one. Sam got VF-1 and I got VF-2. VF-1 jumped out ahead with their impressive Wolf Pack concept and paint scheme.

Among the innovative, first-of-a-kind things we did are the following:

Held classified sessions with intelligence officers, CIC officers, and squadron personnel to work out new tactics (Sam gets full credit for organising and pushing this programme).

Developed a 'skunk works' in one of the first industrial warehouses constructed across from the back gate at Miramar where we developed state-of-the art training programmes for integrating aircrew functions and training programmes for maintenance personnel.

Got Office of Naval Research (ONR) researchers at Berkeley's Business School to help us structure the squadron department organisations to better handle the new CNO personnel programmes coming out at the time and to get better performance overall.

Developed an online computer system to help in scheduling aircrew and maintenance training, and to support supply of spare parts for the 'bureau number sensitive' F-14 systems.

Flew in the Have Doughnut and Have Drill programmes in the Nellis operating area (against captured MiG-17 and MiG-21 aircraft).

Helped develop the TOPGUN programme which was still in its infancy at the same time.

So, it was an exciting time to be at Miramar.

We held a VF-2 AOM at the Miramar O'Club to finalize the VF-2 names etc. After much brainstorming, Ben 'Youssarian' Thompson muttered "Bounty Hunters", and that was it! I added the Bullet call sign and six-gun shoulder patch. Since VF-2 was the first carrier squadron in the Navy on board USS Langley (the Navy's first aircraft carrier), we decided to recreate the original squadron theme.

Prior to the F-14 programme, I had been in VF-162 with Tom Weinel, who was our LSO and a good artist (Tom now runs the Crusader Association Website and email traffic).

Retired Admiral Jackson Tait was a test pilot aboard Langley and then a pilot in VF-2. He was living in Jacksonville at the time VF-2 was standing up. Tom was on the CAG-20 staff at Jax so I asked him to visit Admiral Tait. During his three visits, the original patch and the red white and blue rudder stripes that the squadron carried while on Langley were captured.

Tom did an original design of the current VF-2 colour scheme, which was then tuned up by squadron personnel. We sent two squadron metalsmiths to Grumman's Calverton facility to paint the first fleet aircraft to come to Miramar. Joel Graffman and I went to Calverton and flew it back, and I remember us checking into NY Center as 'Bullet 201, INS direct to Dallas', which was a new capability at the time. A few days after we arrived at Miramar, Joel and I flew the first high performance F-14 demo at Miramar, followed by an all-hands picnic.

The rest of the F-14 story is now history, and all the aircrews and maintenance

FIRST DECADE

This VF-142 Ghostriders F-14A-80-GR Tomcat (159433) sports the AJ tailcode of CVW-8. Shortly after this photo was taken the two units were affiliated with CVW-6, carrying the AE tailcode instead. This photo was taken on April 20, 1975. (Jim Sullivan)

VF-143 Pukin' Dogs' first CAG while operating the Tomcat. This F-14A-80-GR Tomcat was photographed in 1975. (Tailhook Collection)

HALF CENTURY, BABY! FIFTY YEARS OF THE GRUMMAN F-14 TOMCAT

The F-14B Tomcat testbed (157986) as seen in July 1975. (Paul Minert Collection)

FIRST DECADE

The 11th prototype F-14A-45-GR Tomcat (157990), used for non-weapons system avionics tests. Here seen on hangar bay compatibility tests aboard USS *Independence* (CVA-62). (Tailhook collection)

personnel who made it happen should be very proud of their contributions to that success story and the great times together.
Dick Martin, Bullet 1

One of the few Junior Officers selected to fly the Tomcat was Bob 'Hoot' Gibson who was flying F-4 Phantoms off USS *Coral Sea*:

The commanding officer of the squadron came to me one day – and he just happened to be a back-seater, and he just happened to be my back-seater because he had chosen me to be his pilot, so he must have felt I was pretty good because the senior radar intercept officers in the squadron wanted to fly with the more safe pilots – and said, "How would you like to make another cruise?" I'm thinking, "Oh, no, it's time for me to go to shore duty." I said, "Oh, Skipper, I don't know." He said, "In the F-14 Tomcat." I said, "Really?" The Tomcat was just coming to fruition then and was just getting ready to join the fleet. It turned out that they looked at the first two squadrons, and they said, "You know what, we don't have enough junior pilots in these squadrons." They were heavy on more senior pilots. They said, "We need some more relatively junior pilots, so we want three pilots from the West Coast

F-14A-85-GR Tomcat (159625) of VF-24 Red Checkertails in 1975. Like its sister squadron VF-211, VF-24 was the only squadron to transfer directly from the F-8 Crusader to the F-14 Tomcat. VF-24 would receive their first Tomcats on December 9, 1975, among them BuNo 159625. VF-24 would eventually change their name to Fighting Renegades in August 1979. This aircraft was sent to AMARC on January 31, 1991.

It doesn't get any more colourful than this! Great-looking VF-124 Gunfighters F-14A-85-GR Tomcat (159616) in Bicentennial markings, here seen parked at NAS Miramar in November 1975. (Peter Mancus via Jim Sullivan)

FIRST DECADE

F-14A-75-GR Tomcat (159013) of VF-32 Swordsmen in 1975. Like its sister squadron VF-14 Tophatters, VF-32 were a part of CVW-1 and were the second wing to receive the Tomcat in their inventory. Like VF-14, VF-32 transferred from the F-4B Phantom to F-14A Tomcats in 1974. The first Atlantic fleet squadron to transfer to the Tomcat did so at NAS Miramar, as the crews were trained with VF-124, since the training squadron at NAS Oceana (VF-32s homebase), wouldn't receive the first Tomcat till 1976. 159013 would remain with VF-32 for a long time and would eventually shoot down a MiG-23 in the famous Gulf of Sidra incident on May 4, 1989. On August 20, 1990, this aircraft was placed in storage at AMARC and was eventually struck off charge on June 1, 1992.

An F-14A-65-GR Tomcat (158991) of VF-1 Wolfpack parked at NAS Miramar in December 1975. (Paul Minert Collection)

HALF CENTURY, BABY! FIFTY YEARS OF THE GRUMMAN F-14 TOMCAT

and three pilots from the East Coast." The East Coast fighter squadrons were based at Oceana, Virginia, which is right near Virginia Beach.

They were going to pick three pilots that had at least one cruise and were relatively junior. I had a cruise and a half. I wound up being one of the three pilots picked off the West Coast to go to Fighter Squadron 1, which was, along with Fighter Squadron 2, [one of] the first two operational Tomcat squadrons. I joined that squadron, and this time I had a normal turnaround. I joined them in December of '73 and then we left on the first cruise the next September, September of '74.

Capt Bob 'Hoot' Gibson, F-14 pilot and Shuttle astronaut

FIRST FLEET TOMCATS

I was a fighter pilot and I have some great, and somewhat unusual Tomcat memories – I was a member of the VF-124 Cadre that brought the F-14 into the fleet. We were all relatively senior and had collectively literally sold our souls to part of the initial cadre. When I checked in, in January 1973, no aircraft were due till April so got checked out in the A-4 and had great fun with Lyle 'Ho Chi' Bien in the back seat as the duty GCA pilot. He really got quite good. The first F-14 Tomcats were never dull – I once got a master caution on a GCA final, looked over at about 12 caution lights – none of which turned out to be valid. That machine always has a way of getting your blood pumping. For me – coming from two 11-month Gulf of Tonkin cruises in F-4s, just getting into an aircraft that turned (even with the old motors) was the greatest thing since sliced bread, let alone the technology it brought to bear. I was the squadron LSO and waved a field arrestment during that year but never had the pleasure of bringing the Tomcat aboard the ship. [Skip left the Navy and went to Iran as a civilian working for Grumman, flying Iranian Tomcats as an instructor]

Skip 'Thud' Meinhold

FIRST BIG MISSILE SHOOT

I was on the Joint Evaluation Team (JET) at Point Mugu 1972-74 and we did the Weapons System BIS trials. My first flight was in #16 with Smoke Wilson in April 1973 and we were not supposed to even roll the airplane (envelope hadn't been cleared yet). Most of my early hours were in #s 4, 5, 6, 9, 11, 15, and 16. I even had some early flights with Grumman/Hughes test pilots. My first ACM engagement in an F-14 was up in the desert north of Nellis. That was before we started throwing TF30 blades and when we believed the jet wouldn't spin. After the RAG, I moved east with VF-32 and Tom Finta (VF-14) and I ran the first big missile shoot at the Eglin test range. We shot 27 missiles (nine AIM-54s) and didn't return a single drone. Those were the great years!

Rick Gildea, Tomcat RIO

FALL OF SAIGON

In December of 1973, the first cadre of Marines arrived at VF-124 to serve as instructors and as initial aircrews for VMFA-122, the first squadron slated to transition to the Tomcat. VMFA-122 was stationed at MCAS Kaneohe at the time and turned in their Phantoms in July of 1974 to formally begin their transition to the Tomcat. At that time, VF-32 and VF-14 had turned in their Phantoms and were transitioning to the Tomcat at VF-124 before switching coasts to become the first Tomcat squadrons at NAS Oceana making the first Atlantic deployment in June 1975.

The second Marine squadron slated to transition was VMFA-531 which was selected in spring of 1975 while based at El Toro MCAS. However, the decision by the Commandant to withdraw from the Tomcat programme altogether in summer of 1975 resulted in Marines at VF-124 being stranded there. Many remained as instructors. VMFA-122 was reactivated at MCAS Beaufort and equipped with F-4J Phantoms and VMFA-531 returning to El Toro in August of 1975.

VF-1 and VF-2 continued to receive their full complement of 12 Tomcats each by April 1974. Both squadrons were assigned to Carrier Air Wing 14 aboard USS Enterprise which was working up for a WESTPAC deployment in September 1974. That deployment included flying top cover for the evacuation of US personnel from Saigon, South Vietnam in April 1975.

We went to the Tonkin Gulf, and at that point, things were falling apart in South Vietnam. I remember there was a press release that North Vietnam issued that said we were there sabre-rattling and brazen provocateurs is what we were for being in the Tonkin Gulf with this brand-

F-14A-85-GR Tomcat (159616) of VF-124 Gunfighters in 1975. Arguably one of the most colourful Tomcat schemes ever. In celebration of the Bicentennial year 1976, many squadrons had one or more aircraft painted in bright red/white/blue colours. VF-124 was no different. Since there were not many Tomcat units in service in 1976, few Tomcats were seen wearing Bicentennial markings, but VF-124 had received Tomcats as early as 1972, and were training crews for both Pacific and Atlantic fleet units. 159616 would be painted in these bright colours in late 1975, but would enter frontline service in mid-1976.

A F-14A-85-GR Tomcat (159631) of VF-24 Red Checkertails seen parked at NAS Miramar on June 19, 1976. (Tailhook Collection via Bob Lawson)

F-14A-70-GR Tomcat (158985) of VF-2 Bounty Hunters at NAS Miramar in March 1976. At the time both VF-1 and VF-2 had some of their aircraft painted in the Ferris experimental paint scheme. (Paul Minert Collection)

FIRST DECADE

F-14A-80-GR Tomcat (159434) of VF-143 Pukin' Dogs in 1976. The third wing to receive the Tomcat was CVW-6, which previously had VF-84 and VF-41 as its fighter squadrons, both flying the F-4N Phantom from USS *Franklin D. Roosevelt* (CVA-42). On July 27, 1975, CVW-6 was assigned to USS *America* (CV-66) and VF-143 (and its sister squadron VF-142) became a part of the wing. CVW-6 went to sea for a deployment that lasted from March 6 to March 24, 1976, following USS *America* spending almost a year in dry dock. From April 15 to October 25, 1976, CVW-6 was operating in the Mediterranean Sea. The Pukin' Dogs' aircraft always stood out among the other fighter squadrons in the US Navy's inventory, with their blue trim. The use of this colour dates back to when the squadron traded their F3H-2 Demons for F4H-1 Phantoms. In the Demon days, the squadron was designated VF-53 (assigned to CVG-5, thus being the third squadron in the 5 Carrier Air Group) and their aircraft sported a red trim colour. When the squadron received the F4H-1 Phantom it was assigned to CVG-14, and as it was common at the time, that resulted in a redesignation as it was no longer a part of CVG-5 but was now with CVG-14. The squadron's new designation was VF-143 (third squadron of CVG-14). The third squadron in a carrier air group were assigned blue as their trim colour – a tradition which the squadron maintains to this day.

An F-14A-85-GR Tomcat (159612) of VF-32 Swordsmen parked at NAS Oceana in late 1976. Note the red/white/blue bands on the tail and the full-out Bicentennial coloured VF-14 F-14 Tomcat in the background. (Tailhook Collection)

new fighter, the Tomcat. We didn't do a whole lot. We sailed the Tonkin Gulf, we did flight operations in the gulf, just to let them know we were there.

We were supposed to have left and come home, I think, in March of '75, and all of a sudden, it developed that South Vietnam was just going to fall. We were extended an extra month to provide fighter cover for the Fall of Saigon. Over there it was April 29, 1975. Over here, because of the International date line, it was April 30, 1975. That's the day Saigon fell, and that's the day that we launched all the helicopters in to pick up the last few Americans and the last few Vietnamese who had worked with us very closely and a large number of members of their military and their families. I flew fighter cover that day, overhead Saigon, the very last day of the Vietnam War. The helicopters came in and picked everybody up, and they were landing on the rooftops around Saigon, and on the embassy grounds in Saigon. Like I say, I flew one of what we called Combat Air Patrol, or CAP, mission overhead, armed to the teeth, in case they shot any of our helicopters down or shot at us or anything like that, none of which happened. They just wanted to let us get in there, get our people, and get out, so they didn't shoot at us at all.

They called it a combat mission, so I had one combat mission in the F-14 Tomcat. It turned out to be my very last carrier landing because when I came back in and landed after that one, we buttoned everything up and pulled out and headed back to California. I got back from that cruise and then I did go to shore duty as an instructor in the F-14 Tomcat, but I didn't want to be there. I wanted to be a test pilot, but I wound up working as an instructor in the F-14 Tomcat for about nine months before that happened.
Capt Bob 'Hoot' Gibson

THAT LEARNING CURVE

My Tomcat memories are indelibly inscribed on the brain – checking into VF-1 just after they completed their first deployment, as part of the group of first nuggets to go to the Turkey. I was a brand new lieutenant, junior grade, relieving a lieutenant commander in the billet of airframes branch officer – because the squadron had more than 15 lieutenant commanders and above at that time. We were learning to always save gas, especially since we flew the airplane without drop tanks on deployment, with 1+45 cycles. Getting it in the air was always a chore, with the AEs being the magicians who made it happen – circuit breaker drills on start-up, during troubleshooting, on the cat. Wipeouts where you just made sure the outboard spoilers 'winked' and didn't go full up, since they might stick there... always hard to get off the ground, but once you

HALF CENTURY, BABY! FIFTY YEARS OF THE GRUMMAN F-14 TOMCAT

F-14A-70-GR Tomcat (158979) of VF-1 Wolfpack seen in May 1977 with the experimental Ferris paint scheme. (Michael Grove via Paul Minert Collection)

did, it flew like a champ. At that time, in the fleet, it was 'unspinnable', so you could, and did, just about anything with the flight controls. We learned, shortly after, that that was not the case. Periodic groundings, that came too frequently, were part of that learning curve.
Vice Admiral Marty 'Streak' Chanik

Continuing the operating practice of having two fighter squadrons per carrier air wing, Phantom sister squadrons began transitioning together at VF-124. VF-14 and VF-32 transitioned to the Tomcat at Miramar in 1974 and then headed to NAS Oceana to become the first east coast Tomcats followed by VF-142 and VF-143 in 1975. VF-41 and VF-84 transitioned in 1975. Meanwhile, VF-24 and VF-211 were transitioning at Miramar by 1975.

With the Marines out of the Tomcat programme, Grumman was experiencing funding issues that were resolved by selection by Iran to purchase the F-14 Tomcat to help defend their country against the incursions by Soviet high-flying MiG-25 Foxbats from the northern border and longstanding threat from Iraq on the western border. The Shah, himself a pilot, sat in an F-14 Tomcat cockpit in July 1973. Iran would eventually become a customer, purchasing 80 Grumman F-14A Tomcats and 633 Hughes AIM-54 Phoenix missiles for $2 billion. The Iranian Air Force saw the Tomcat as more than a fighter/interceptor, it was viewed as a vital component to integrate its powerful long-range radar to cover gaps in radar coverage in the mountainous border areas. The Iranian purchase of 80 Tomcats and their assistance in securing financing for Grumman saved the F-14 Tomcat programme. Soon, Iranian aircrews arrived at VF-124 to learn how to operate the Tomcat.

Cdr 'Hot Dog' Brown, a former F-8 pilot and LSO serving at Pt Mugu flying the F-14 Tomcat became the Officer in Charge of the Navy operation inside Iran to help train the Iranian aircrews and maintainers. Navy aircrews ferried the Tomcats to Iran in small batches until 79 of the 80 ordered had been delivered (one remained in the US for developmental purposes and was never delivered). The first group of Iranian pilots to transition to F-14 Tomcat at VF-124 in 1976 were Mohammad Farahvar, Kazem Heidarzadeh, Mojtaba Zanganeh and Iraj Khoram.

Paul Miles gives his perspective as a young naval aviator at Miramar during the heady days of arriving while the F-8 Crusader and F-4 Phantom ruled the roost and provided aircrews to flesh out the community and influence the development of tactics, techniques and procedures as well as continue the fighter legacy:

While it seems obvious today that the F-14 was the heir to the F-4's title of premier Navy fighter, there was a tremendous amount of influence from the F-8 Crusader community as well – especially in the early days. VF-124, which had been the F-8 Fleet Replacement Squadron (FRS, but really known as 'the RAG'), became the F-14 RAG while VF-121 continued to train Phantom crews. Unfortunately, in transitioning, VF-124 gave up the

FIRST DECADE

This F-14A-95-GR Tomcat (160379) of VF-41 Black Aces is seen parked at NAS Oceana on May 12, 1977. (Jim Sullivan)

F-14A-85-GR Tomcat (159614) of VF-211 Checkmates in 1976. VF-211 (with sister squadron VF-24) were the only ones to transfer directly from F-8 Crusaders to the F-14 Tomcat. VF-211 was a part of CVW-21 while flying the Crusader, but would transfer to CVW-9, which was left without fighter squadrons when VF-96 and VF-92 were disestablished in late 1975. CVW-9 was deployed aboard USS Constellation (CV-64), its first deployment with the Tomcat, from April 12 to November 21, 1977. This made it the fourth carrier air wing to be equipped with the F-14 Tomcat.

call sign 'Gunfighter' and assumed the questionable call sign of 'Hoppy'. 'The Fighting Hoppies' just didn't have a good ring to it. Based on the squadron's insignia, we called ourselves the 'Book-busters' for a while. To make up for the lack of inspiration in call sign, VF-124's instructor cadre was fleshed-out with a bunch of F-8 guys (and Marines in expectation of flying the Tomcat, but that's another story).

Among the characters in the LSO shop at VF-124 in 1976 where I had my first 'collateral' duty were 'Cowboy' Brotherton, 'Bean' Barrett, and the immortal 'Bug' Roach (who now flies Harleys in Heaven, I'm sure). It was hard to get any serious work done in that office.

My first fleet squadron was VF-24, descended from one of the great MiG-killing F-8 squadrons (as an aside, I always wanted one of the old VF-24 guys to explain our call sign, 'Pageboy'?? We finally changed it to 'Renegade'). The other ancestor of VF-24 was VF-96. Yes, Duke Cunningham and Willy Driscoll's VF-96. How the Navy chose to preserve the VF-24 Red Checkertails and disestablish the VF-96 Fighting Falcons must have been an interesting story… the F-8 won that 1v1. But I wish they had kept VF-96's call sign ('Showtime'!).

We had four F-8 pilots in VF-24 after the transition: 'Buzz' Johnson, 'Worm' Ringwood, 'Action' Jackson, and 'PF' Hoffman. AJ and PF had made VF-24's last F-8 deployment on USS Hancock, and I don't think they got a single F-8 night trap after they left the RAG. That day-only business changed when they climbed into the F-14, and they had someone watching over their shoulder, too. To switch to a 30-ton, twin-tailed, double-barrelled, two-seated, all-weather wing-swinger was quite a leap, but they made it look easy.

Later on, more Gator drivers, as they finished their attitude-check assignments to other communities, joined the Tomcat world. 'Moon' Vance became VF-24's XO/CO after 'influencing' the S-3 community as a RAG instructor. Rear Admiral 'Punchy' Gillchrist restored Miramar's Fighter Wing from the doldrums. Certainly, the TARPS programme benefited immensely from the photo RF-8 guys, not least of whom was 'Hoser' Satrapa, who officially was a recce pilot (but we all know better since he had flown the F-8 over Vietnam). Each of those guys deserves a book of his own.

I've always thought one of the main reasons that the F-14 community maintained a fair amount of high-speed colour over the years was because of the early F-8 influence. The F-8 guys considered themselves to be the wild stepchildren of Naval aviation, and many of the Phantom guys agreed with them. There was something about flying solo and surviving a tour in the Gator that just gave them permission to ignite their hair. They brought many fine, long-standing Naval Air traditions with them: the Mutha Trophy, the Tomcat (nee: Crusader) Ball, El Centro gunnery dets, the Mt. Signal Café, 'Dead Bug' and a healthy respect for the ramp.

Philosophy from some of my F-8 heroes: As we were trying to solve all of the Navy's problems from the vantage point of the Junior Officer Bunkroom, 'Moon' Vance reminded me of what was important in life. "Relax, Kid. You could be flying Fudds." Moon began his flying career in the Grumman E-1.

I asked Hoser, "What's the after-takeoff checklist in the F-8?" Actually, it was more like 'Hoser' saying, "Kid, ask me what's the after-takeoff checklist in the F-8!" "Okay, Hoser, what's the after-takeoff checklist in the F-8?" "Gear up, wing down, light up!" (I'm sure

FIRST DECADE

The first time the Tomcats of VF-14 Tophatters saw a major change in their paint scheme was in 1977. The red chevron on the vertical stabilizer was replaced by a far more subtle red stripe. This CAG bird (159428) was captured at NAS Oceana on October 20, 1977. (Jim Sullivan)

An F-14A-65-GR Tomcat (158625) of VF-101 Grim Reapers on the ramp at NAS Oceana on October 20, 1977. (Jim Sullivan)

HALF CENTURY, BABY! FIFTY YEARS OF THE GRUMMAN F-14 TOMCAT

This F-14A-85-GR Tomcat (159599) of VF-32 Swordsmen was photographed at NAS Oceana on October 20, 1977. CVW-1 had a brief shakedown deployment aboard USS *Dwight D. Eisenhower* (CVN-69) from November 7 to December 13, 1977, and the aircraft of VF-32 proudly display the carrier name on the vertical stabilizer. This aircraft crashed on March 6, 1982, when the arresting gear cable failed on USS *Dwight D. Eisenhower*. At the time the aircraft was in service with VF-143. (Jim Sullivan)

A flight of F-14A-85-GR Tomcats (NG-104/159628, NG-103/159630 and NG-102/159632) of VF-211 Fighting Checkmates in flight while deployed aboard USS *Constellation* (CV-64) from April 12 to November 21, 1977. (Bob Lawson)

33

FIRST DECADE

An F-14A Tomcat during carquals aboard USS *Enterprise* (CVN-65) on March 2, 1978. Notice the Ferris paint scheme. (Bob Lawson)

F-14A-90-GR Tomcat (159828) of VX-4 Evaluators in 1977. The Tomcat was not only finding its way into front line fighter squadrons and training squadrons in the latter part of the 1970s, but also the test and evaluation squadrons. The late 70s saw experimentation with aircraft colours. The US Navy had a tradition of painting its aircraft in bright flashy paint schemes, but that tradition was coming to an end as the 70s were drawing to a close. The Ferris scheme, introduced and patented by aviation artist Keith Ferris, was tested by both VX-4 and several frontline fighter squadrons. Although it never became standard, it certainly was a good indicator that the tides were changing in the US Navy as the 80s began.

An F-14A-95-GR Tomcat (160387) of VF-41 Black Aces parked at NAS Oceana on March 11, 1978. (Don Linn)

somewhere there are some examples of the F-8 oxygen mask mod, complete with fake hose and cigarette port.) So I asked Hoser (well, you know how it goes), "What do you do after you bolter in the F-8?" "Put out your cigarette and get serious!" "Hoser, why did you carry two hand-grenades with you over 'Nam? What good are only two grenades?" "Well, Kid… after you throw the first grenade, you can throw rocks for a long time before you need the other one."

I was fortunate that when I began flying the Tomcat as a student in August 1976, panic had not actually set in among the operational leadership – yet. The F-14 programme itself was in turmoil: three airplanes had been lost in a year to 'thump-bang' catastrophic engine failures; the Marine Corps had decided the F-14 was unaffordable and had dropped out of the programme, resulting in cancellation of the air-to-ground weapons programme and a big jump in the plane's unit cost; the fleet's reliability was abysmal; and cost-overruns on the programme were threatening its very existence. I think Navy headquarters was hoping that during this period of commotion, the fleet would just quietly bring the planes onboard, do its job, and stay out of the news for a while. But it was not to be.

A few months before my first F-14 flight at VF-124, two VF-124 F-14s crashed within days of each other, and

FIRST DECADE

THE FIGHTER MAFIA

As the F-14 was entering service, controversy over fighter design was raging in the Pentagon – primarily due to influence of the 'Fighter Mafia' led by legendary tactician and theorist Colonel John Boyd who had made a name for himself, first at the Air Force Fighter Weapons School at Nellis as a leading tactics instructor, and then at Eglin AFB where he joined with Tom Christie to develop energy manoeuvrability (EM), a way to characterise and compare fighter performance. That led to its use in designing the F-15 Eagle and ultimately the F-16 Fighting Falcon by virtue of the Lightweight Fighter competition. The F-14 Tomcat was no lightweight fighter but it was still a revolutionary leap ahead from the venerable F-4 Phantom.

Nevertheless, the Fighter Mafia, which also included Pierre Sprey, Everest Riccioni and Franklin 'Chuck' Spinney were not happy about the cost and compromises they felt were evident in the F-15 Eagle and F-14 Tomcat. They advocated for a light, simple and affordable fighter that could prevail in performance against the hordes of Soviet fighters that, it was postulated, would overwhelm the relatively few heavyweight US fighters – particularly over the focal point of the Cold War in Europe, the Fulda gap.

When the Air Force missionised the F-16 into the ground-attack role in January 1975, they were livid. They used their influence to get the Department of Defense (OSD PA&E) to sponsor a Joint Test and Evaluation (JT&E) to evaluate air combat tactics and missile technology at Nellis AFB using F-14 Tomcats and F-15 Eagles equipped with Sparrow and Sidewinder missiles as the Blue Force and aggressor F-5E aircraft equipped with AIM-9L all-aspect Sidewinders as the Red Force.

This JT&E was designated Air Combat Evaluation/Air Intercept Missile Evaluation (ACEVAL/AIMVAL) and it was intended to evaluate quality (heavy expensive fighters) vs quantity (lightweight affordable fighters). It also examined the impact of forward quarter infrared missiles such as the AIM-9L.

The Navy Tomcats designated to participate in ACEVAL/AIMVAL were brand new aircraft delivered to VX-4 (the Navy's Operational Test and Evaluation (OT&E) Squadron based at Pt Mugu). Lieutenant Commander Joe 'Hoser' Satrapa was selected to be the Officer in Charge (OinC) of the VX-4 Detachment operating out of Nellis AFB.

Satrapa had flown the F-8 Crusader initially over Vietnam and then the RA-5 Vigilante. Selected to join VX-4, the OPs O took him out to humble him in a F-4 Phantom only to be dominated by Satrapa. After a quick transition training syllabus, Satrapa was introduced to the Tomcat which he mastered quickly. He pressed for 'his' Tomcats to be painted in the distinctive Heater-Ferris splinter paint scheme pioneered by artist Keith Ferris and pilot 'Heater' Heatley on VF-74 Phantoms. The AIM/ACE Tomcats were also equipped with VTAS Helmet Mounted Sights (HMS) in order to target the advanced high off boresight Short Range Missile (SRM) being examined in the AIMVAL portion of the JT&E.

The Blue Force aircrews were expressly forbidden from any ACM between the F-15s and F-14s due to international interest in both airframes. The Navy had handily outflown the Air Force at Andrews AFB while demonstrating both aircraft for the Shah in 1973 so the flag officers overseeing AIM/ACE wanted no repeat that would threaten international sales of the F-15. However, there were other F-15 aircraft at Nellis not part of Blue Force and not bound to any such orders.

The F-15 Eagle was still relatively new to operational units with first F-15B having been delivered in 1974. The Air Force was anxious to market it to Japan, Israel and Saudi Arabia and after losing the competition to sell fighters to Iran, it did not want the F-14 to become a distraction.

Despite the warnings, Satrapa and his wingman arranged a little sporting encounter with an F-15 squadron not assigned to AIM/ACE to size up each other's mounts, figuring they could escape notice. Up till then, the F-14 had yet to fight the F-15. When it happened, Hoser and his wingman both prevailed – bringing back exciting camera footage of his opponent with the pipper on the canopy validating a dramatic up-close guns kill.

The word leaked out to AvWeek who reported on the results and shortly thereafter, an Air Force general burst into the Blue Force spaces demanding the film and making all sorts of threats. Hoser already had a personal copy of his kill safely stashed away and it survived the backlash. It became a treasured memento on his wall and circulated wildly even before the Internet.

In **Hoser's** own words, here is his recollection:

Now, this is no ****! Towards the end of the ACE/AIMEVAL, things had heated up between the Eagle and Turkey pilots. At the Nellis O'Club many innuendoes and challenges had been thrown out as a result of the high profile dog fights between the Tomcat/Eagle Blue Force and the F-5Es. The Blue Force F-15 drivers were threatened with a court martial, flying rubber dog **** outta Hong Kong and having their birthday taken away if they even thought about locking horns with ACEVAL Tomcats.

When the test sorties were finally over, a couple of F-15 instructors in the 415th training squadron took the bait. 'Turk' Pentecost and I were a section. 'Turk' was not nearly as cocky, arrogant and boisterous as D-hose, but just as aggressive, smart, devious and just as good a stick. We briefed a very wide hook, an altitude split of 10,000ft and a radar sort at 25nm by Bill 'Hill Billy' Hill and 'Fearless' Frank Schumacher. All pre-merge heat and radar missiles didn't count. It was GUNS only at the merge. The wide hook enabled Turk and D-hose to split the fight into (2)1v1's, with one Turkey high, one low and lots of lateral separation.

As Hill Billy and D-Hose closed for a 250ft, guns kill on their Eagle, the comm went like this:

D-hose: "Where are you Turk?"
Fearless: "Right above you Hoser."
D-hose: "We got two cons! Who's out front?"
Turk (mildly offended): "Who do ya think?"
Both Eagles were gunned, "knock it off"

was called, and the Tomcats RTB'd with a 500 knot, 6.5g, half second break at Nellis… cuz that was our salute and tribute to our fine VX-4 maintenance personnel.

Knowing the gun camera film would be destroyed by the Nellis photo lab, it was covertly sent to a secret contact at Grumman for processing. 'Bout a month later, December 6, the door slams open and General Knight, with two of his staff, doggie wobble heads, entered demanding to know "who and where are Hoser and Turk?" Falcon (JW Taylor), OinC, stepped up asking if he could be of assistance. The general responds with, "Your fighter jocks have no idea how their playful antics affect important political decisions!" Well, as General Knight proceeded to explain, Japan had contracted for 21 F-15s, but an article in Aviation Week had talked about the F-14 being superior to the Eagle. With gun camera film to prove it; Japan was considering buying F-14s instead.

The General told JW he wanted ALL copies of the gun camera film, the TVSU/VCR tapes, and audio recordings on his desk by 0900 the next day. He was obviously pissed when he arrived, but as a result of the humility and contrition displayed by Turk and D-hose, he was satisfied that his mission was accomplished. Of course, D-hose and Turk didn't want to embarrass the F-15 community, and they never mentioned the incident again… UNTIL NOW! A few months later at a VX-4 at JW's, D-hose sez, "Hey Falcon, I know ya got a copy of that 16mm gun film, how 'bout it?" JW bugs for a few and returns with film I have in my hand right now.

PS: The 8" x 10" single frame of the 16mm gun film on my bulkhead in my ' war room' shows a F-15 thru a F-14 HUD, radar lock, at 250ft, Vc zero, pipper on the pilot's helmet, gun selected, No X over the 'G' – master arm on – half detent on trigger depressed (which activates gun camera and opens the gun gas purge doors), with… zero rounds remaining… good thing!

The ACE/AIMEVAL JT&E ran for several years concluding in 1978. The Fighter Mafia felt vindicated that the Blue Force F-14s and F-15s ended up in mutually assured destruction when they took the fight to the merge with the Red Force carrying forward aspect missiles like the AIM-9L. It was only a matter of time before the Soviet Union caught up to the US technology which had been consistently 20 years ahead.

A principal finding was that the necessity to produce illumination for the Sparrow until impact, which resulted in the Red Force being able to launch their all-aspect Sidewinders before impact – resulting in mutual kills. What was needed was Phoenix-type multiple-launch and terminal active capability in a Sparrow-size airframe. This led to a memorandum of agreement (MOA) with European allies (principally the UK and Germany for development) for the US to develop an advanced, medium-range, air-to-air missile with the USAF as lead service. The MOA also assigned responsibility for development of an advanced, short-range, air-to-air missile to the European team; this would become the British ASRAAM.

The F101DFE engine shortly before being installed in the F-14B Tomcat testbed (157984). (US Navy via Craig Kaston)

FIRST DECADE

The ninth prototype (157988) F-14A-40-GR Tomcat, pictured in November 1979. The ninth aircraft was used for evaluation of the AN/AWG-9 radar. (Tailhook Collection)

within a few hundred yards of each other, in the landing pattern at NAS Miramar. I was on the platform during night field carrier landing practice, 'writing book' as a fledgling Landing Signal Officer (LSO), when one of our birds fell from the pattern. On board were a former prisoner of war and his instructor RIO. A friend of mine and fellow F-14 student, Randy Wilt, lost control on his second fight in the airplane due to asymmetric flaps. Four memorial services in three days. Shortly thereafter, we all got to watch the film of the first F-14 flat spin, which ended with a splash in the Chesapeake Bay near the Patuxent River Naval Air Test Center.

None of this dampened my enthusiasm for the F-14 of course. I was young and bulletproof. I would occasionally get to see an F-14 do the 'Scamp departure' from Miramar, going straight up, and be in awe of such a powerful machine. The F-14 was the coolest jet on the planet. The instructors didn't seem worried, either. The old-heads talked about how troubled the F-8 and the F-4 had been in their early days. They said we would

the loss-rate. Thus, the prohibitions began.

The Scamp departure promptly disappeared. Because of Randy Wilt's crash, flap transitions had to be performed at or above 800ft, and had to be wings-level. As we encountered more engine problems, the use of afterburner was prohibited and a 4g-limit was imposed (except for emergencies or actual combat!). That lasted for most of the fleet for about a year, until engines modified with containment were installed. During that period, F-14 students were faced with trying to fight the wily A-4 using military power and 4gs... good luck! Then we began finding metal chips in the wingsweep actuators, so manual wingsweep was prohibited for a while.

Like all of my classmates, I had expected to be assigned to one of the four squadrons that were transitioning from the Phantom to the Tomcat at that time. But one of the nuggets in VF-24, which had finished transition, had ejected from his second F-14 and had become the 'Forty Million Dollar Man'. The leadership decided he was now too infamous to fly the F-14 and needed to be replaced. So, upon graduation I was sent to VF-24.
Cdr Paul 'Kid' Miles

VF-14 and VF-32 transitioned to the Tomcat at Miramar in 1974 and headed to NAS Oceana to become the first east coast Tomcats followed by VF-142 and VF-143 in 1975. VF-41 and VF-84 transitioned in 1975 and soon thereafter, VF-101 Grim Reapers stood up as the east coast RAG in 1977. Meanwhile, VF-24 and VF-211 transitioned at Miramar by 1975 followed by VF-114 and VF-213 by 1976 and followed by VF-51 and VF-111 in 1978. By 1980, 14 Fleet Tomcat squadrons were operating from both coasts in addition to the two RAGS and VX-4 as well as dedicated test aircraft at Pt Mugu and the Naval Air Test Center at NAS Pax River.

Rear Admiral Gillcrist, Commander FITAEWING at Miramar during the latter part of the decade recalled:

The US Navy has had a running battle with certain elements in our government (DoD, the Congress and the other armed services) over the last 25 years or more over whether we need carrier battle forces in the first place. So, as OP-50, I spent a great deal of my time entreating other senior naval officers to use instead, the expression 'maritime air superiority' (MAS). George Haering (GS-18) a former CNA Analyst and head of the Strike Warfare Branch in OPNAV was the counterpoint to John Boyd and the Fighter Mafia. Although not an aviator, he got into the F-14 cockpit as often as he could, becoming the most vocal MAS advocate and touting the virtues of the Tomcat in public media such as the influential Armed Forces Journal.

The Tomcat era had well and truly arrived but troubling issues with the TF30 engines and overall readiness persisted, drawing press attention.

simply learn how to work around the problems until the Navy fixed them, no big deal.

I did my obligatory supersonic run on my first flight, and full-afterburner takeoff on my second. I got to do intercepts against an SR-71 with a Marine RIO in my back seat, fired the gun, went to the boat, and learned both exhilaration and humility in air combat training. In fact, I got to do everything in the syllabus. But the guys after me were not all so lucky.

The F-14 was not just another Navy fighter. In particular, its 40-million-dollar price tag made losses that the F-8 and F-4 programmes had endured without fanfare become unacceptable. Something had to be done to reduce

THE BIG STICK

The fourth prototype (157983) F-14A-15-GR Tomcat at NAS Pt Mugu, CA. This aircraft was used for AIM-54 evaluation from 1973, when this photo was taken. (Tailhook Collection)

The AIM-54 Phoenix was unique in that it was developed as a weapon system integrated with the AWG-9 radar. The Navy had been developing air-to-air missiles for use in defending the aircraft carrier from Soviet bombers carrying air-to-surface missiles as far back as 1951. As this threat increased during the Cold War, the Navy began formulating plans for a fleet defence fighter that could carry multiple long-range missiles and stay on station for a considerable length of time (up to six hours 150nm from the carrier) using a TF30 turbofan for efficient fuel flow although without an afterburner.

This requirement evolved by 1959 into the Douglas F6D Missileer carrying an AN/APQ-81 radar and Bendix AAM-N-10 Eagle long-range missiles. The Missileer was subsonic and not designed to 'dogfight'. Its dubious ability to defend itself led to cancellation by 1960.

Robert S. McNamara was appointed as Secretary of Defense in January 1961 and by June, he had forced a shotgun marriage between the Air Force and

THE BIG STICK

This F-14A-60-GR Tomcat (158616) from NATC was captured on display at NAS Patuxent River in August 1973. The aircraft is demonstrating its capability to carry four AIM-54 Phoenix missiles. (Paul Minert Collection)

Navy to develop the Tactical Fighter Experimental (TFX). The Navy would have to see their fleet defence fighter needs met by the TFX design. Boeing and General Dynamics were selected out of six competitors by 1962. In November 1962, McNamara selected the General Dynamics design even though the Boeing design had been recommended by the Evaluation Board earlier in 1962.

McNamara had his way and the Air Force began developing the F-111 into an all-weather strike and interdiction aircraft capable of low level supersonic flight. The Navy still wanted a Fleet Air Defense (FAD) fighter so General Dynamics brought in Grumman to make the F-111 carrier capable and integrate the AWG-9 weapon system. This variant was called the F-111B. The first F-111A prototype flew on December 21, 1964 followed by a F-111B on May 18, 1965. The first initial production F-111A aircraft arrived at Nellis AFB on July 17, 1967 and were assigned to the 428th Tactical Fighter Squadron. By 1967, the F-111B was flying at NAS Patuxent River undergoing carrier suitability. Seven prototypes were built, but by 1967 the Navy had serious concerns. Both Congressional Armed Services Committees (House and Senate) voted to not continue with the F-111B in May 1968, three months after McNamara left office.

However, the AWG-9 and AIM-54 Phoenix were ready for integration in another aircraft and that was to be the F-14 Tomcat. To meet the Navy FAD requirement, the AWG-9 could track up to 24 different targets simultaneously and assign firing order numerics automatically. It could launch AIM-54s against six different targets simultaneously. This capability revolutionized the outer air battle and carried on a platform such as the Tomcat, with ability to reach and maintain distance CAP stations upwards of 200nm from the carrier battle group, it gave the Soviet regimental bomber planners serious worries. According to a Backfire aircrewman, they considered themselves nothing more than kamikazes with the prospect of trying to achieve a launch location against a carrier.

The AIM-54 was a large missile weighing in at 1,000lb and capable of achieving Mach 5. It could reach an altitude of 100,000ft where, in a loft mode, it travel for unprecedented ranges before tipping over and using its own terminally active radar to complete an intercept upwards of a hundred miles away. The ability to launch six Phoenix against six different targets was unprecedented and became a force multiplier.

SIX-ON-SIX

As the F-14 gang at Pt Mugu were aware (sometimes painfully) PMA-241's deputy for weapons trials was Clyde Tuomela. I came back from a flight and had a message that he wanted to see me. Clyde said to me 'Swoose' (as in Snead, the PMA at the time) was getting a lot of pressure from Congress to demonstrate the six-on-six shot: "He wants YOU to do it ASAP, but don't screw it up."

As the senior pilot of the Joint Evaluation Team (JET) and the Flight Test Officer of the Naval Missile Center, I probably could have opted for the test, but Swoose designating me was a convenient cop out. Jack Hawver and I had many discussions within the

F-14A-120-GR Tomcat (161444) of VX-4 Evaluators in 1986. This aircraft tested the possibility of landing aboard an aircraft carrier with a six-pack (six AIM-54 Phoenix missiles). The aircraft itself went on to be upgraded to F-14A+ standard in May 1986. It would crash on April 17, 1996, near NAS Oceana; both crew ejected and survived the crash.

JET team, and with the Hughes people both at Mugu and at Conoga Park, as to what the test was going to look like. We (and the Hughes crews) had fired several multi-target shots before (up to 4v4), and their parameters were taken into consideration. Once we decided, Jack and I 'flew' simulations on every AWG-9 simulator that was available in the country. We then briefed the PMA on what we proposed. Part of the work up also included discussions with the test conductors and the targets people to see if it was possible to do a six-target presentation.

The formation consisted of one BQM-34E at Mach 1.2, three BQM-34Cs at Mach 0.9, and two QT-33s at Mach 0.7. They were to be in a line abreast at the 30-mile 'open fire' with the AWG-9 prioritising the targets, making the supersonic target automatically the #1 priority, since it was the greatest threat. During our simulation we discovered that if we shot it first, we would not have had six missiles tracking at the same time. So after the initial detection at 58 miles, Jack reset the priority so six missiles would all be heading down range towards their targets at the same time.

The eighth prototype (157987) F-14A-35-GR Tomcat at NAS Patuxent River, MD, in April 1974. The aircraft was used for Navy evaluation tests and was attached to NATC. It is seen here equipped with the AIM-54 Phoenix. The aircraft was destroyed when one of its engines caught fire while parked at Pax River on May 13, 1975. (Tailhook Collection)

THE BIG STICK

An F-14A-60-GR Tomcat (158616) from NATC here seen carrying a AIM-54 Phoenix missile on the wing-mounted hardpoint in July 1978. (Paul Minert Collection)

F-14A-90-GR Tomcat (159853) of VX-4 Evaluators on display on October 16, 1982. (Craig Kaston via Paul Minert Collection)

Per a preflight agreement, I fired the first and last missile from the front cockpit and Jack fired the other four using the RIO launch button, getting them all off in 38 seconds. At that range, the Phoenix missiles began their climbs towards 100,000ft as I looked up; the six contrails looked like SA-2 smoke trails over downtown Hanoi during an Alpha Strike! The missiles all carried telemetry packages in lieu of warheads to provide accurate measurements of performance.

The first missile was a direct hit on a BQM-34C. The missile fired at the BQM-34E took the miss distance-scoring pod off the wing of the drone. Both QT-33s were hit in the empennage area. When they slowed down for recovery, they lost control and spun in short of San Clemente Island. Of the other two BQM-34Cs, one had a missile within lethal range and the other experienced an internal malfunction before the Phoenix could get to it, but not before demonstrating that the AWG-9 could guide six missiles concurrently.

In retrospect, the fact that the operation was accomplished at all, let alone within two months' time with only one dry run, was a tribute to all who participated in the 'six-on-six', which only happened that one time. It was certainly my privilege to have been the shooter.

The videos of the actual firings were taken/recorded/telemetered to the ground by an experimental system on an F-4 piloted by Roger Box, soon to be my relief as the Flight Test Officer, and subsequently, my relief as CAG-14.

I have a few other stories to tell, but I'll get to that later.
John 'Smoke' Wilson, Tomcat pilot

THE BIG STICK AT SEA
A Tomcat flown by pilot Lt Ed Riley and RIO Lt Scott Lamoreaux from VX-4 loaded with six AIM-54C missiles trapped

HALF CENTURY, BABY! FIFTY YEARS OF THE GRUMMAN F-14 TOMCAT

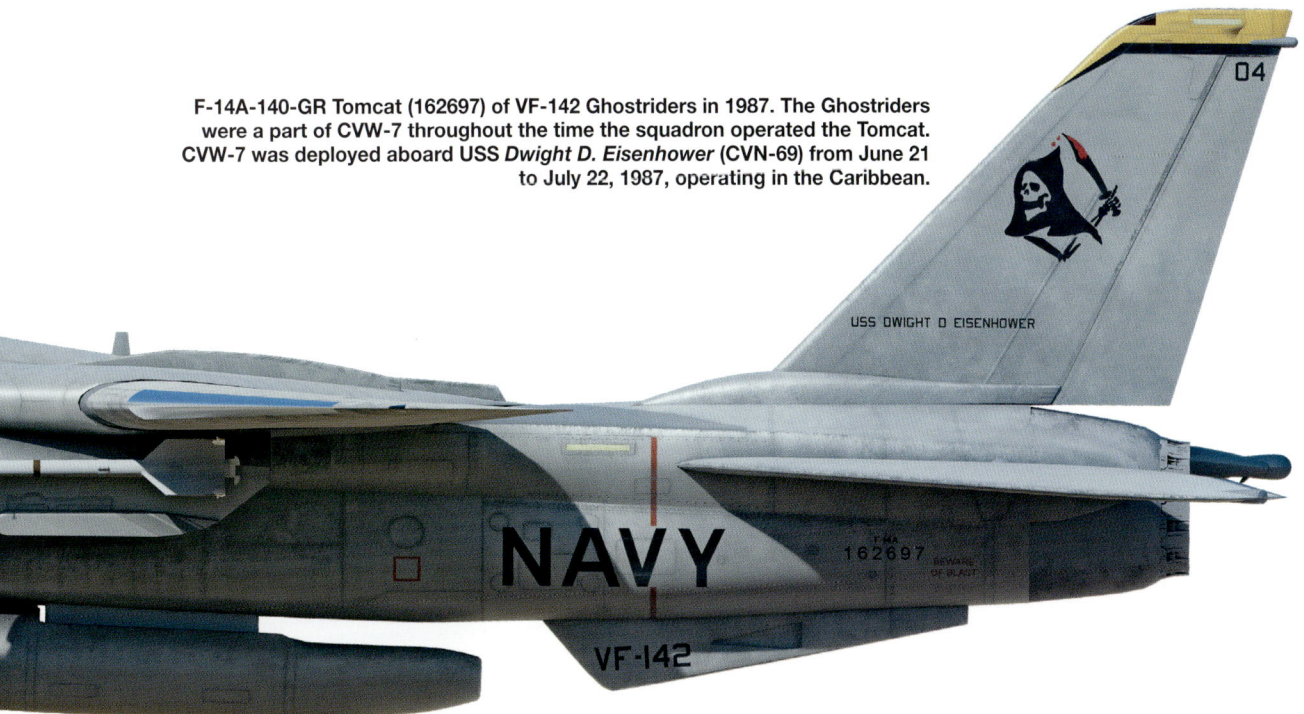

F-14A-140-GR Tomcat (162697) of VF-142 Ghostriders in 1987. The Ghostriders were a part of CVW-7 throughout the time the squadron operated the Tomcat. CVW-7 was deployed aboard USS *Dwight D. Eisenhower* (CVN-69) from June 21 to July 22, 1987, operating in the Caribbean.

A rare shot of a F-14A-60-GR Tomcat (158617) of PMTC on October 27, 1985, carrying an AIM-120 AMRAAM missile. Successful tests were done by the PMTC to shoot the AIM-120 from a Tomcat, but as a Tomcat RIO put it: "We have a Phoenix missile, why would we want a Diet-Phoenix missile?" (Paul Minert Collection)

A F-14A-130-GR Tomcat (161867) of PMTC on display in October 1993, carrying an AIM-54C Phoenix missile. (Paul Minert Collection)

aboard USS *Constellation* (CV-64) after launching from NAS Pt Mugu on June 30, 1984. As part of the AIM-54C OPEVAL, operational suitability and operational effectiveness had to be determined during operational testing (OT) and that included getting a statistically significant number of 'captive carry – cats and traps' aboard a carrier. To accomplish this, over a period of two years, Tomcats with multiple loadouts of AIM-54C Missiles got exposed to the carrier environment before they were shot in various scenarios to prove that they would still reliably perform after being exposed to the stresses involved in carrier operations.

The Navy had learned the hard way over Vietnam that the demanding carrier environment exacts a heavy toll on aircraft and missile reliability. The Ault Report revealed many deficiencies with missile reliability and aircrew training resulting in the creation of TOPGUN and more attention being paid to missile reliability and manufacture.

So, the question of 'why' gets asked regarding a loadout of six Phoenix missiles, due to urban legend that it is not practical off the boat due to fuel remaining at Max Trap. The main reason we did it was, during operational testing you want to verify that every condition which could be experienced during normal operations is checked; to verify that it indeed does work or if any special restrictions or operational factors need to be considered. This information then makes it into the NATOPS and Tactical Manual. To verify it, an OT Pilot 'flies it' rather than verifying through analysis only.

Since the technical evaluation (TECHEVAL) is considered the engineering verification to specification, the operation evaluation (OPEVAL) considers fleet operational tactics for effectiveness and suitability – the criteria

THE BIG STICK

F-14A-90-GR Tomcat (159863) of VF-301 Devil's Disciples in 1994. CVWR-30's days of operating the Tomcat were numbered in 1994, but VF-301 still participated in an exercise where live missiles were fired at drone targets. Three AIM-54 missiles were launched from VF-301 jets. The squadron was disestablished on December 31, 1994.

F-14A-85-GR Tomcat (159626) of VF-213 Black Lions in 1995. This colourful CAG bird of VF-213 operated off the deck of USS *Abraham Lincoln* (CVN-72) from April 11 to October 9, 1995. Curiously the squadron's modex numbers were actually in the 1xx range (notice the single tail on the Lion), but the CAG bird was given the 213 modex (for obvious reasons). This aircraft is today on display at NAS Fallon, NV.

F-14A-140-GR Tomcat (162709) of VF-201 Hunters firing an AIM-54. (US Navy via Craig Kaston)

HALF CENTURY, BABY! FIFTY YEARS OF THE GRUMMAN F-14 TOMCAT

A F-14B-120-GR Tomcat (151435) of VF-103 Jolly Rogers fires an AIM-54C over the Mediterranean on September 24, 2002. (US Navy)

for success is often not the same. Normally this means that in TECHEVAL, many times, engineering analysis is used after test flights verify specific test points in a matrix of capabilities to be proven. OPEVAL will typically concentrate on more 'edge of the envelope' tests to verify many of the test points that were analysed but not flown.

I had flown multiple cross-country flights accumulating over 20 hours of flight time with the six Phoenix/two Sidewinder loadout, and to prepare for this CV landing, a regular bounce workup with various loadouts including 6+2 missile loadouts was accomplished and handling qualities at the heavy loads were explored. Particular attention was paid to 'in-close wave off' and potential 'bolter' technique.

It was decided that a Case III straight in approach to the trap with enough fuel to return to Pt Mugu would be used. Knowing that the Tomcat would be 'trick or treat' on the ball, a dedicated A-7 tanking aircraft was available to assist if required, to rendezvous and pass enough fuel for a second try. In addition to the landing, the maximum weight takeoff 'cat shot' was of equal importance. Full afterburner catapults could be a dicey situation if a burner blowout or a stall with the TF30 engines was encountered at maximum weight. Proper technique and early identification and application of the right controls were absolutely required to successfully fly away.

The question of who should fly the flight caused some discussion within the ranks of the pilots and RIOs at VX-4 at the time. The OPEVAL Operational Test Directors (OTDs) wanted a representative fleet crew and not just more experienced operators. Since I (Lt Ed 'Dragon' Riley)

and Lt Bill 'Kato' Nevius were the Co-OTD team conducting the OPEVAL, it was decided to go with an experienced pilot and a RIO with less experience in the F-14. I had over 1,500 hours in the F-14A and over 400 traps (300+ on CV-64). Lt Scott 'Scooter' Lamoreaux was a very experienced RIO in the F-4, but had less than 100 hours in the F-14A and this would be his first trap in the Tomcat.

The operational test crew was aware that landing with six Phoenix was a rare event, however the tactical significance of this flight was potentially a 'real world' requirement (known as the 'Doomsday' loadout). Getting the maximum number of Phoenix missiles airborne as quickly as possible in a Fleet Air Defense (FAD) scenario had been war gamed at WEPTAC and it was determined to be a clear discriminator making a difference against superior numbers of attackers during the Cold War era.

How better to do this than use the maximum loadout capability of the Tomcat loaded with the new AIM-54C that was proving to be effective against air-to-surface missiles at 100,000ft/Mach 4+ as well as low-flying cruise missiles and the attacking aircraft platforms at long range. With the largest warhead of any air-to-air missile and kill radius unmatched, the Tomcat with six Phoenix missiles was in a class by itself.

With all the preparation to make this a safe yet operationally realistic event, in the end it went exactly as planned with a successful trap (OK, three wire)/hot pump/and AB cat shot and return to home base. To answer the question of the viability of carrying six Phoenix around the ship: sure – why not, if the tactical situation dictates?

Ed Riley, Tomcat pilot

TARPS

TARPS

The Tomcat community was busy enough with the Fleet Air Defense mission at the height of the Cold War when the Navy decided to add a tactical reconnaissance capability. This was to be an interim measure pending development of a dedicated F/A-18 variant for use by the Navy and Marine Corps, replacing the RF-8 and RA-5 aboard carriers and RF-4 in Marine Corps service. A Tactical Aerial Reconnaissance Pod System (TARPS) was developed by the Naval Air

It was first flown on BuNo 157984 (Tomcat #5) with the pod mounted on the engine nacelle where the drop tank was normally carried. The pod was ultimately mounted on station 5 (between nacelles and offset to the right). The first production TARPS Tomcat was BuNo 160696. 'Hoot' Gibson had completed Test Pilot School (TPS) and was assigned to conduct the first flights with the TARPS pod.

CERTIFYING TARPS

My dad had been a test pilot and an aeronautical engineer, so I'm sure there was a bunch of hero worship, and he was my hero. I wanted to be an aeronautical engineer, and I wanted to be a test pilot. I actually had a little bit of trouble getting to TPS because the Navy had said, "F-14 Tomcat training is so expensive that once you get into the Tomcat, you can't come out of it." Only they had let one of my squadron-mates go the year before to TPS, and then I guess maybe they made the rule after he went. They said, "We're not going to let anybody get out of the F-14 Tomcat. Once you're in it, that's all you're going to do." I really wanted to go to Test Pilot School.

It was a one-year course, and I've never worked harder in my life than TPS. College was not quite as difficult, even astronaut training wasn't as difficult as Test Pilot School. I did very well at TPS and went to flying test flights in the F-14 Tomcats at NAS Patuxent River; I was assigned a major new project for the Tomcat, and that was the first reconnaissance version of it. I got to do first flight in that and all the structural demonstration, which involves high-G, high Mach number, 6.5gs at one point, 1.65 Mach, rolling turns and things like that. Did all the envelope expansion, structural demonstration to certify the TARPS pod as ready for the fleet.
Capt Bob 'Hoot' Gibson

Sixty-five TARPS Tomcats were planned to allow three TARPS aircraft per TARPS squadron. Unlike the RF-8 and RA-5 which carried no armament (to minimise weight and allow for maximum speed, essential for a photo reconnaissance aircraft to enter a threat zone flying straight and level to capture the desired images and survive), the Tomcat maintained full weapons capability (on the shoulder stations) while carrying the TARPS – allowing it to be self-escorting.

The TARPS pod contained three camera stations carrying a two-position 6in focal length KS-87B frame camera in the forward bay, a 9in KA-99 panoramic camera in the second bay with 1,000ft of film (each frame was up to 9 x 36in) and an AAD-5 digital IR line scanner in the rear bay. A TARPS configured jet had a TARPS CPS control panel in the rear cockpit, allowing the RIO full control of camera operation.

The photo reconnaissance mission was not received well by all of the Tomcat community. They were more interested in ACM or the all-important Fleet Air Defense mission. They almost universally preferred shooting down MiGs (or bombers), or training for that role, to taking pictures. As Capt Monroe 'Hawk' Smith, skipper of the VF-213 Black Lions recalls, his junior officers were resistant to the idea even though he himself had lobbied for VF-213 to be the TARPS squadron in Carrier Air Wing 11. The first TARPS jet arrived in January 1980 fresh from the factory and was assigned MODEX 216.

VF-124 stood up the initial TARPS syllabus at Miramar training both east and west coast squadrons before VF-101 stood up its syllabus in early 1982. Each TARPS squadron received three TARPS configured aircraft, three pods, additional maintainers and intelligence support personnel as well as having four aircrews trained at the RAG.

The first TARPS deployment was with VF-84 on the east coast in 1981, followed by VF-211 on the west coast. It was not long after fleet introduction that TARPS forced a rethinking of employment of Tomcats 'over the beach' and knowingly into threat envelopes. By 1981, it was generally felt that Tomcats should not go 'feet dry' into hostile missile engagement zones due to large size, inadequate countermeasures and missile warning gear that could only detect the SA-2 and SA-3. It did not have the capability to detect and use electronic countermeasures against the SA-6 and other newer surface-to-air missiles.

When the conditions in Lebanon deteriorated, the 6th Fleet Commander began tasking TARPS missions daily to surveil the Bekaa Valley. These missions were flown at supersonic speeds and routinely drew AAA and MANPAD fires in response. In a crash effort, the Naval Air Warfare Center Weapons Division developed an ALQ-167 ECM (Electronic Countermeasures) pod configured to jam the SA-5 and SA-6 SAM radars found in Syria. The 'Bullwinkle' pod was based on the proven DLQ-3 pod and mounted on a forward Phoenix pallet forward of the TARPS pod. Concurrently, an Expanded Chaff Adapter (ECA) was integrated into the adjacent Phoenix pallet providing additional expendables. Although the ALR-67 was planned for incorporation into the F-14A+, an interim solution was provided by modifying commercial Fuzzbuster radar detectors in pairs in the front cockpit adjacent to the pilot's HUD. A simple red light would flash if the aircraft was illuminated by a SAM radar associated with the deadly SA-6.

TARPS had now given the Tomcat its first prolonged combat exposure as they flew predictable daily low level photoreconnaissance missions through the Bekaa Valley. To achieve the required 'spot size' with the KA-99 camera, the Tomcats flew at 3,000ft, which put them at high risk of suffering AAA damage from barrage fire. However, the TARPS Tomcats from three squadrons, VF-143, VF-31 and VF-32, suffered no losses or damage

The first time the TARPS pod was taken on a deployment was when VF-84 deployed three TARPS-capable aircraft on USS Nimitz (CVN-68) from August 1, 1981, to February 12, 1982. Here's AJ-221/161138 and AJ-223/161141 seen in flight over the Mediterranean. (Bob Lawson)

Development Center at Warminster and flown on the A-7 before it was decided that the Tomcat was more suitable to carrying the enormous 2,000lb pod which also had a huge drag count.

The pod was mounted between the engine nacelles offset to the starboard side. Although it could be mounted on any Tomcat, it needed electrical and environmental connections to operate along with the TARPS specific controller installed in the rear cockpit and operated by the RIO.

TARPS

F-14A-110-GR Tomcat (161141) of VF-84 Jolly Rogers in 1981. VF-84 were the first squadron to deploy the TARPS pod. The squadron was part of CVW-8, which was deployed in the Mediterranean aboard USS *Nimitz* (CVN-68) from August 3, 1981, to February 12, 1982. Three aircraft in the squadron were TARPS-capable. The TARPS-capable aircraft had modex numbers in the 22x range. It became common practice for squadrons that deployed TARPS capable aircraft to have the modex numbers in the 12x or 22x range (although not always the case, as seen on some of the following pages, some squadrons had their aircraft modex numbers running continuously, from 100 or 200, and then simply reserved the highest modex numbers for the TARPS birds). This aircraft was struck off on March 9, 1999. Today it is preserved at NAF Atsugi, Japan.

F-14A-110-GR Tomcat (161147) of VF-31 Tomcatters in 1982. VF-31 became the second Atlantic fleet squadron to take the TARPS pod to sea. At the time VF-31 were part of CVW-3, deployed aboard USS *John F. Kennedy* (CV-67). The deployment lasted from January 4 to July 14, 1982, and it took CVW-3 to the Mediterranean. As mentioned elsewhere, it was common practice among squadrons to have the TARPS-capable aircraft fitted with the highest modex numbers. So it was with VF-31 but in this case the TARPS birds were 210 through 214.

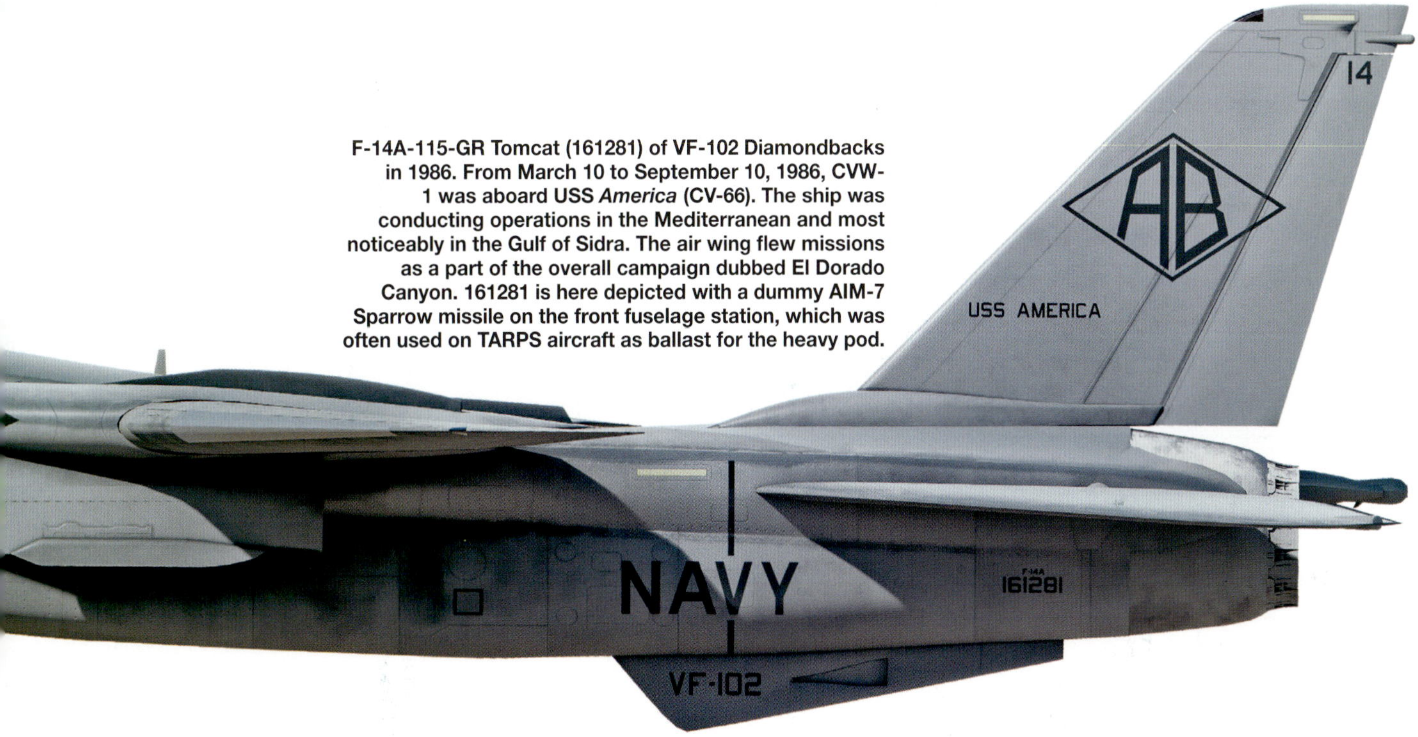

F-14A-115-GR Tomcat (161281) of VF-102 Diamondbacks in 1986. From March 10 to September 10, 1986, CVW-1 was aboard USS *America* (CV-66). The ship was conducting operations in the Mediterranean and most noticeably in the Gulf of Sidra. The air wing flew missions as a part of the overall campaign dubbed El Dorado Canyon. 161281 is here depicted with a dummy AIM-7 Sparrow missile on the front fuselage station, which was often used on TARPS aircraft as ballast for the heavy pod.

TARPS

F-14A-65-GR Tomcat (158620) of VF-202 Superheats in 1988. Both Atlantic fleet reserve squadrons had TARPS-capable aircraft in their inventory at some point. VF-202 received their TARPS birds in 1987 and flew them until the squadron was disestablished on December 31, 1994. The TARPS-capable aircraft were then passed on to VF-201 where they would remain in service till that squadron traded their F-14 Tomcats for F/A-18A+ Hornets in January 1999. The aircraft went on to continue its service with VF-154 in Iraq in the early 2000s. The aircraft crashed in southern Iraq on March 31, 2003, due to mechanical failure. Both aircrew were rescued.

TARPS-capable F-14A-125-GR Tomcat (161621) of VF-154 Black Knights in 2000. In 2000 161621 was the CAG bird of VF-154, assigned to CVW-5. Traditionally CVW-5 has had some very colourful aircraft and this one was no different (despite the rest of the squadron being painted in the standard Tactical Paint Scheme – TPS). Notice that the TARPS mission is indicated just above the BuNo below the horizontal stabilizer. 161621 was no stranger to being adorned with bright colours, having once been assigned to VF-111 as 'Miss Molly'.

HALF CENTURY, BABY! FIFTY YEARS OF THE GRUMMAN F-14 TOMCAT

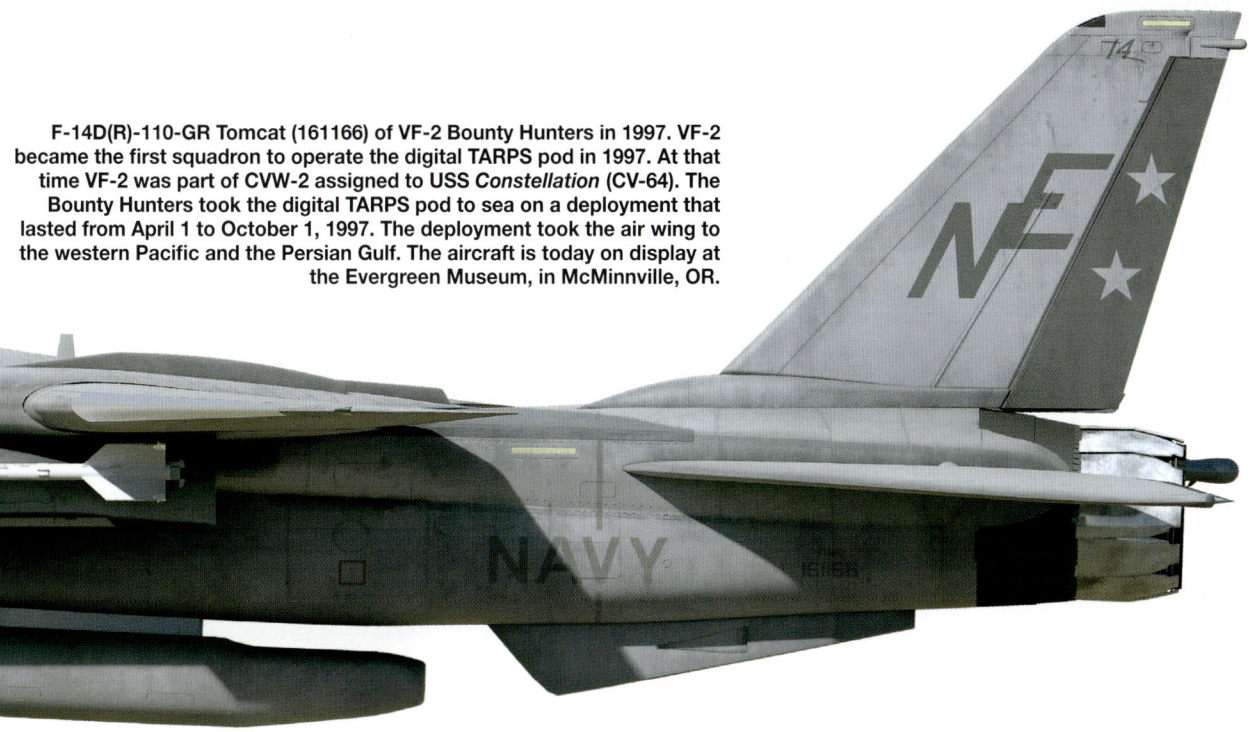

F-14D(R)-110-GR Tomcat (161166) of VF-2 Bounty Hunters in 1997. VF-2 became the first squadron to operate the digital TARPS pod in 1997. At that time VF-2 was part of CVW-2 assigned to USS *Constellation* (CV-64). The Bounty Hunters took the digital TARPS pod to sea on a deployment that lasted from April 1 to October 1, 1997. The deployment took the air wing to the western Pacific and the Persian Gulf. The aircraft is today on display at the Evergreen Museum, in McMinnville, OR.

A TARPS-capable F-14A-110-GR Tomcat (161138) of VF-84 Jolly Rogers seen in flight in late 1981/early 1982. (Bob Lawson)

from hostile fire. VF-143 flew 45 combat TARPS missions off USS *Eisenhower* in the fall of 1983. USS *John F. Kennedy* and *Ike* with VF-31 taking over combat TARPS responsibilities VF-32 aboard USS *Independence* conducted combat TARPS over Grenada before joining *Kennedy* on station, culminating in the Air Wing Strikes on Lebanese positions resulting in the loss of an A-6E Intruder and an A-7E but no loss or damage to the speedy Tomcats.

Rear Admiral Jerry Tuttle, Commander Task Force 60/Battle Force 6th Fleet was in command of the carrier forces arrayed against the Lebanese insurgency and had a vested interest in the results of the daily TARPS missions. He requested better cameras for the Tomcats to allow them to fly at higher altitude and get the same results. NAVAIR procured four KA-93 36in focal length Long Range Optical (LOROP) cameras which arrived at NAS Oceana in early 1984 for deployment with VF-102. NAVAIR also procured KS-153 LOROP cameras as well. The LOROP cameras remained forward deployed in theatre and were cross decked between off and ongoing carriers.

The TARPS mission remained unpopular with some Tomcat aircrews and with maintenance control. Some squadrons kept the pods installed to give experience to aircrews and maintainers; other squadrons installed the pod only for tasked missions. Some squadrons only let Syllabus trained aircrews fly TARPS whereas others broke up the four aircrews and had the trained aircrew train their respective pilot or RIO. Some squadrons established TARPS as a Dept with a lieutenant commander in charge, whereas others put a lieutenant in charge in the Operations Dept. Regardless, TARPS became a meaningful and high visibility mission that proved to be more than an interim solution.

In 1985, a F/A-18(R) was flying at the Strike Test Directorate at NAS Patuxent River with cameras inserted where the M61 Vulcan cannon would normally reside. The design was supposed to allow removal and reinstallation of the gun. The problem that surfaced was the infrared line scanner imagery was inferior to the results of same camera in the TARPS pod. Since TARPS Tomcats and pods were in short supply and relegated to fleet units only, the NAS Oceana NAVAIR rep (NAESU) asked VF-102 if they could fly to Pax River and conduct side by side flights over a resolution target located at nearby Webster Outlying Field.

Lt Cdr Mike 'Mikey' Franklin and Lt Dave 'Hey Joe' Parsons were selected to conduct the flights and headed to Pax River shortly after the request was made. The idea was to fly side by side profiles in formation at various altitudes and then land to swap cameras to determine whether it was the camera or the aircraft at the root of the problem. Turns out it was the aircraft. The TARPS pod has a door that opens to allow the AAD-5 infrared line scanner to have no filters or reflections from glass. The F/A-18(R) utilized a piece of very expensive 'black glass' to provide a smooth aerodynamic surface. The glass was constructed to allow IR imagery to be gathered but was apparently filtering the IR spectrum and causing fuzzy results. After a few prototypes were flown, the F/A-18(R) concept was deferred until a later date.

Meanwhile, the Navy realised that TARPS would have to continue in the photo reconnaissance role indefinitely. In fact, after realising that having only three TARPS configured Tomcats per squadron was problematic in light of actual experience, the requirement was laid down for all F-14D Tomcats to have the internal modifications to carry the TARPS pod.

Additional upgrades were in store for the TARPS pod too, resulting in a digital upgrade to the KS-87B serial camera.

TARPS IN ACTION

Meanwhile, the Air Force and Marine Corps were still operating the RF-4C Phantom as their primary photo reconnaissance platform by the mid-1980s. The Air Force had migrated most of the assets to the Air National Guard and Reserve units but still maintained the Replacement Training Unit (RTU) and active duty units at Bergstrom AFB near Austin, Texas. In 1986, they sponsored a Reconnaissance Air Meet (RAM 86) at Bergstrom – inviting any interested parties to compete; this drew TARPS units from NAS Oceana and NAS Miramar. The last Naval Air Reserve

RF-8 Crusader unit VFP-206, which was nearing its retirement, participated along with the Marine Corps RF-4B unit (also nearing retirement) and the Australians sent a contingent of F-111 fighter-bombers equipped with cameras. The competition focused not only on aircrew performance, but intelligence personnel skills and maintainer aspects as well.

Perhaps because of the recent release of the blockbuster movie Top Gun, featuring the Tomcat, and their recent participation in Operation Eldorado Canyon earlier in 1986, the Tomcats from VF-102 arriving at Bergstrom drew considerable media attention, even making the cover of the Sunday paper in full colour.

The RAM 86 photo reconnaissance missions were all low level and opposed by USAF F-15 Eagle and F-16 Falcon fighters. The mission was not successful if the photo recce bird did not detect the attack and execute a defensive manoeuvre but no dogfighting was allowed. However, the enterprising VF-102 aircrews asked, 'Can we shoot back?' The umpires were shocked but agreed that if the Tomcats did not dogfight, but found themselves with a firing solution, they could declare the intercepting fighter dead. There was a lot a scoffing afterwards until Lt Chuck 'Bug' Hunter bagged an F-15 and then an F-16. Kill markings soon appeared on both VF-102 Tomcats as Lt 'Basic' Bob Wright also scored against the incredulous USAF interceptors. Chuck ultimately 'shot down' the three-star general who commanded the governing Air Force, who was out for sport and did spot Chuck in trail of 'Basic', who he was trying to target.

Interestingly, CAOC planners for Desert Shield initially overlooked the presence of TARPS squadrons aboard USS *Saratoga*, USS *Ranger* and USS *John F. Kennedy* and gave them no tasking except occasional forays to image shipping in the southern part of the Red Sea. TARPS pods were uploaded for the missions and downloaded immediately afterwards. Things changed after the balloon went up and Desert Storm was initiated in mid-January 1991. Planners and strike leads suddenly woke up to fact that their nice satellite imagery was immediately out of date once strike ensued and the plethora of RF-4 assets were suddenly overtasked or needed too much fuel and escorts to go deep into Iraq and cover the target sets.

Then the Israelis exacerbated the situation by pressuring the US to up their game in the search for the elusive Scud missile sites in the central and western desert regions of Iraq. Suddenly, TARPS was the most viable solution to meeting the demand for daily monitoring of suspected Scud operating areas. Turns out the RF-4C Phantom planners had postulated that surveilling the triangular-shaped Scud basket areas would take pairs of RF-4C Phantoms escorted by F-15C fighters, requiring multiple aerial refuellings.

The Battle Force Red Sea CAOC liaison, Lt Cdr Alex Hnarakis, who shuttled back and forth between USS *John F. Kennedy* and CAOC in Saudi Arabia, asked what it would take for TARPS to conduct the mission. Working literally on the back of an envelope, Lt Cdr Dave Parsons calculated that a pair of TARPS Tomcats could cover not only the triangular target set in a single sortie, self-escorting, but could also cover all the demands of the strike leads for pre- and post-strike imagery in a roughly 90 minute flight. Working with the friendly USAF tanker rep Capt Mark Hasara, who was a visitor to the ship, he discerned that a KC-135 would be able to provide a topoff prior to 'fencing in' and even wait for us on our exit points.

Tanker missions were considered support flights garnering only a single point for an Air Medal but Mark told the author that penetrating the border gave them double credit so the tanker crews would be more than happy to oblige us by leaving their orbits and taking us right up to the border where we would detach and accelerate to conduct our mission.

The loss of an F-14A+ in the first week of Desert Storm gave mute testimony that the Tomcat still lacked adequate ECM/DECM capability.

Desert Storm TARPS missions were flown with an ALQ-167 pod and ECA to optimise protection, but the answer was the ALQ-165 Airborne Self Protection Jammer (ASPJ) which was developed for incorporation into the F-14D. However, ASPJ was experiencing protracted development and suffering schedule delays with associated cost overruns. More troublesome was the system's less than optimal performance in testing, with convoluted testing metrics resulting in considerable Congressional distress which ultimately resulted in Congress stopping funding of ASPJ.

An early TARPS-capable F-14A-105-GR Tomcat (160925), parked at NAS Fallon on June 18, 1982. (Don Linn)

An F-14A-65-GR Tomcat (158631) from NATC at Patuxent River, MD, in the early 80s. (Tailhook collection)

SECOND DECADE

Transition to the Tomcat by the remaining Phantom units was well underway by 1980. At NAS Oceana, VF-101 was a fully operational second FRS supporting the east coast Tomcat community. VF-11 Red Rippers and VF-31 Tomcatters transitioned to the Tomcat in 1980 with the remaining four Phantom squadrons shortly thereafter.

LIFE IN THE RED RIPPERS

After completing my first tour flying the F-4J Phantom with Fighter Squadron 33 (VF-33), followed by DIFDEN (non-flying) orders to the US Naval Academy as a company officer, in 1979, I got orders back to the fleet to fly the Phantom again, this time with the Red Rippers of Fighter Squadron 11 (VF-11)! I was ecstatic! Even better, after arriving, I found out that the squadron would be transitioning to the F-14 Tomcat after deployment.

And so, after F-4 refresher training with VF-171 at NAS Oceana, I reported to VF-11 where I made one Mediterranean cruise with the Red Rippers on board

Another experimental camo scheme that was tested in the early 1980s. This F-14A-110-GR Tomcat (161135) of VF-101 Grim Reapers was captured with this unique paint job on May 2, 1981. (Paul Minert Collection)

HALF CENTURY, BABY! FIFTY YEARS OF THE GRUMMAN F-14 TOMCAT

Same Tomcat, 158631, in November 1980. (Paul Minert Collection)

A Fighting Renegade going vertical over the Arabian Sea in 1983. This F-14A-105-GR Tomcat (160889) was captured by Cdr David 'Bio' Baranek. (David Baranek, Tailhook Collection)

the USS *Forrestal* (CV-59) flying the F-4J again! I was welcomed into the Ripper Ready Room and quickly became a Red Ripper!

Our motto was:
Here's to us – The Red Rippers!
A damn bunch of
Gin drinking,
Bologna slinging,
Two-balled,
He-man bastards!

The squadron insignia was a boar's head taken from a gin bottle atop a shield featuring a bard sinister and two balls – hence the reference in the motto.

We had a great time at sea and ashore! One of our favourite drinking songs was The Silver Tongued Devil and I.

IN NEED OF A SUPERHERO

I joined the world famous Red Rippers of VF-11 in December 1980 as an ensign along with a handful of other pilots and RIOs who, like me, had just completed initial F-14 training syllabus at VF-101. We were, in fact, the first Tomcat-qualified aircrew in VF-11, as the existing Red Ripper aircrews were still in the RAG working through their Phantom-to-Tomcat transition.

Our arrival coincided with the acceptance of the squadron's first F-14A aircraft. Though the Tomcat was still a new, state-of-the-art fighter in 1980, these Tomcats were among the initial block aircraft and had already gone through one or more major upgrades to bring them closer to the standards of current production models. These jets were not very reliable, and to make matters worse, the VF-11 maintenance personnel were mostly Phantom-experienced and still learning how to work on the far more complex Tomcat. In short – the squadron missed a lot of scheduled sorties in those early Red Ripper F-14 days.

Since this was my first squadron, I had no baseline for comparison as to what made a good squadron or bad squadron. After a few months, though, I realised that my former RAG classmates from VF-101 were accumulating far more flight time in their new squadrons than I was in VF-11. If one measured VF-11's performance against other Tomcat squadrons of that day, there was only one place where the Red Rippers excelled: we clearly out-stayed and out-spent all other squadrons at the Oceana O'Club… by a very wide margin. The Rippers' reputation was a bit colourful due to our social antics at the club.

One Friday morning, in the spring of 1981, I found myself on the flight schedule for an in-house 1v1. We were told to 'brief and hold' because there were no aircraft ready to fly. This was a common occurrence in those days, and it was becoming more and more clear – even for a new guy like me – that the Red Rippers had a very long way to go.

THE ORIGIN OF RIPPERMAN

After the flight brief, the four of us sat in the ready room shooting the breeze, keeping our fingers crossed that the

SECOND DECADE

F-14A-90-GR Tomcat (160325) of the 72nd TFS based at Shiraz AB in 1980. Over the course of numerous conflicts with Iran's neighboring country Iraq, no fewer than 159 aerial victories were won by Iranian F-14 Tomcats. The kills were made with every kind of missile in the Iranian inventory, including the AIM-54 Phoenix. Notably, on more than one occasion individual AIM-54s damaged or shot down more than one aircraft when they exploded. On one occasion no fewer than three MiG-23s were shot down by a single AIM-54 on January 7, 1981. Throughout the 1980s the IRIAF's Tomcats would be painted in the depicted desert camo scheme. This particular aircraft was likely captured by Iraq forces during the Iran-Iraq war. The fate of the aircraft is unknown.

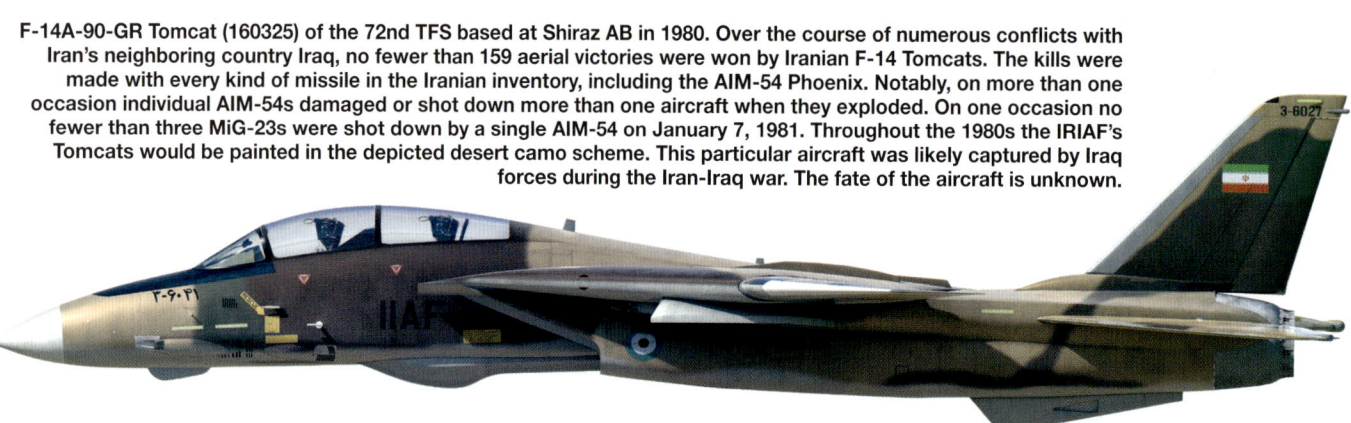

F-14A-95-GR Tomcat (160365) of the Tactical Fighter Base 8 at Mehrabad AB in 1996. During the mid-1990s, the IRIAF Tomcats were painted in a new grey/blue camouflage scheme. The Iranian F-14 Tomcats remain active to this day. Although access to parts is severely restricted, reverse engineering and parts salvage from unairworthy Tomcats keeps a number of the jets flying.

A F-14A-95-GR Tomcat (160384) of VF-84 Jolly Rogers parked at NAS Oceana on May 24, 1982. CVW-8 was deployed aboard USS *Carl Vinson* (CVN-70) on the carrier's maiden deployment that lasted from April 15 to June 7, 1982. (Don Linn)

maintenance folks downstairs would pull off a miracle and produce a couple of jets. I related the tale of my date from the last night when I had seen the new movie Superman. As I described the impressive special effects in the movie, I joked about how neat it would be to fly whenever you wanted – without relying on the VF-11 Maintenance Department. All four of us had fun expanding on this concept, and the idea of Superman eventually morphed into Ripperman. We all laughed – and the conversation moved on to other things… probably about getting to the bar early if the flight was eventually cancelled. Which it was.

Now that I had some time to kill, I used it to pay a visit to the PR shop, home of the Parachute Riggers who take care of the aircrew's flight and survival gear. The PRs had ample quantities of red material on hand, so I cut off a 5ft swath and tied it around my neck, a la Superman… or in this case, Ripperman. Wearing my green flight suit and new red cape, I walked into the squadron's operations office, where several fellow JO's were hanging out, and asked, "Well… what do you think?" Privy to the earlier ready room discussion, one of the JO's said, "It's fine, Mean Jim, but it's no good for protecting your secret identity… we can tell it's you." Still with the scissors in hand, I grabbed the end of the cape and cut off a four-inch wide strip, cut out two eyeholes, and then donned the admittedly very crude mask. "Well?" I asked. "Perfect!" they all said.

Since there wasn't much else to do that afternoon, we spent a few minutes planning Ripperman's first public appearance – in the O'Club, of course. At the last minute, I decided to augment the rudimentary costume by adding flight gloves and an 'R' on the back of the cape (using 1in masking tape… very professional).

RIPPERMAN'S PUBLIC DEBUT

Happy Hour at the Oceana O'Club was its usual busy, 'happening' place. I immediately set the skit in motion by taking a seat at the main bar, next to an unknown (and unsuspecting) young lady. I was in the mild-mannered secret identity mode, having a beer and being my normally quiet, reserved self. A few minutes later, Lt Eric 'Sodbuster' Benson walked in and, as we had briefed, he began talking to the young lady who was sitting next to me. Though Sodbuster is typically a very charming fellow, he purposely set out to annoy the young lady, and was doing a very good job of it. Sodbuster insisted on lighting her cigarette, even though she'd made it very clear she wanted nothing to do with him.

Though the young lady might have liked me to intervene on her behalf, I excused myself from the bar, explaining that I wasn't feeling very well. In the empty dining area of the club, I removed my glasses and pulled the Ripperman costume from my flight suit pockets. With mask, cape and flight gloves on, Ripperman kicked open the double doors to the main bar, effectively creating the commotion and grand entrance that was planned and desired.

The bar became very quiet, and all eyes were on Ripperman, who immediately walked up to the Sodbuster-annoyed maiden. "Is this person bothering you?" Ripperman asked. The young lady didn't really know what to do at this point… probably trying to deduce who was the lesser of these two evils. Having made up her mind, she said, "Well, yes, he is bothering me". Per the script, Ripperman grabbed Sodbuster by the front of his flight suit and, with one hand, lifted him up onto the bar. Actually, Sodbuster jumped onto the bar, but the illusion was fairly well pulled off. Ripperman then pushed Sodbuster over the bar, successfully vanquishing the damsel's unwanted suitor.

A close up shot of F-14A-95-GR Tomcat (160390) as seen on April 9, 1982. The Su-22 kill markings were originally painted on the tail, but were since moved to the fuselage below the canopy. (Paul Minert Collection)

160390 at NAS Oceana on April 28, 1984. The aircraft is still carrying the kill marking on the forward fuselage. (Paul Minert Collection)

This F-14A-85-GR Tomcat (159604) of VF-32 Swordsmen at NAS Oceana on April 30, 1983. (Jim Sullivan)

SECOND DECADE

VF-51 Screaming Eagles had a long tradition of colourful paint schemes; this F-14A-70-GR Tomcat (158983) was seen parked at NAS Miramar in January 1984. Later the same year CVW-15 would embark aboard USS *Carl Vinson* (CVN-70) on a deployment to the Indian Ocean and Westpac. (Paul Minert Collection)

Regrettably, Ripperman adlibbed for a moment, grabbing the young lady's cigarette from her hand and said, "Ma'am you really shouldn't smoke – it's not good for you." Knowing his flight gloves were made of fire-retardant Nomex, Ripperman snuffed the cigarette out on the palm of his hand. It should be noted that Nomex is flame-resistant, not heat-resistant. Superheroes may be super strong, but not necessarily super smart. Ripperman's alter ego sported a burn scar on the palm of his left hand that endured for several weeks.

Showing no visible signs of pain – and anxious to get back on script – Ripperman turned his attention to a group of VF-11 JOs who were, as planned, sitting around a large, round, and very heavy hatch-cover table. One JO held up a beer bottle with his hand covering the label. "What kind of beer am I drinking, Ripperman?" This was an important question – it was the first time Ripperman's name was uttered in public, and therefore the first time everyone in the bar actually knew who this masked marvel really was. Starring intently at the bottle, Ripperman announced, "Budweiser", causing the JO to exclaim, "Holy shit, he's got X-ray vision!"

Disturbed, no doubt, by the profanity, Ripperman took a deep breath and starting exhaling in the direction of the table of Ripper JOs – about 20ft away. On cue, the JO's all fell out of their chairs, pulling the heavy hatch-cover table on top of them. Wow… Ripperman has super breath, too.

Ripperman then exited through the doors from whence he arrived – his premier performance lasting all of about 90 seconds.

Several minutes later, with my glasses back on and Ripperman's cape, gloves, and mask stowed safely away, I returned to my seat. The bar was still abuzz with what had just transpired, Sodbuster had returned, but the young lady had disappeared. She never came back. Sodbuster exclaimed, "Mean Jim, you

As the 1980s progressed, paint schemes increasingly lacked colour. This F-14A-115-GR Tomcat (161296) of VF-1 Wolfpack is indicative of the move toward the TPS, still with the large insignia but all markings in dark grey on a gull grey background. CVW-2 was assigned to USS *Kitty Hawk* (CV-63) for a single deployment that lasted from January 13 to August 1, 1984. This photo is taken in that timeframe. (Tailhook Collection)

HALF CENTURY, BABY! FIFTY YEARS OF THE GRUMMAN F-14 TOMCAT

A F-14A-95-GR Tomcat (160389) of VF-84 Jolly Rogers at NAS Oceana on April 28, 1984. (Jim Sullivan)

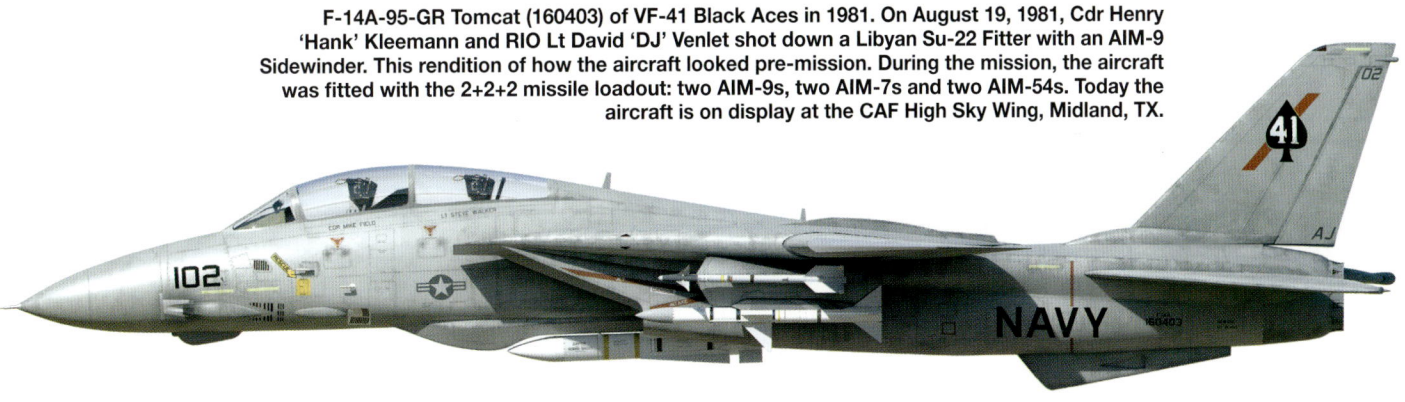

F-14A-95-GR Tomcat (160403) of VF-41 Black Aces in 1981. On August 19, 1981, Cdr Henry 'Hank' Kleemann and RIO Lt David 'DJ' Venlet shot down a Libyan Su-22 Fitter with an AIM-9 Sidewinder. This rendition of how the aircraft looked pre-mission. During the mission, the aircraft was fitted with the 2+2+2 missile loadout: two AIM-9s, two AIM-7s and two AIM-54s. Today the aircraft is on display at the CAF High Sky Wing, Midland, TX.

F-14A-95-GR Tomcat (160390) of VF-41 Black Aces in 1981. This aircraft was crewed by Lt Lawrence 'Music' Muczynski and RIO Lt James 'Amos' Anderson on August 19, 1981. Like Hank and DJ's 160403, this aircraft also shot down an Su-22 Fitter of the Libyan Air Force and also with an AIM-9 Sidewinder. At the time of the mission that day there were no crew names on the canopy rails; both names and the Su-22 silhouette on the tail were added afterwards. VF-41 were at the time a part of CVW-8 operating from the deck of USS *Nimitz*. The deployment lasted from August 3, 1981, to February 12, 1982. The aircraft would crash on October 25, 1994, while attempting to land on USS *Abraham Lincoln* (CVN-72). Pilot Lt Kara Hultgreen was killed – the first female pilot in the US military to die in a crash. RIO Lt Matthew Klemish survived.

SECOND DECADE

This Pukin' Dogs F-14A-120-GR Tomcat (161426) displays markings of time to come. The colours were on the way out and replaced by far more subdued markings. However, this aircraft has retained the high visibility insignia and standard markings. The photo was taken at NAS Oceana on April 28, 1984. (Jim Sullivan)

An F-14A-120-GR Tomcat (161418) of VF-142 Ghostriders on April 28, 1984. Here seen parked at NAS Oceana, this VF-142 Tomcat displays the markings that would remain virtually unchanged for the rest of the squadron's service period. If it ain't broken, don't fix it! (Jim Sullivan)

HALF CENTURY, BABY! FIFTY YEARS OF THE GRUMMAN F-14 TOMCAT

F-14A-85-GR Tomcat (159610) of VF-32 Swordsmen in 1989. On January 4, 1989, Cdr Joe Connelly and RIO Cdr Leo Enwright (flying in AC-207 depicted here) and Lt Hermon Cook and RIO Lt Cdr Steven Collins (flying AC-202, 159437) was scrambled to intercept two Libyan MiG-23s that were heading directly toward USS *John F. Kennedy* (CV-67). Two AIM-7M sparrows were fired, but when they failed to guide the MiG-23s got closer. In the following dogfight, one MiG-23 was shot down with an AIM-7M (by AC-202) and the second was destroyed by AC-207 with an AIM-9. Both Libyan pilots ejected from their stricken aircraft, but were not recovered by Libyan forces. After the mission, a black MiG-23 silhouette was added just above the modex number on both AC-207 and AC-202. 159610 was later upgraded to F-14D standard and is today on display at the National Air and Space Museum, Udvar-Hazy Center, Washington D.C.

The Su-22-killing F-14A-95-GR Tomcat (160403), here seen sporting the modex number 101 in May 1984. The kill marks are gone, but the other markings remain virtually identical to when the incident in the Gulf of Sidra happened in 1981. (Paul Minert Collection)

missed it… Ripperman was here!" While I was acting as if I had no idea what Sodbuster was talking about, Sodbuster added thoughtfully, "Hey wait a minute… you're never around when Ripperman is." Followed by an immediate, "Naaah… that's ridiculous."

EPILOGUE
Though the Ripperman stunt was intended to be a one-time only event, squadron leadership embraced the gimmick and Ripperman became a bonafide collateral duty passed on from generation to generation in the Rippers. Ripperman stories abound, and maybe a half-dozen or so may actually have some shred of truth to them.

The Ripperman saga has a happy ending. Within two years, the Red Rippers had completely turned their fortunes around, winning the Atlantic Fleet Battle E and Safety S. Even Sodbuster and I survived… Sodbuster ended up in command of the VF-41 Black Aces and returned (repeatedly) to the scene of the crime as Commanding Officer, NAS Oceana. I (eventually) grew up to command the VF-103 Jolly Rogers and later became CAG, Carrier Air Wing 11.

Even Ripperman survived. Forty years (and some several dozen JOs) after his first appearance, Ripperman is still serving Naval Aviation and the world famous Red Rippers.
Capt 'Mean' Jim Green

VF-31 was sister squadron to VF-11 during their transition to Tomcats. The Navy transitioned Phantom squadrons through the RAGs in pairs, spreading the aircrews across several classes (typically three). The squadrons would add new members as well during this timeframe. Here is **Scott 'Stewie' Stewart's** recollection:

LIFE IN VF-31
My Tomcat adventure began in the F-14 RAG where aspiring Tomcat 'replacements' (student was not used) cut our teeth on Tomcat legends named Moon, Rogie, Zobes, Bump, Sammy, Hey Joe, and Hoser. It was here that we learned how to fly our country's best fighter jet, a ridiculously powerful $50 million airplane and it was here that we joined an elite group of Naval Aviation warriors whose close camaraderie reminded us that being in a Tomcat squadron was like being in a motorcycle gang – except your mother was proud of you!

The first Tomcat 'motorcycle gang' I joined was the Tomcatters of VF-31. Our MEJO (Marginally Effective Junior Officer) fraternity was a club where 'all for one' and 'one for all' was the order of the day. We were led by Hulk, Market and Wigs. The MEJOs were blessed with superstars like Traps, Fozzie, Lil Mac, Moons, Dirt and Monk. All would go on to command F-14 squadrons, some aircraft carriers with Traps and Fozzie going on from there to flag rank.

We witnessed the birth of major modern day terrorism on the United States, when 241 Marines perished in a terrorist attack on their barracks while they slept on a quiet Sunday morning. From the decks of the JFK, we flew over the 'friendly skies of Beirut' on combat TARPS missions. We stood Alert 15 and five watches in four-hour shifts each night, and by flashlight wrote letters home to our loved ones while listening to a Walkman strapped into the cold, dark, spacious F-14 cockpit.

We launched to intercept Cold War enemies flying aircraft named Badgers and Bears. Our experiences were preserved by George Wilson in Supercarrier. When we returned home, we shot Phoenix missiles off the northern coast of Puerto Rico, earned our coveted TOPGUN patches and frolicked in the Oceana O'Club with Tasha and Ripperman.
Capt Scott 'Stewie' Stewart, USN (ret)

VF-41 and VF-84 were aboard USS *Nimitz* in the North Arabian Sea off the coast of Iran in early 1980, sharing the hangar with eight RH-53D Sea Stallion helicopters allocated for Operation Eagle Claw, the attempt to rescue US hostages held in the Embassy in downtown Tehran. The ambitious mission was led by the nascent Delta Force and Navy Tomcats would be called upon to deal with the Iranian Tomcats should they attempt to interfere.

Although the mission was planned to be executed under cover of darkness, Carrier Air Wing 8 was given targets to attack to cover the raid involving daylight flights. To prevent confusion and allow recognition, the Tomcats were painted with special orange and black recognition stripes. The attempted mission in April 1980 was aborted when several helicopters suffered failures and

SECOND DECADE

Throughout the 1980s two dedicated fighter squadrons per wing was the norm. Above USS *Carl Vinson* (CVN-70) are two F-14A Tomcats of VF-51 (161343) and VF-111 (161243) flying in formation with an E-2C Hawkeye of VAW-114. This photo was taken during a deployment to the Westpac and Indian Ocean that lasted from October 13, 1984, to May 24, 1985. (Tailhook Collection)

F-14A-75-GR Tomcat (159428) of VF-33 Tarsiers in 1984. While the standard paint schemes of fleet squadrons had changed from the colourful markings of the 70s to more subdued paint schemes, the aircraft of the Tarsiers' CO were still painted in a very colourful paint scheme throughout the early 80s. This particular aircraft was nicknamed 'The Batmobile' likely due to the black/yellow colour combination, which was only carried by this jet during a deployment aboard USS *America* (CV-66) that lasted from April 24 to November 14, 1984. The Batmobile didn't get many flight hours however, as it was damaged on June 17, 1984, when the port landing gear collapsed as the aircraft was recovering aboard USS *America*. 159824 was repaired, but only after spending a long time in the lower deck of CV-66, jokingly referred to as the 'Bat Cave'. The aircraft went back into service only to be damaged again on January 4, 2004. After that incident the aircraft was struck off charge.

An F-14A-85-GR Tomcat (159589) of VF-33 Starfighters captured at NAS Oceana on April 28, 1984. (Jim Sullivan)

This F-14A-70-GR Tomcat (158978) of VX-4 Evaluators was seen in this temporary paint scheme in June 1985. (Paul Minert Collection)

SECOND DECADE

An F-14A Tomcat firing an AIM-54 Phoenix. From August to September 1977, IIAF crews were training in AIM-54 loading and firing qual at PMTC prior to delivery of Tomcats and AIM-54s to Iran. (US Navy via Craig Kaston)

Two IRIAF F-14A-95-GR Tomcat (3-6063/160361) in flight over the Iranian Desert in the late 80s. (Paul Minert Collection)

the forces were recalled. Unfortunately, a helicopter collided with a C-130 in poor visibility while taxiing at the Desert One in the Iranian desert. Consequently, no US Tomcats ever tangled with their Iranian opponents.

Although Tomcats saw their first use in an operational theatre during 1975, covering the withdrawal of US personnel from Saigon, no aerial engagements occurred involving the VF-1 and VF-2 Tomcats operating off USS *Enterprise*.

Ironically, the first aerial engagement for the Tomcat and use of the AIM-54 Phoenix occurred over Iran. On September 17, 1980, First Lieutenant Fereydoun 'Ferry' Mazandarani fired an AIM-54 Phoenix at an Iraqi MiG-23 that had penetrated Iranian airspace, downing it in a massive fireball. Tensions were high between the two countries over border issues and Saddam Hussein, ruler of Iraq, had been making aggressive moves on the ground and in the air.

HALF CENTURY, BABY! FIFTY YEARS OF THE GRUMMAN F-14 TOMCAT

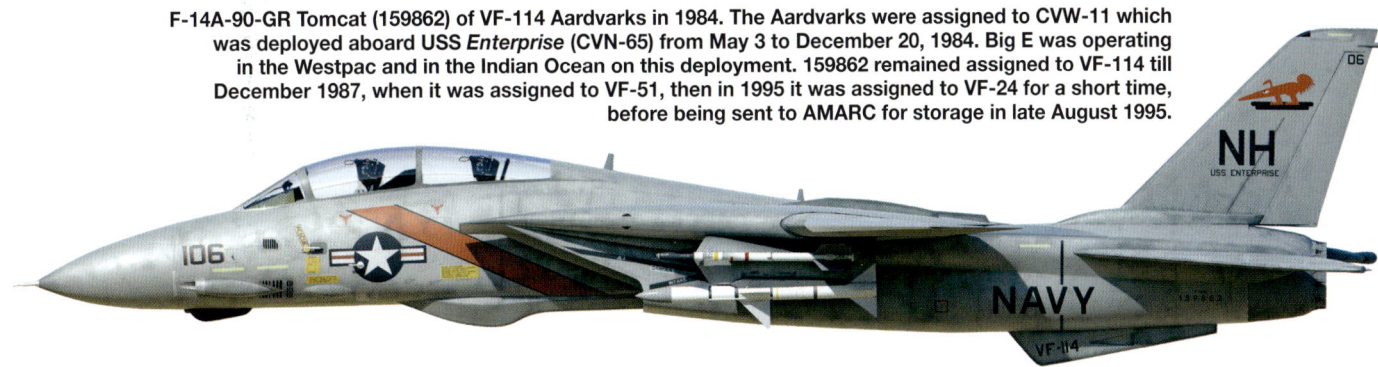

F-14A-90-GR Tomcat (159862) of VF-114 Aardvarks in 1984. The Aardvarks were assigned to CVW-11 which was deployed aboard USS *Enterprise* (CVN-65) from May 3 to December 20, 1984. Big E was operating in the Westpac and in the Indian Ocean on this deployment. 159862 remained assigned to VF-114 till December 1987, when it was assigned to VF-51, then in 1995 it was assigned to VF-24 for a short time, before being sent to AMARC for storage in late August 1995.

Tomcats were used to augment ground radars to cover gaps in coverage in mountainous terrain. The Iranians had drawn first blood in the air and the two countries soon after initiated a protracted eight-year slugfest that ultimately ended in a draw. Tomcats were active from the start and proved themselves again and again, claiming upwards of 160 Iraqi aircraft downed with several pilots achieving ace status. Mazandarani himself claimed 16 victories while flying the Tomcat from 1980 to 1988, downing five in the first three months of the conflict from September to December 1980 using the AIM-54. Due to the embargo imposed by the US, the Iranians had to make do with whatever spares they had on hand and even improvise.

USS *Independence* CV-62 made its last deployment with Phantoms in 1980 with the VF-102 Diamondbacks and VF-33 Starfighters. Upon return in April 1981, they turned in their F-4J Phantoms and entered VF-101 to begin their transition – receiving their first F-14A Tomcats in the fall of 1981. VF-102 received three brand-new Block 110 Tomcats equipped for TARPS that still smelled like new cars. The rest of the Tomcats for both squadrons were Block 100 updates fresh from NARF Norfolk.

In the summer of 1981, the Navy drew first blood for the American Tomcat when two VF-41 Tomcats were fired upon in the Gulf of Sidra by a Libyan Su-22. The Tomcats easily turned the tables on the Fitters, downing both with Sidewinders before withdrawing and returning to USS *Nimitz* (CVN-68). The Gulf of Sidra would continue to be a hot spot throughout the 80s with the Libyan dictator continuing to foment trouble and sabre rattle over his so-called 'Line of Death' that he proclaimed to be his inviolate territory in the Gulf of Sidra. The US Navy contested that claim at behest of the White House and continued to conduct Freedom of Navigation Operations.

IMPOSSIBLE TO EXPLAIN

I spent the summer of '81 as a 'nugget' in the RAG at Oceana and no time in my life has ever compared. Most on the base were still flying F-4s and those of us flying to Tomcat were being instructed by those who had made the first cruises; Snort, Wheatley, Mountain, Magic, etc. The XO was Jay Johnson who would eventually be CNO. During this summer as well as most of my first tour, I never related my pay to flying. I was having a great time and for whatever reason I also got paid.

Joe Dalton and I had rented a place across the street from the beach down on 73rd Street and that summer, along with all our rag buds, lived the fighter pilot's life. After a week of flying we headed to the O'Club on Friday for a happy hour that included strippers and countless rolls of the dice to see who would be buying the round. The club closed at 2am, usually while we were talking to some very bad looking women who claimed it was their first time ever to the Oceana O'Club.

Every Saturday that summer we picked up the party at the beach house the next morning. Without a plan, someone always showed up by noon with a keg and the JOs would start to arrive. Regulars included Dan 'Vegas' Cannan, Jim 'Luca' Anderson, Steve 'Slugo' Vaughn, Dane 'Swede' Swanson, Frank 'Falcon' Logan, Phil 'Toastee' Melfa, Frank 'Ely' Whitney, John 'Guido' Tartaglione, Scott 'Spanky' Francis, along with many, many more. Sunday was for recovering and we kicked it off Monday morning at 101's hangar with some bad coffee so we could do it all again.

I've been away from the Navy for years and now find those days as a fighter pilot are impossible to explain to anyone who has never experienced it. As the Tomcat went into retirement I didn't feel old; I feel fortunate to have been part of something truly special.
Steve 'Wojo' Witkowski, Tomcat pilot

THE DIFFERENCE A 'D' MAKES

I went through the VF-101 RAG with Lt Tony 'Eagle' Reade in 1981 en route to VF-33, which was transitioning from the F-4 Phantom. We were part of the fresh inputs and got crunched in the ramp on our missilex (missile exercise) hop, then hit a jinking bogey with a 40-degree Target Aspect Sparrow launch. RAG students got to shoot a missile back then as a sort of graduation exercise from intercept phase.

I then went to VF-33, and was tagged with a 'no-notice' graded COMPLEX MISSILEX during workups with Mike 'Scotch' Hamele. The Wing Readiness cell tasked us with simultaneous launch from sister squadron VF-102 and us, with Air Wing observers in the lead. The radar crapped out at the rendezvous, came back on the climb out with BIT indicating a waveguide pressure problem. "No problem," I tell Mike, "on the turn-in, set nothing less than 95% throttle and don't worry who has the lead." It was power down, power up, BIT check, radar on at 12nm (observer cleared us with… "lock cleared to arm, cleared to fire"). I took a pulse lock, got a hot trigger light, and shot! Boola Boola!

Reserve squadrons would hang onto their high visibility markings for a little longer than the frontline squadrons. In August 1985 the high visibility colours were singing their swansong, and this F-14A-70-GR Tomcat (158989) was likely among the last of VF-302 to carry their signature yellow chevron. (Paul Minert Collection)

SECOND DECADE

F-14A-125-GR Tomcat (161620) of VF-154 Black Knights in 1984. VF-154 were among the last frontline fighter squadrons to trade their F-4 Phantoms for F-14 Tomcats. The first Tomcats arrived in October 1983 and CVW-14 (which had VF-21 and VF-154 assigned) was deployed aboard USS Constellation (CV-62). The first deployment lasted from February 20 to August 24, 1985, and took VF-154 along with the rest of CVW-14 to the Westpac and the Indian Ocean. 161620 is on display at the Selfridge Military Air Museum, Mt. Clements, MI.

F-14A-90-GR Tomcat (159853) of VX-4 Evaluators in 1984. Stationed at NAS Pt. Mugu, CA, VX-4 had a long history of testing aircraft and ordnance. The squadron had operated virtually every fighter aircraft in the Navy's inventory, and during the time when the squadron operated the F-4 Phantom, Vandy 1 appeared: an all black aircraft sporting the Playboy bunny on the tail. When the squadron received the F-14 Tomcat the tradition was continued. However, the squadron didn't permanently operate an all-black Tomcat, but one of the squadron's aircraft was painted for special occasions, which caused the paint scheme to vary quite substantially. 159853 was painted as depicted here for the retirement ceremony of the F-4 Phantom. The paint was a watercolour and was washed off soon after the ceremony was over. The aircraft was retired on June 1, 1992, and sent to AMARC for storage.

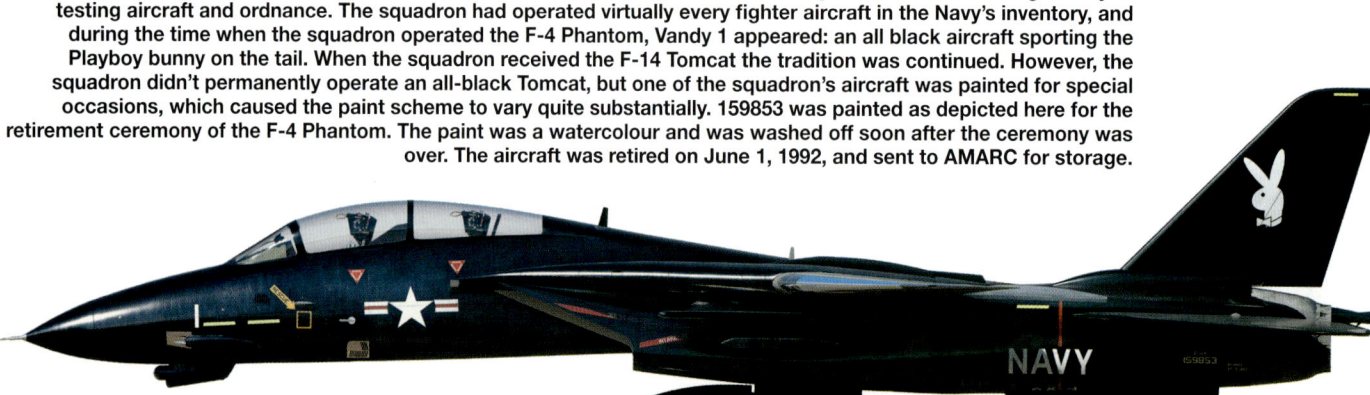

F-14A-75-GR Tomcat (159427) of VF-33 Starfighters in 1986. In retaliation for the Libyan terrorist bombing of a discotheque in Berlin on April 5, 1986, Operation El Dorado Canyon was commenced. F-111Es of the 48th TFW and EF-111s of the 20th TFW flew from bases in the United Kingdom to attack five different targets in Libya. VF-33 were a part of CVW-1 stationed aboard USS America (CV-66) which was in the Gulf of Sidra at the time of the attack. F/A-18 Hornets and A-6 Intruders would attack targets in Libya while VF-33 and VF-102 flew CAP missions to protect the attacking aircraft. The deployment would last from March 10 to September 10, 1986.

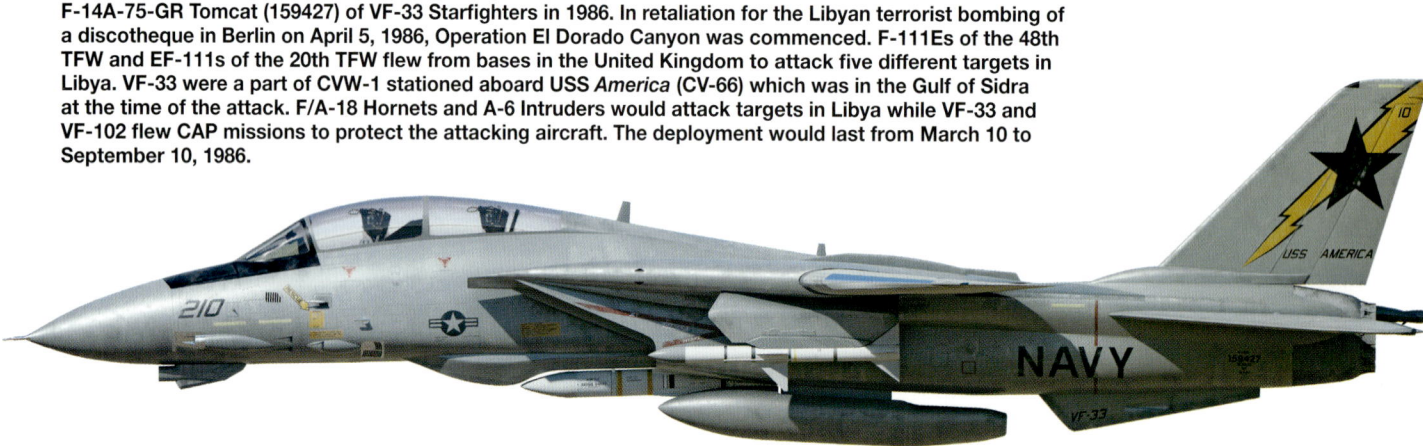

F-14A-135-GR Tomcat (162589) of VF-124 Gunfighters in 1987. VF-124 was the Fleet Replacement Squadron for the Pacific Fleet from August 1972 until it was disestablished on September 30, 1994. Throughout its active duty, the squadron would operate colourful aircraft which were displayed at air shows both domestically and abroad. This was one such aircraft. It would eventually serve with frontline fighter squadrons throughout the 1990s, but return to training duty when it joined VF-101 on December 19, 1995.

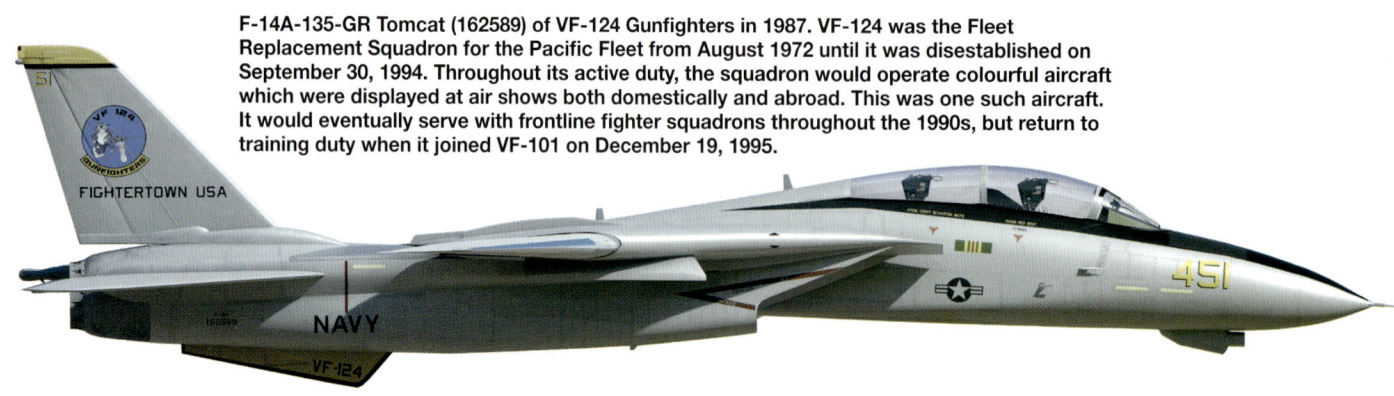

HALF CENTURY, BABY! FIFTY YEARS OF THE GRUMMAN F-14 TOMCAT

F-14A-70-GR Tomcat (158992) of VF-301 Devil's Disciples in 1986. This aircraft of the Pacific Fleet Reserve squadron VF-301 is here seen sporting a full-fledged TPS. In the mid-80s some squadrons carried markings in a lighter shade of grey than the background camouflage colour. The home base of the two fighter squadrons of CVWR-30, was NAS Miramar, CA. This aircraft was sent to AMARC for storage on February 28, 1991.

F-14A-140-GR Tomcat (162711) of VF-202 Superheats in 1987. Neither VF-202 nor its sister squadron VF-201 were shy about showing where they were from. Both squadrons' home base was NAS Dallas, where the HQ of RCVW-20 was located throughout their period of active service. When VF-202 was disestablished on December 31, 1994, their aircraft went on to VF-101 Grim Reapers. This aircraft was struck off charge on September 15, 1997, from VF-101. 162711 was the last F-14A Tomcat produced. All subsequent Tomcats off the production line were either A+/B or D models.

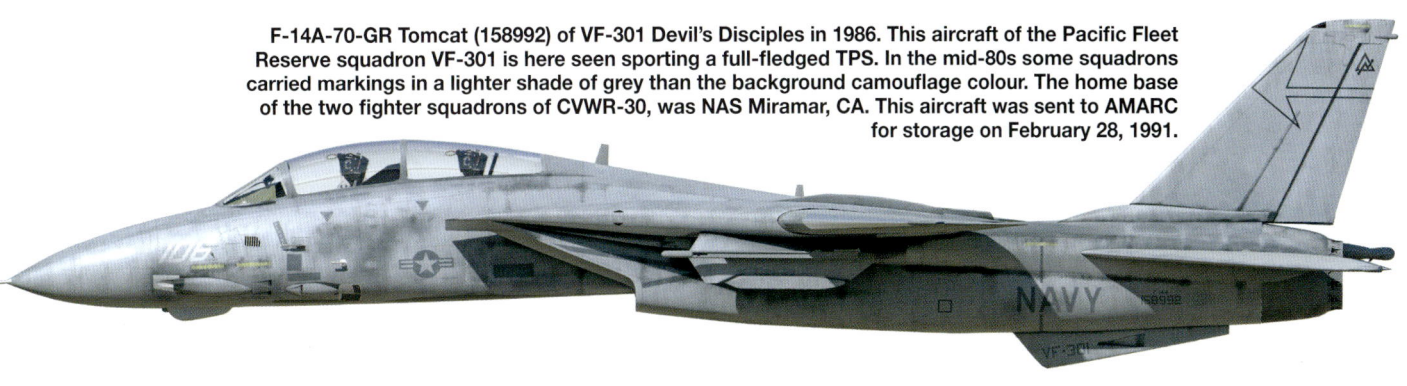

F-14A-125-GR Tomcat (161608) of VF-21 Freelancers in 1987. On August 8, 1987, two aircraft from VF-21 were flying CAP over the Persian Gulf when an Iranian F-4E Phantom appeared, zeroing in on an American P-3 Orion flying a patrol mission. The event took place in the early morning and the area was covered in low clouds. Dust particles from the surrounding deserts rendered radars almost useless, so the F-4 Phantom crew never noticed the two F-14 Tomcats that were passing overhead. Lt Cdr Robert Clements flew the lead F-14 and when the F-4 Phantom failed to turn away from the Orion, Clements fired an AIM-7 missile at it. The missile climbed in front of the Phantom, but didn't detonate. Three more missiles were fired at the Phantom from both Clements' jet and that of his wingman Lt 'Bear' Ferran. Those missiles were registered by the Iranian F-4 Phantom which made a run for it, but turned sharply away from the Orion. The last missile fired by Clements detonated close to the Phantom, but it wasn't till the Iranian crew landed safely that they could see how close they had come to being shot down. Parts of their aircraft's tail were missing and most of it was damaged. The depicted aircraft may not be the one involved in the incident, as it has not been possible to find records showing which specific airframes were involved in the engagement.

F-14A-115-GR Tomcat (161279) of VF-191 Satan's Kittens in 1988. VF-191 was disestablished on March 1, 1978. However, the squadron would briefly reappear on December 1, 1986, as a part of the newly established CVW-10. The intention was to make the squadron operational with the F-14A Tomcat and then upgrade them to the ultimate version of the Tomcat: the F-14D. As it would turn out, only 55 F-14Ds were built (or upgraded), which resulted in VF-11 and VF-31 receiving the F-14D while VF-191 and sister squadron VF-194 were disestablished once more, on September 30, 1988. The aircraft of VF-191 were sent to VF-24 and VF-211.

SECOND DECADE

An F-14A-130-GR Tomcat (158632) of VF-201 Hunters in August 1985. (Paul Minert Collection)

F-14A-70-GR Tomcat (158984) of VF-302 Stallions in August 1985. (Paul Minert Collection)

With the hook down, this F-14A-70-GR Tomcat (158999) of VF-301 Devil's Disciples is preparing to trap aboard an aircraft carrier, as a part of the squadron's carquals. This photo was taken from the backseat of another F-14 by RIO Jan Jacobs (Lt Cdr Jan Jacobs, USNR via Paul Minert Collection)

We did Battle Group workups under legendary Rear Admiral J O Tuttle and flew our butts off. We'd land, hit the head, do maintenance and LSO debriefs with a quick stop at CVIC, head back to the ready room for a sandwich and cup of coffee thanks to SDO having refreshments ready for the crews cycling in and out of jets all day, then the brief for the next launch (contact E-2 on button 2, GO!).

I met my wife thanks to BuNo 159428, the VF-33 'Batmobile', and Eagle's persistence in getting per diem for an aircrew to attend the NAS JAX airshow.

Later, after Test Pilot School and postgraduate study at Monterey, I got to conduct initial flight tests on the F-14D's APG-71 radar in the PMTC A-3, then join VF-11 in their transition to the F-14D. What a difference! In the F-14A, we couldn't keep up with an F/A-18 going downhill for a supersonic AMRAAM shot. In the F-14D, we had to throttle back on the bug out so the mixed section could keep together!

I then went to NAVAIR for a tour in the F-14 Class Desk working for Capt T-Bear Carson (on the shortlist of two of the best bosses I ever had). Working with AIR-4.3 Flight Clearance folks (OK, sometimes going toe-to-toe) to keep the structural issues (read fatigue life) in check. In those days, Lt Cdr Phil 'Rowdy' Yates carried the torch for DFCS and then made it a reality. It was rewarding to see what can happen when OPNAV, AIRLANT/AIRPAC, PMA, and NAVAIR all agree... thus preserving millions in funding to do safety, logistics, and operational enhancements that enabled the F-14 to retire with the dignity she enjoys today. It might have been flying a desk, but our entire team had the mission of working for the fleet.

I wanted TACAIR as an NFO so that I had some role to play in how the airplane was operated, rather than just working a system. My flying experience is a credit to the pilots I flew with and to the generation of pilots and RIOs that blazed that trail.
Mark 'Psycho' Suycott, Tomcat RIO

MEANWHILE, ON THE WEST COAST
My logbook shows "No Further Flights This Command VF-124" on January 22, 1981, after completing the F-14 type course. On January 25, 1981, I flew towards the east coast as a new pilot with VF-114. I had already been approached by my detailer with the opportunity to join VF-114 asap. The squadron was preparing for another pre-deployment work up aboard USS America and needed a pilot. I was that pilot.

The Aardvarks had the reputation as a squadron of high achievers, grooming officers for higher rank and positions of leadership. Orange flight suits, gloss black helmets adorned with Zot (the aardvark character from the B.C. comic strip) and F-14s marked with an orange slash, I was joining the Cold War and would make two deployments with the 'Varks.

In between deployments, I was selected by my squadron to attend the

HALF CENTURY, BABY! FIFTY YEARS OF THE GRUMMAN F-14 TOMCAT

An F-14A-125-GR Tomcat (161609) of VF-21 Freelancers during a training flight for the TOPGUN class in September 1985. VF-21 had recently transitioned to the F-14 Tomcat and it wouldn't take long before the squadron's pilot made use of their training during the 'Tanker War'. (David Baranek)

One of NASA's F-14A-60-GR Tomcats (158613) in August 1986. The aircraft were primarily used for spin recovery research. (Paul Minert collection)

An F-14A Tomcat of VF-33 Starfighters in flight in 1987 just prior to the deployment where CVW-1 took part in Operation El Dorado Canyon. (Bob Lawson)

Navy Fighter Weapons School, TOPGUN, for the intensive five weeks course. I was crewed with Lt John 'Breeze' Martin and BuNo 159862 was one of the jets the squadron made available for our use. The majority of our TOPGUN sorties were flown in this aircraft.

This was the aircraft we flew against 'the types' of the Constant Peg programme. Extensive briefings on the programme and signing incredibly binding documents of secrecy permitted our participation. On March 30, 1982, our Tomcat joined up with a Mig-17 for 1v1 dissimilar air to air combat. After swallowing hard, making a few quips with Breeze on the intercom, it was "Fight's On!". We flew three sorties on this day.

"No Further Flights This Command VF-114" is stamped in my logbook next to the date; April 27, 1983. I had flown my last flight with VF-114, the day the squadron returned to NAS Miramar at the completion of an eight-and-a-half-month deployment aboard USS Enterprise. My faded collection of squadron, 'Centurion' and Tomcat patches are a small reminder of my time flying the F-14, serving my country and flying in defence of freedom and democracy.
Anytime Baby!
Lt Kevin 'Sully' Sullivan

In late 1981, a new instructor reported to VF-101 who would revitalize the community in more ways than one. The Commanding Officer of VF-101, Cdr Dave Frost, had pulled strings to get none other than Lt Cdr Joe 'Hoser' Satrapa assigned to the Grim Reapers from a career ending assignment to VAQ-33 at Key West. Although the given reason was to establish the TARPS Syllabus to support the East Community, Satrapa had another task in mind. Although his experience over Vietnam flying the RA-5C Vigilante certainly qualified him to introduce the TARPS capability and develop a syllabus based on the existing VF-124 syllabus, he also brought his prowess in aerial gunnery with him from his initial days in the fleet flying the F-8 Crusader. With permission of Cdr Frost, Satrapa devoted every spare minute to revamping and energizing the Gunnery Phase including launching each class with a Patton style speech replete with uniform and slides. Word spread throughout the community and his presentations were soon standing room only events. More importantly, the results on the banner were spectacular. RAG students were soon routinely achieving Century Banners (over 100 hits). Satrapa also scrounged gun cameras and film to help students improve their performance on the banner.

Meanwhile, the Soviet threat loomed large as the Cold War continued unabated. The long-anticipated TU-22M Backfire bomber had been unveiled in 1980 during a Warsaw Pact exercise and then showed up in June 1981 off the coast of Norway followed by an appearance in the North Pacific in September and October of 1982 meeting

SECOND DECADE

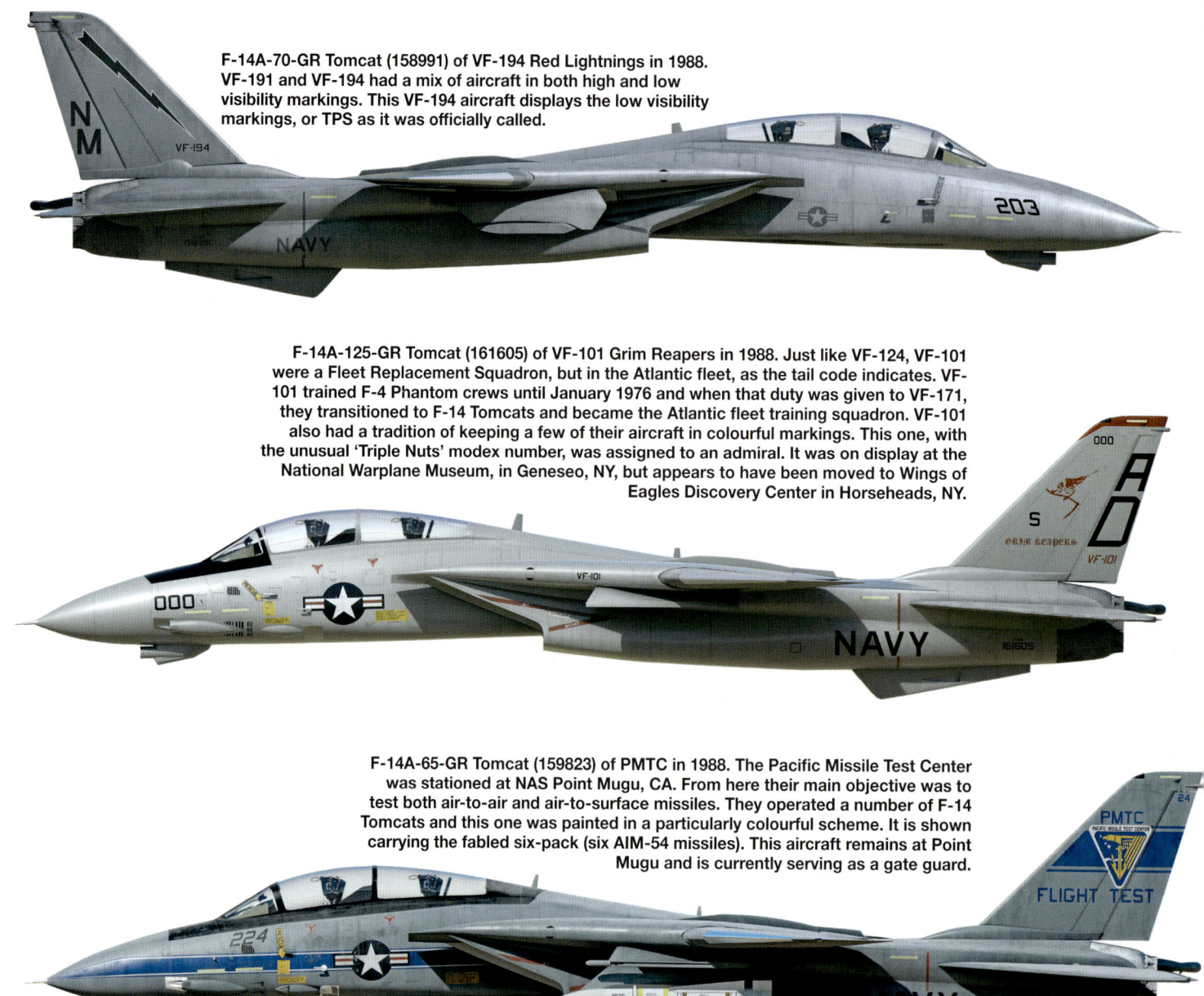

F-14A-70-GR Tomcat (158991) of VF-194 Red Lightnings in 1988. VF-191 and VF-194 had a mix of aircraft in both high and low visibility markings. This VF-194 aircraft displays the low visibility markings, or TPS as it was officially called.

F-14A-125-GR Tomcat (161605) of VF-101 Grim Reapers in 1988. Just like VF-124, VF-101 were a Fleet Replacement Squadron, but in the Atlantic fleet, as the tail code indicates. VF-101 trained F-4 Phantom crews until January 1976 and when that duty was given to VF-171, they transitioned to F-14 Tomcats and became the Atlantic fleet training squadron. VF-101 also had a tradition of keeping a few of their aircraft in colourful markings. This one, with the unusual 'Triple Nuts' modex number, was assigned to an admiral. It was on display at the National Warplane Museum, in Geneseo, NY, but appears to have been moved to Wings of Eagles Discovery Center in Horseheads, NY.

F-14A-65-GR Tomcat (159823) of PMTC in 1988. The Pacific Missile Test Center was stationed at NAS Point Mugu, CA. From here their main objective was to test both air-to-air and air-to-surface missiles. They operated a number of F-14 Tomcats and this one was painted in a particularly colourful scheme. It is shown carrying the fabled six-pack (six AIM-54 missiles). This aircraft remains at Point Mugu and is currently serving as a gate guard.

Tomcats from USS *Enterprise* that rose to intercept them as they hunted for the Carrier Battle Group. The Backfire's supersonic capability presented a significant challenge to Tomcats defending a Carrier Battle Group. The Phoenix was the only counter to the large Backfire raids being anticipated.

Both communities began looking at revising tactics to extend the outer air battle to tackle this threat. The last phase of FRS training was devoted to addressing it. At NAS Oceana Dr Glen Wheless, PhD, a former VF-14 RIO, became the guru of the 2F112 Domed Simulator which replicated the Tomcat's AWG-9 and simulated the latest Soviet attack profiles and ECM capabilities. This was the province of the RIO who ran the tactics from the rear seat giving SA to the pilot and directing the intercept. The concept of Vector Logic was introduced to positioned the Tomcats in a pie-shaped defensive grid with Tomcats and tankers arrayed out to 200 miles to tackle the Soviet regimental-size raids against the carrier.

Soon, even more complex tactics were devised such as Chainsaw and Sawtooth to extend the outer air battle to distances as far as 1,000 miles away from the carrier. The goal was to intercept the Backfires and Tu-16 Badgers well before they could launch their air-to-surface missiles. This is why the Tomcat was integrated with the AIM-54 Phoenix with capability to track 24 targets simultaneously and launch up to six Phoenix at different targets at once.

The Iran-Iraq border skirmishing had escalated into a hot war harkening back to World War I, with back and forth attrition-style battles with trenches and seesaw exchanges of territory. Saddam Hussein thought Iran was in a vulnerable state after the revolution that disposed the Shah. Many of the best Iranian pre-revolution military leaders who did not escape to exile had been cashiered or jailed or executed. The remaining leadership that comprised the Islamic Republic of Iran Air Force (IRIAF) were of unquestioned loyalty to the Ayatollah and Islamic Republic. The Iranian Tomcat community had to be reconstituted after war with Iraq broke it. One of the most talented Tomcat pilots, Major Jalil Zandi, was condemned to ten years in prison and threatened with death due to accusations of disloyalty by his commanding officer, Lt Col Abbas Babei. Babei was notorious for brutal repression and retaliation against anyone suspected of disloyalty to the Islamic Republic. Outbreak of war saved Zandi as none other the Air Force commander demanded his release.

The lessons learned from the rushed and less than successful strike against Hezbollah were profound and far reaching. The Secretary of the Navy, John Lehman, himself a Naval Aviator actively drilling as a reservist with A-6 squadrons at NAS Oceana, was involved in every aspect of examining the events

HALF CENTURY, BABY! FIFTY YEARS OF THE GRUMMAN F-14 TOMCAT

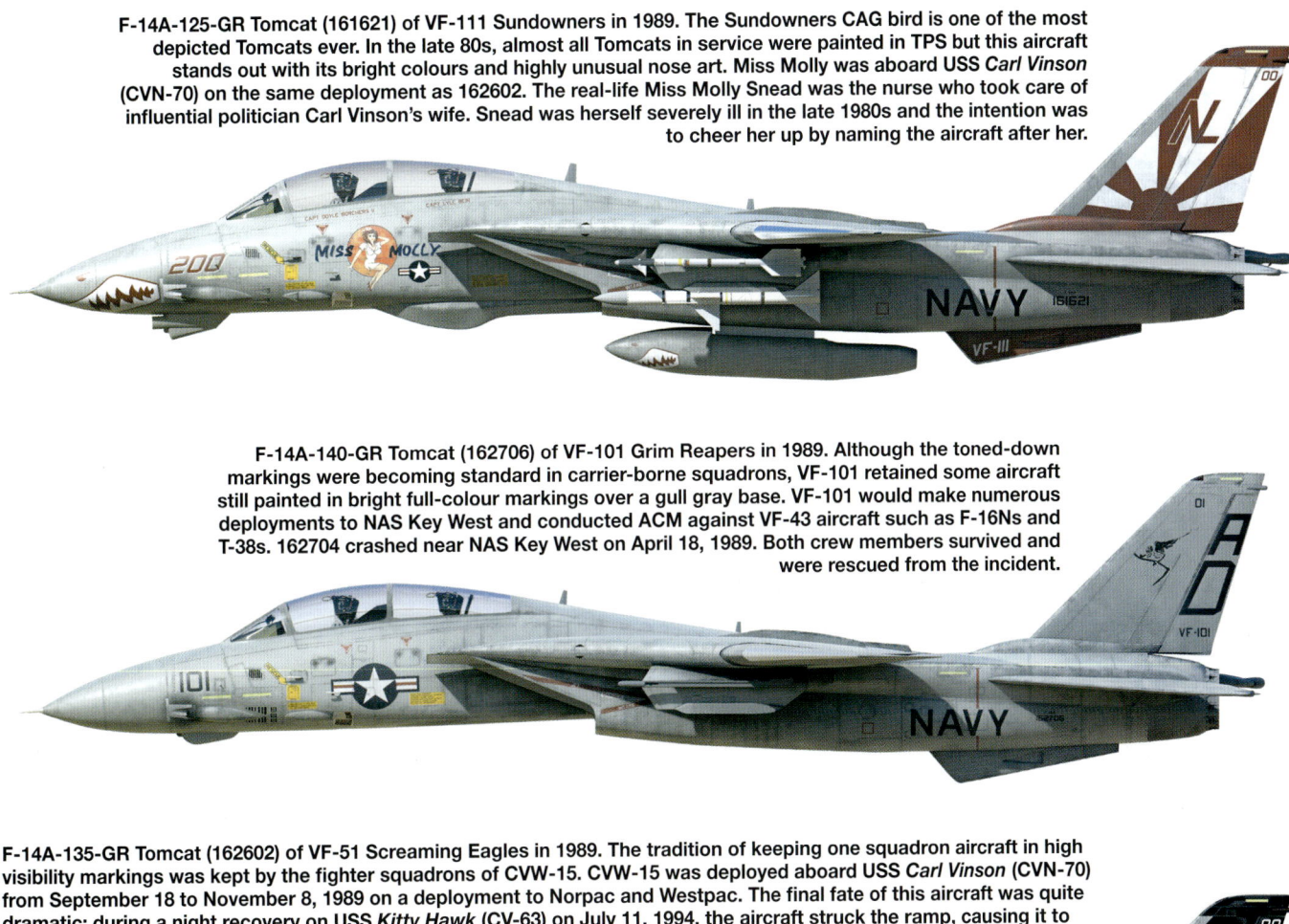

F-14A-125-GR Tomcat (161621) of VF-111 Sundowners in 1989. The Sundowners CAG bird is one of the most depicted Tomcats ever. In the late 80s, almost all Tomcats in service were painted in TPS but this aircraft stands out with its bright colours and highly unusual nose art. Miss Molly was aboard USS *Carl Vinson* (CVN-70) on the same deployment as 162602. The real-life Miss Molly Snead was the nurse who took care of influential politician Carl Vinson's wife. Snead was herself severely ill in the late 1980s and the intention was to cheer her up by naming the aircraft after her.

F-14A-140-GR Tomcat (162706) of VF-101 Grim Reapers in 1989. Although the toned-down markings were becoming standard in carrier-borne squadrons, VF-101 retained some aircraft still painted in bright full-colour markings over a gull gray base. VF-101 would make numerous deployments to NAS Key West and conducted ACM against VF-43 aircraft such as F-16Ns and T-38s. 162704 crashed near NAS Key West on April 18, 1989. Both crew members survived and were rescued from the incident.

F-14A-135-GR Tomcat (162602) of VF-51 Screaming Eagles in 1989. The tradition of keeping one squadron aircraft in high visibility markings was kept by the fighter squadrons of CVW-15. CVW-15 was deployed aboard USS *Carl Vinson* (CVN-70) from September 18 to November 8, 1989 on a deployment to Norpac and Westpac. The final fate of this aircraft was quite dramatic: during a night recovery on USS *Kitty Hawk* (CV-63) on July 11, 1994, the aircraft struck the ramp, causing it to break apart and catch fire. Both crew members ejected successfully but while the RIO landed on the forward part of the ship, the pilot landed in the flames. He was rescued, though not without injury.

that had transpired and instituted immediate changes to command and control in order to address issues that pervaded the chain of command and to address tactical shortcomings in weapons, protective countermeasures and mission planning. The Tomcat Community received attention as part of the overall revamping of Naval Aviation's ability to deal with the Soviet style Integrated Air Defence System (IADS) that was present in various hotspots in which carrier-based strike aircraft would have to operate.

Both Syria and Libya had received the latest technology SAM systems, notably the deadly 2K12 Kub (NATO SA-6 Gainful) that had given the Israelis a nasty surprise in 1973 and was not detected by the Tomcat's dated Vietnam vintage ALR-45/50 Radar Warning Receivers (RWR) or the ALQ-100/126 DECM countermeasures. The solution was to upgrade the ALR-45/50 to the latest ALR-67 being installed in the A-7E Corsair and A-6E Intruder, which allowed them to detect the SA-6 Straight Flush illuminator and guidance radar and employ HARM radar homing missiles against the search/track radars associated with the system. The F-14A(PLUS) was planned to incorporate the ALR-67 but the existing Tomcat F-14A community needed a solution immediately. NAVAIR responded with commercial automotive radar detectors marketed as Fuzzbusters.

A pair of Fuzzbusters were installed on the pilot's glareshield flanking the HUD and modified with a single red light to indicate the presence of the SA-6 search/track radar. Coverage was only for the forward quarter which was deemed the most critical aspect, but it was ready within months of the Lebanon debacle. Special teams were deployed to NAS Oceana to install the Fuzzbuster mounting brackets and power connectors into the deploying squadrons.

Even more worrisome was the export of the Soviet S-200 Angara (NATO SA-5 Gammon) surface-to-air missile (SAM), a strategic SAM developed to protect key cities in the Soviet Union. Designed to take out US strategic bombers such as the supersonic B-58 Hustler as well as the high-flying U-2 reconnaissance aircraft at great distances, it had unprecedented range of almost 200nm. Syria became the first country to receive the SA-5 in 1982 and soon had eight launchers deployed in three locations protecting Homs, Dumayr and Damascus. Due to the system's complexity, specialists from the Soviet Union were on site operating the SAMs much as they had done in Vietnam and Egypt in the 1970s.

The SA-5 launchers situated at Homs could target aircraft flying directly

SECOND DECADE

An F-14A-120-GR Tomcat (161419) of VF-101 Grim Reapers doing carquals on USS *America* (CV-66) on May 16, 1988. (Don Linn)

above the carriers operating in the Eastern Mediterranean in addition to sorties near or over Lebanon. This was a significant challenge to the TARPS Tomcats operating in the Beqaa Valley with no capability to detect or jam the SA-5 Square Pair tracking and guidance radar. NAVAIR turned to the experts in electronic countermeasures at China Lake and Pt Mugu. The answer was reconfiguration of the WRA modules in the existing DLQ-3 pod used for ECM training by VAQ-33 and VAQ-34. These pods were routinely modified to represent the latest in Soviet jamming techniques and have an existing airworthiness pedigree from NAVAIR.

It was a relatively simple matter to develop a variant that could jam the SA-5 Square Pair and/or the SA-6 Straight Flush radars. The modified DLQ-3 variant was designated the ALQ-167 pod and mounted on a Phoenix pallet on the starboard forward station. They were distributed to TARPS squadrons only, along with an innovative modified Phoenix pallet carrying four additional ALE-39 chaff/flare buckets thereby tripling the amount of expendables carried by TARPS Tomcats. The additional buckets were mounted in a module that replaced the LAU-93 Phoenix launch rail and was called the Expanded Chaff Adapter (ECA).

To further help TARPS Tomcats survive the Beqaa Valley gauntlet, NAVAIR procured medium- to high-altitude cameras that had same resolution at 30,000ft as the KA-99 had at 10,000ft. A limited number of KA-93 LOROP (Long Range Optics) cameras were rushed to NAS Oceana. Two were installed in VF-102 TARPS pods just prior to their 1984 deployment and an OPEVAL was underway as the squadron sortied from Norfolk in April. Although expected to utilise the KA-93 LOROP, ECA and ALQ-167 with the Fuzzbusters, the situation in Lebanon cooled considerably and USS *America* passed by the area and entered the Suez Canal for an Indian Ocean deployment.

In 1983, the last remaining Phantom squadrons at Oceana had transitioned to the Tomcat. VF-74 and VF-103 gave up their Phantoms and began their Tomcat legacy.

VF-103 SLUGGERS

I joined the VF-103 Sluggers in July 1983. The squadron had just transitioned from the F-4J to the F-14A and was a mix of F-4 guys new to the Tomcat and experienced Tomcat aircrew. I was a junior lieutenant commander who was a 'retread' (NFO-pilot transition) with over 1,000 hours in the backseat of Phantoms. I'd been to TOPGUN and had been an F-4 RAG instructor. In spite of this experience, it was a double transition for me.

First task of interest was a TRANSLANT (crossing the Atlantic Ocean). The fighter squadrons (VF-103 and VF-74) had each left four aircraft behind when Saratoga (CV-60) had departed Mayport. We launched about 2am on April 11, 1984 and rendezvoused with three KC-135s south of Cape Cod and headed east. It was a long flight (8.9 hours). That's a long time to stay strapped into a Martin-Baker. I'd brought a couple of PB&Js (peanut butter and jelly sandwiches) to munch on. The first one was delicious, but I dropped the second to the cockpit floor. It wasn't found until the next 210 day on the seat. Landed in Rota late afternoon. The only incident of interest on the flight was when one of the Sluggers lost an engine mid-Atlantic at 27k. He started a descent with a wingman. Got the engine restarted on the way down and rejoined. No more excitement that flight.

That cruise lasted until October 10, 1984 and was affectionately called the 'Loveboat Cruise' due to preponderance of port calls. We flew typical ops in the East Med off the coast of Lebanon and FON (Freedom of Navigation) ops in the Gulf of Sidra off of Libya but 'endured' lots of port calls involving skiing in the Italian Alps, a solo trip to Vienna and a real familiarity with the joys of bella Napoli which is a common port visit for carriers in the Med.
Lt Cdr Larry Neal, Tomcat pilot

Terrorism continued to make headlines in 1984 and 1985 with multiple groups trying to grab the spotlight and outdo each other in terms of violence and destruction. In 1985 a faction of the Palestinian Liberation Organization (PLO) called the Palestinian Liberation Front (PLF) was responsible for seizure of the cruise ship *Achille Lauro* as it sat pier side at Alexandria, Egypt. Brandishing AK-47 assault rifles, four terrorists who had been posing as passengers forced the captain to head to sea with 97 passengers as hostages.

While at sea, the terrorists executed an elderly Jewish passenger confined to a wheelchair and dumped his body in the sea after their demands for release of 50 Palestinian prisoners held in Israel were ignored. USS *Saratoga* was deployed to the Med with VF-74 and VF-103 onboard. VF-103 Sluggers were tasked to obtain

TARPS imagery of the *Achille Lauro* for a Special Operations rescue attempt. The White House had authorized SEAL 6 to the area in USAF C-141 Transports. They needed up to date imagery of the cruise ship. The TARPS LOROP camera was used to image the ship from a standoff altitude.

The head of the PLO, Yasser Arafat, interceded before a rescue could be attempted and negotiated release of the hostages at Port Said. The terrorists disappeared. However, intelligence sources revealed that they were at Almaza Air Base near Cairo and planning to leave Egypt with the mastermind of the PLF, Abu Abbas, on an Egyptair 737 and thereby escape to Tunis, a known safe haven for the PLO and headquarters for the PLF faction. Delta Force and SEAL Team 6 were positioned to capture the terrorists if they could be diverted to an airfield where they could be surrounded and forced to surrender. The problem was how to get the airliner to comply. The answer was the F-14 Tomcat.

While the *Achille Lauro* hijackers were plotting their escape, USS *Saratoga* was monitoring the situation while heading to a planned port call in . As night ensued, the *Saratoga* launched Tomcats from VF-74 and VF-103 to set up four BARCAP (Barrier Combat Air Patrol) stations between Egypt and Tunisia to intercept air traffic thought to be Egyptair 2843 (registered as SU-AYH)

Lt Cdr Larry Neal (with Lt Cdr Gantt as RIO) was airborne with a TARPS pod in Clubleaf 214 (BuNo 161134) on the night of October 10, 1985.

Elsewhere, the Cold War was still ongoing with NATO Exercise 85 in full swing. USS *America* was tasked to participate and conduct operations deep inside Vestfjord in Norway thereby protecting it from Soviet Tattletales, submarines and aerial surveillance. Ocean Safari 85 was the largest peacetime Naval exercise in history with an unprecedented 160 warships from ten allied and coalition partners participating.

The exercise began on August 28 with ships departing Norfolk simulating a resupply of Europe and protection of the Sea Lines of Communication. A Surface Action Group (SAG) led by USS *Iowa* (BB-61) broke off and transited the northern GIUK gap transmitting as if it was the *America* Carrier Battle Group to draw Soviet attention from the actual CVBG as it penetrated a cordon of Soviet ships and subs arrayed across the Iceland to Scotland passage. Additional warships were dispatched to the North Sea, the Norwegian Sea, the Baltic Sea and the Straits of Denmark. NATO aircraft particularly USAF and RAF assets willingly fulfilled the role of adversaries.

Bets were laid so the Carrier Battle Group had to contend with snooping Soviet submarines, surface ships and aerial reconnaissance arrayed across the GIUK gap to detect the passage to Norwegian waters. Secretary Lehman planned to join the carrier in the North Sea due to the UK's persistent claims that the 'big carrier' concept was past its prime and not survivable. The Soviet response was not confined to the GIUK gap, a SAG centred around the flagship *Groznyy* (NATO Kynda class) was dispatched to the English Channel to watch for an end around move en route to the Mediterranean.

The *America* Carrier Battle Group cover and deception plan began before the assorted ships left the Hampton Roads Operating Area. The Soviet Union sent the very best they had, the *Lira* CCB-516 (NATO Balzam Class) Intelligence Gathering Ship (AGI) to await departure of the USS *America* and follow her to the publicly announced exercise. Carrier Air Wing 1 flew aboard uneventfully in the sunny afternoon in August flying over the *Lira* as it followed the *America*. Cover and deception tactics had been refined

As night fell, *America* was joined by USS *Eisenhower* which began interweaving and increasing speed before splitting and changing light patterns. The *Lira* was left behind as USS *America* headed eastwards unescorted. USS *Iowa* headed to her assigned passage broadcasting prerecorded emissions as if she was the USS *America*. The Soviet ships and subs awaiting the arrival of USS *America* were hampered by heavy seas and the prowling Tu-95RTs (Bear D) aircraft were stymied by the USS *America* operating in EMCON conditions under a heavy overcast.

Near the end of the decade the first F-14A(PLUS) variants arrived at NAS Oceana.

Two F-14A-135-GR Tomcats (NJ-451/162591 and NJ-453/162593) of VF-124 Gunfighters over the SoCal coastline in 1989. (Tailhook Collection)

The first Bombcat! F-14B-125-GR Tomcat (161608) 'FLIR Cat' of VF-103 Sluggers at NAS Oceana in spring 1995. (Don Linn)

THE BOMBCAT

The Tomcat had an underdeveloped air-to-ground capability inherent in its design thanks to initial interest and participation of the Marine Corps. For decades, this capability lay dormant, and the Tomcat community disdained the notion of dropping bombs. Desert Storm changed that prevailing attitude and consideration of incorporating a range of air-to-ground strike capability began taking shape in the Block 1 Strike Upgrade which was planned to provide a precision EO/IR sensor to enable dropping of precision bombs (i.e. Laser Guided Bombs or LGB) and HARM capability.

The Tomcat faced a significant challenge in maintaining relevancy and incorporating strike capability. The danger of being relegated to the B Team and potentially being stood down altogether loomed large. After 20 years in fleet service, the Tomcat was seemingly doomed. It barely survived the budgetary cuts of 1994 and unless something miraculous occurred before summer of 1995, many felt it would be retired as early as 1997. Then the miracle happened.

The most needed capability was a Forward Looking InfraRed (FLIR) targeting pod that would enable the Tomcat to guide precision weapons. It could carry Laser Guided Bombs (LGB) but not guide them. The USAF LANTIRN Pod had been flown at Pax River by Lt Cdr Alex Hnarakis prior to his becoming XO of VF-103. Capt Dale Snodgrass at Fighter Wing One saw the opportunity to demonstrate the LANTIRN on a fleet aircraft. Martin Marietta was willing to

HALF CENTURY, BABY! FIFTY YEARS OF THE GRUMMAN F-14 TOMCAT

This F-14A-95-GR Tomcat (160394) of VF-41 Black Aces was used in ground-attack testing from April 1994 to April 1995, hence the nickname 'Strikecat'. This aircraft crashed shortly afterwards as it took off from USS *Theodore Roosevelt* (CVN-71) on May 22, 1995. Both crew were rescued. (Paul Minert Collection)

The LANTIRN pod on 161608. (Don Linn)

provide the expertise to provide the software needed on their nickel and arranged for the loan of a USAF pod.

The Program Office was told in no uncertain terms not to support this unsolicited effort by the so-called Horner Mafia then in charge of the purse strings. However, Vice Admiral 'Sweet Pea' Allen, Commander of Naval Air Force Atlantic Fleet was keenly interested in getting the Tomcat the precision capability it needed to replace the A-6E Intruder. Prior to assuming his position, he had been in the Pentagon and presided over the demise of the A-6E Intruder. It was a tough call with him being an A-6E B/N himself.

He gave his blessing in the fall of 1994 for VF-103 to participate in a proof of concept experiment using a LANTIRN pod to guide LGBs. Fairchild, the maker of the Tactical Information Display (TID) and the AWG-15 store management system provided the requisite hardware in the loop (HWIL) to enable Martin Marietta

Close up of the noseart of 161608. (Don Linn).

BOMBCAT

F-14A+-155-GR Tomcat (163411) of VF-24 Fighting Renegades in 1990. The idea of dropping bombs from the F-14 Tomcat had been on the table almost since the aircraft was conceived. Prototype 10 was used as a test platform for dropping dumb bombs, and VF-32 had on several occasions dropped freefall practice bombs. In November 1990 however, two VF-24 Tomcats became the first to drop live bombs during Integrated Air Wing Training at NAS Fallon. The aircraft were painted in experimental schemes and named the 'Thief of Baghdad' (depicted here) and 'Camel Smoker'. Tensions in the Persian Gulf region were rising at the time, which undoubtedly was the reason behind the names. The scheme was likely applied in watercolour paint so it could be easily washed off should it become necessary to deploy on short notice. 163411 would suffer a grim fate as it disintegrated in supersonic flight on March 15, 1993. Both crew were killed.

F-14B-125-GR Tomcat (161608) of VF-103 Sluggers in 1995. The 'FLIR cat' was the LANTIRN testbed, making test flights from the Northrop Grumman test facility from March 1995, and on June 14, 1996 the new F-14 Strike Fighter was unveiled to the public. VF-103 were the first squadron operating the type to deploy aboard an aircraft carrier, when CVW-17 deployed aboard USS Enterprise (CVN-65) from June 28 to December 20, 1996.

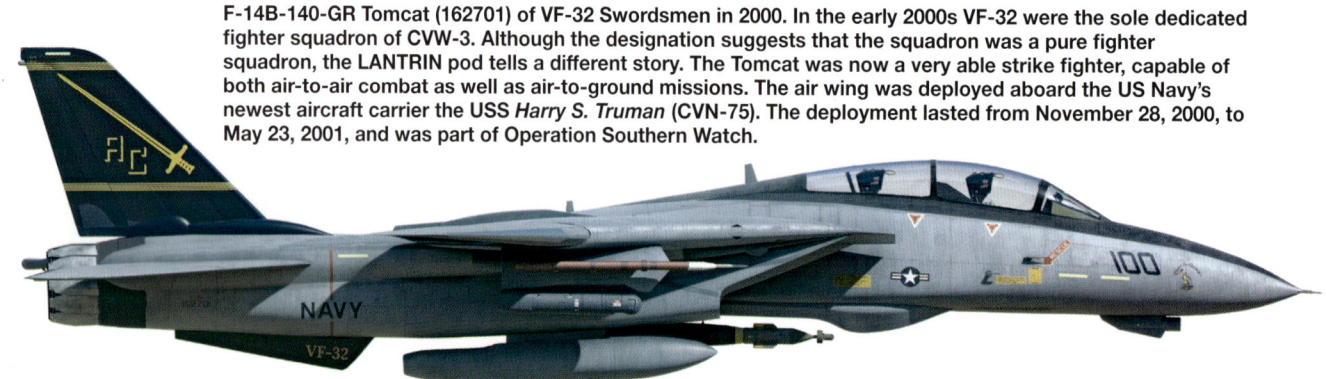

F-14B-140-GR Tomcat (162701) of VF-32 Swordsmen in 2000. In the early 2000s VF-32 were the sole dedicated fighter squadron of CVW-3. Although the designation suggests that the squadron was a pure fighter squadron, the LANTRIN pod tells a different story. The Tomcat was now a very able strike fighter, capable of both air-to-air combat as well as air-to-ground missions. The air wing was deployed aboard the US Navy's newest aircraft carrier the USS Harry S. Truman (CVN-75). The deployment lasted from November 28, 2000, to May 23, 2001, and was part of Operation Southern Watch.

Systems Engineer, Monty Watson to fine tune the software so that the Tomcat could be integrated to drop LGBs without ever being integrated into the AWG-9 software which was a miracle in itself.

By spring of 1995, a VF-103 F-14B Tomcat was configured with a hand control salvaged from the A-12 programme and equipped with a Fairchild chip developed to test F-14D components on a F-14A. Its existence was remembered by Jim Ruliffson of Whitney, Bradley & Brown (WBB) and it enabled the digital LANTIRN pod to be mounted on an analogue aircraft. It was an innovative solution and it solved the critical issue of time.

A traditional integration would have taken several years and been too late to save the Tomcat from obscurity. Then Hnarakis with RIO Lt Cdr Larry Slade flew the Strikecat and dropped numerous LGTR (Laser guided training rounds) at nearby Dare County achieving perfect hits. Next was to go full scale live drops at the Vieques Target Range. There was no question that the rapid innovation experiment was a success and Vice Admiral Allen was briefed. A miracle had occurred and now NAVAIR was energized to start procuring pods and integration kits. Within a year, VF-103 would deploy in summer of 1996 as the first LANTIRN-equipped Tomcat squadron.

Just as importantly, a very quiet effort was underway to give the Tomcat an important mission complementary to LANTIRN. A young Lt Brian Brurod had convinced his skipper in VF-41 to allow him to train with the Marines as a Forward Air Controller (Airborne) of FAC(A). The Marines had pioneered the role of the FAC(A) and had a syllabus at Marine Aviation and Weapons Tactics Squadron – One (MAWTS-1). Brian got himself trained and become the leading advocate and expert in flying FAC(A). Before the decade was out, he would become the CVW-8 expert and conduct the Combat Baptism of the Tomcat in the FAC(A). His skipper, Cdr Joe Aucoin backed him to the hilt as VF-41 used it in their SCAR missions over Kosovo.

LANTIRN CAPER

As a career F-4 Phantom driver, I never had the privilege of flying the Tomcat operationally, but I did get to pick up number 19 (later lost at Pax in a flat spin) at the factory while stationed at Pax River after attending Test Pilot School. Shortly thereafter, I got surprise orders to TOPGUN as CO in April of 1975, which gave me the opportunity and obligation to truly understand the aircraft and its formidable weapons systems through the demanding ground and air syllabus at the 'Gun' School.

Subsequent to a fleet CO tour of an F-4 squadron, I attended the Naval War College and used the TOPGUN background to coauthor a classified study of the Tomcat weapons system vs the Backfire threat – focusing on offensive and defensive ESM/ECM systems. This was during the height of the Cold War War-at-Sea tactical and training renaissance. The text was incorporated into the TOPGUN War-at-Sea training (TopScope) as the primary text, which was very gratifying to me.

After that assignment, I had a tour in the Pentagon as the fighter analyst in OPNAV followed by the plum job as Deputy Program Manager (DPM) for Advanced Development in the F-14 Program Office. This put me basically in charge of the F-14A+ (later redesignated as the B model) and the F-14D and its unique upgraded weapons system. After daily detailed engineering discussions of system capability and architecture with Navy and Grumman engineering staffs, I felt that I knew the jet as well as anyone could without flying it for a living. When I retired in 1986 as a captain with 24 years of service and three years of intimacy with the Tomcat, little did I know that this was to continue in my retired profession as well.

Upon retirement, I became a defence consultant as a founding partner of Whitney, Bradley & Brown, Inc. and continued to work systems integration on the Tomcat in support of the ASW-27C, AWG-15 upgrades and IRST, but the most gratifying and transformational work came in 1994 when the LANTIRN caper began to unfold. When the word came that the Block 1 Strike upgrade funding had been sacrificed in the latest round of cuts, I had already been working with Martin Marietta on integration of their USAF-developed LANTIRN pod onto the Tomcat presuming a 1553 data bus being present as part of the Block 1 upgrade. Without the databus, the pod was incompatible with the jet and a nonstarter. I specifically remember to this day the momentous meeting with Dan Fischoff of Martin Marietta in which he said: "We need to figure out a way to get LANTIRN on the jet without having to incorporate it into the software build!"

That was an epiphany/eureka moment for me – I realised that I knew exactly how to do it and didn't know why I hadn't suggested it before… Fairchild had built a 1553 translator for a classified programme that I had been involved in as DPM and it had all the relevant data needed by the LANTIRN pod for stabilization and pointing accuracy. Dave 'Hey Joe' Parsons had just joined the WBB team with his extensive AIM-9X systems integration experience and after hashing over the integration issues, we jumped in my car and raced up to the Fairchild plant near Germantown to chase down the actual article and see if it was in working condition. It was and we then we proceeded to brief the integration concept to Capt Bob 'Velcro' Riera who had recently taken over the job as PMA-241. After hearing our unorthodox concept, he turned to his lead software engineer, Gary Stuart, and asked if it would work. His reply was "I'm afraid it will…"

That's when we knew we had a winning concept, but there was no money to demonstrate its feasibility. We convinced Martin Marietta to fund their effort, but needed a Tomcat and without funding the program office was helpless to assist until OPNAV's cumbersome budget process could respond, which would be too late.

In the fall of 1994, we turned to COMNAVAIRLANT, Vice Admiral Allen. He had been a staunch advocate for F-14 Precision Strike in his prior tour at OPNAV and was holding his former OPNAV staff cohorts to their promise to make sure the Tomcat was provided with this capability after the decision to retire the A-6 was made. He jumped on the chance to demonstrate the capability and show it to OPNAV despite their reluctance to support it.

As AIRLANT, he could authorize use of one jet for this purpose and he directed his staff to cooperate with us to demonstrate LANTIRN on the Tomcat. By spring of 1995, a VF-103 jet was getting 'shacks' with LGTR and inert LGBs. By any measure, the demo was wildly successful and OPNAV and NAVAIR were able to respond accordingly making it an official programme in record-breaking fashion and fielding the first LANTIRN pods with VF-103 in something like 223 days. We didn't stop there as additional capability was inserted through Tomcat Tactical Targeting (T3) and Fast Tactical Imagery (FTI) followed by JDAM integration; all at relatively low cost and in record time.

The ultimate proof of success was on deployment as the Tomcat quickly became the heavyweight strike capability for the airwing first over Iraq in OSW, then in Bosnia, Kosovo, then in Afghanistan and over Iraq.

I hold to this day in high esteem a letter from the then-Commodore of Fighter Wing, Capt Mark 'Clem' Clemente, who stated I had done more for the F-14 and Tomcat community after I retired then I ever did on active duty.
**Capt Jim 'Cobra' Ruliffson (aka 'Ruff'), USN (ret)
TOPGUN Plankowner and CO, test pilot, CO VF-21, PMA-241 DPM**

'WE NEED TO MAKE THIS HAPPEN'
In the June 5, 1992 edition of Aerospace Daily, the lead article lead with the headline "Navy pilots anxious to apply Gulf War lessons; expand planes roles". In the article, the wish list included "LANTIRN pods for the F-14". Norm Augustine, the CEO of Martin Marietta sent a note to his vice president of business development stating, "We need to make this happen."

The note was sent to me to work. At the time, I was Manager of Advanced Programs for LANTIRN. This started a three-year labour of love which resulted in a sole source procurement of LANTIRN pods for the F-14. LANTIRN had undergone its operational test and evaluation in Desert Storm on the F-15E. During Desert Storm, the Air Force dropped over 90% of the laser guided bombs during the conflict. The A-6 was facing retirement, and the NITE Hawk pod on the F/A-18 lacked long range capability and most did not have laser designators.

We saw the inherent beauty of the F-14 as a precision strike aircraft. It had outstanding range, loiter, and weapons carriage capability. It could easily carry the LANTIRN targeting pod on several stations. Many observers felt that the Navy would never really go forward with the programme since the F-14 was planned for retirement starting in 2003, and that significant funding was going toward F/A-18 improvements. Others felt that even if the Navy programme went forward, they would never put an 'Air Force pod' on their jets.

Because of the importance of the programme, we enlisted assistance from many people within Martin Marietta and outside consultants. We hired Whitney, Bradley & Brown (WBB) of Vienna, Virginia to assist first with a Concept of Operations for the F-14 with LANTIRN, and to help with obtaining support from the various stakeholders within the Navy and OSD. The core team for getting LANTIRN on the F-14 was myself, Monty Watson (a brilliant systems engineer), Jim 'Ruff' Ruliffson (who had been a TOPGUN plankowner, test pilot and later TOPGUN CO as well as PMA-241 lead for the F-14D with intimate knowledge of the F-14 weapons system), and Dave 'Hey Joe' Parsons (a Tomcat RIO fresh from Pentagon Requirements Officer duty as weapons integration expert and knowledge of the budget process) from WBB. Ruff had the inspiration of how to integrate the digital (1553) LANTIRN pod onto to the analogue F-14A/B with no significant modification based on his work on flying F-14D digital components on Pax River F-14A models.

The planned F-14 strike upgrade programme had gone through many different iterations during the three years between concept and contract. First, Grumman attempted to turn the desire for precision strike into new F-14D production, augmented with new computers and software. This programme had a price tag of over $3bn, and was unaffordable within the limited budgets for Naval Aviation. This programme was never initiated, and the Navy decided in early 1994 that targeting pods would not be procured for the Tomcat. They came up with two 'low cost' alternatives that would cost about $300m – one was the integration of JDAM only, and the other was a radar upgrade called 'two box mod' that was intended to provide a modest SAR capability for air to ground targeting. Both would take years to go through development and lengthy developmental flight testing. We needed a solution that was much quicker or risk losing the $300m remaining for Tomcat upgrades.

We went on the offensive throughout 1994 to show that neither of these

BOMBCAT

An F-14B Tomcat of VF-103 Jolly Rogers equipped with a LANTIRN pod is here seen dropping a GBU-24 bunker buster bomb in late 1996. This was the first time an F-14 Tomcat had dropped the GBU-24. (US Navy via Craig Kaston)

upgrades could compare to the true precision strike capability of the LANTIRN targeting pod. These points were effectively made by operations analyses and CONOPS briefings, but we still had to make the system affordable and short cut the developmental flight testing.

Thanks to Ruff's prior PMA-241 work, we made the connection with Fairchild, who had produced a small number of systems for the F-14B which translated the analogue signals into MIL-STD-1553B format. We enlisted Fairchild to produce what we originally called the Precision Strike Processor. This box fit in the port console of the F-14 RIO station, and included a hand controller left over from the A-12 parts bin. We got permission from the Air Force to borrow two LANTIRN targeting pods, and came up with a plan to incorporate weapon delivery software into the LANTIRN pods. We obtained internal funding to modify the LANTIRN pod software, and incorporate an INS/GPS capability (which obviated the need for boresight kit development) to wrap up the precision strike solution. OPNAV and NAVAIR stonewalled the proposal and told PMA-241 not to support us. So, on November 8, 1994, we briefed Vice Admiral Allen – COMNAVAIRLANT on our concept to obtain permission to use a fleet F-14B Tomcat for a proof of concept demonstration. As a result of the meeting, he gave us the green light to proceed, and within six months we had a fully integrated precision strike solution on the aircraft.

We were fully supported by the Fighter Wing Commodore, Capt Dale 'Snort' Snodgrass, who assigned former Developmental and Operational Test (DT/OT) to support us in crafting out a series of flights to demonstrate the concept. Lt Cdr Dana 'Devo' Dervay was the Fighter Wing Coordinator and a flight crew of Cdr Alex 'Yogi' Hnarakis (XO VF-103) and Lt Cdr Larry 'Rat' Slade from VF-103 were instrumental in shaping the initial flights so no formal DT/OT would be required if the proof of concept worked.

Rat Slade and Hey Joe Parsons worked with Fairchild to determine what displays would be incorporated into the Tactical Information Display (TID) using their components resident at the Fairchild Germantown facility. Fairchild produced the displays and importantly, the AWG-15 weapons control panel so shipping a LANTIRN pod to their facility enabled us to connect all the components including the hand controller obtained from the defunct A-12 programme. Our Air Force liaison from Air Combat Command (ACC), a F-15E Strike Eagle WSO (Maj 'Doogie' Halvorsen) helped us determine what controls were necessary leveraging their experience.

By March 1995, the pod and hand controller were installed in a VF-103 F-14B Tomcat named the FLIRCAT. VF-103 then performed several laser guided training round (LGTR), and inert and live LGB deliveries with the modified F-14 at nearby Dare County 'shacking' the target repeatedly. In fact, confidence was so high that Snort, who flew on some of the flights, directed that the FLIRCAT conduct live LGB tests at Vieques, PR. Those drops were impressive and we knew the concept was workable. We worked with the Navy to produce a videotape of the results, and we and the Navy started obtaining support from the combatant commanders and fleet commanders around the world with Snort flying to the Middle East to personally brief the component commanders. The race against the clock to beat the next budget cycle was intense but Vice Admiral Allen advocated for immediate procurement and deployment of the F-14 LANTIRN. Now being called the Bombcat. PMA-241 was now told to support the effort and Capt Bob 'Velcro' Riera put his best team on getting the contract in place to begin procuring LANTIRN pods and controllers.

In June 1995, a Commerce Business Daily announcement came out stating that a contract would be awarded to Martin Marietta to install LANTIRN on the F-14. On the cover of the June 30, 1995 edition, I wrote a note saying, "We made this happen", and sent it to Norm Augustine. This will always be the most important accomplishment of my career, because of the positive impact that the LANTIRN capability had on the F-14 community and Naval Aviation. Notably, VF-103 was about to deploy and took the first LANTRIN pods to sea – validating their effectiveness in combat over Iraq during Operation Southern Watch (OSW).
Dan Fischoff aka 'Micro Shark'

LANTIRN

Whenever I am approached to discuss the F-14 LANTIRN programme, I often forget to mention the personal and professional commitment needed for success. The brief narrative below could not possibly communicate the extent that at least 50 individuals put into establishing the credibility of the LANTIRN weapon system for the F-14. Within the span of six months, these individuals put their lives on hold, their careers in jeopardy, and established a can-do team atmosphere rarely duplicated in a lifetime. I am filled with pride having worked with these folks and to say that I had a part in bringing a tremendous weapons capability added to the Tomcat.

As an engineer, I'm sure my recollection of this effort is technically biased. I offer this brief narrative to help the warfighters appreciate the set of technical challenges (not to mention miracles) that occurred in order to bring this capability to bear. The single word I have often used to describe the effort is 'crusade'. We were challenged to do more than was thought could be done in less time than could be imagined. In retrospect, the effort exemplifies the US naval aviation spirit – without which, I am sure we would have failed. Daily, I reminded myself and the team that this capability would save lives and that the guys (and gals) going into harm's way deserved the very best capability we could provide.

Here's my recollection of how the challenge was presented to me...

"Let's install LANTIRN on three versions of the Tomcat." Sounds great! We need it to feel like it's integrated into the avionics. Sure, why wouldn't you? Oh, by the way, two of the aircraft configurations (A and B) don't have digital data bus and the one that does (D) – we really can't afford to touch the aircraft software. Ouch! And we'll need to flight demonstrate the capability in a couple of months. Yeah, right! And, when we are successful, the fleet will need to be outfitted quickly (less than a year) so that they can show the Hornets, Strike Eagles, and Vipers how precision strike is supposed to be done! Holy shit! So began the crusade.

A quick assessment of where the F-16/F-15E LANTIRN capability was and needed to become for the F-14 found several shortfalls. The FLIR system was great but needed to grow to include many functions that are typically part of the aircraft avionics integrated system. For instance, the INS on the Tomcat was not accurate enough to support precision strike accuracy requirements nor was GPS fully available. GPS alone doesn't support good attitude reference (needed for pod pointing). We quickly concluded an EGI configuration was needed (along with GPS antenna provisions). Without aircraft software changes, it became necessary to add the LGB ballistic computations into the LANTIRN software suite.

Finally, the current aircrew controls and displays presented far too much a challenge to useful pod command/control without frustrating the AWG-9/-15 functions. Therefore, we needed to add a LANTIRN Control Panel (LCP) to the configuration mix. Now, how to display the great LANTIRN imagery? The PTID was close to being installed operationally, so we had the answer for the RIO. Displaying the imagery for the pilot was arguable at first, but the weapon delivery functions require the front-seater to fly-to align the bomb to the desired along-track heading and press the pickle button. So we decided we would have to add 'fly-to' symbology to the pod video and plumb the video into the existing front seat display. The remaining challenge was to find a way to install all of this new equipment and get the aircraft wired to support the new equipment. With the help of JD White, we peered through mountains of NADEP drawings and defined a wiring installation approach.

In September 1994, we met with industry and defined our team. Fairchild Defense and Litton Guidance and Control participated by providing prototypes of the LCP and the EGI.

In October 1994, we briefed the concept approach to the USN (Vice Admiral Allen COMNAVAIRLANT) and were encouraged to refine the details and present the demonstration plan within the next month. The go/no-go decision was made in mid-November. The demonstration timeline was established for March/April timeframe. COMFITWINGLANT (Capt Dale Snodgrass) established the stretch objective of dropping LGBs during a workup at Roosevelt Roads, Puerto Rico at the end of April 2005. That meant that the LMC, LG&C, and Fairchild teams had a little over three months to design and fabricate the prototype hardware and generate all of the new software changes to support the demonstration.

In Feb 2005, we began one week of system integration at the Fairchild facility while the demo aircraft (VF-103 MODEX 214) wiring was being modified to receive the LANTIRN system components. We began aircraft install and checkout toward the end of February, with first flight testing toward the second week of February. After a couple weeks of flight testing, we began workups to drop the LGTRs – the first self-designated weapons on the F-14. By the early April timeframe, inert LGBs were being self-designated by the Tomcat. Now for the real-thing – live bombs. We deployed to Rosie Roads and dropped GBU-16s on the Vieques range.

Seeing that tank target disappear in a ball of fire was proof that the Tomcat was ready for lethal night eyes!
Monty 'Python' Watson, Lockheed Martin engineer

THE DEMO

In December 1994, I joined VF-103 as XO for CO, Cdr Steve 'Snotty' Schlientz. Among the first things he asked was, "Yogi, I have something I need you to do." "Sure Skipper, I'm your XO. What do you need?" Snotty said, 'AIRLANT, Vice Admiral Allen has arranged for and secured NAVAIR approval for a demonstration of the Martin Marietta LANTIRN Targeting FLIR pod on a Tomcat. Martin Marietta is doing this on their dime, outside the Navy's normal acquisition process but they do not have an airplane or crew. In coordination with FIGHTERWING, AIRLANT has asked VF-103 to provide the airplane, crew and fuel for some flying to work with the Martin Marietta engineers on this "science project".

Lt Larry 'Rat' Slade, one of our super Lt RIO's with VX-4 Operational Test experience has been working a couple months on this and there are a few more months of planning and aircraft modifications before first flight. I

The LANTIRN pod is seen being carried by a F-14A-140-GR Tomcat (162696) of VF-211 Fighting Checkmates on September 21, 2000. The squadron had recently returned after a deployment aboard USS *John C. Stennis* (CVN-74) as a part of Operation Southern Watch. The deployment lasted from January 7 to July 3, 2000. (Paul Minert Collection)

specifically want you as the pilot because of your developmental test experience from your Patuxent River tour in the mid-80s. "Sounds great Snotty, I'll get with Rat and start ramping up." Snotty said, "I chose you and Rat because if this works, I don't want the acquisition system to claim that 'fleet guys can't test' and then do years of testing including duplication of what you guys do in this demonstration. I figure you guys will apply the planning, methodology, logical buildup and risk mitigation you learned in the test world."

We were told not too long afterwards that somewhere higher up it was determined we were not allowed to call our well thought out written plan a test plan, nor the flights test flights. We could care less, pressed ahead and called it a demo plan and demo flights (looks like a duck, walks like a duck… whatever). Snotty was a visionary and clairvoyant!

After a few months of hard work by VF-103, led primarily by Rat, and a very small Martin Marietta team led by Monty Watson, we started flying BuNo 161608 in March 1995. LANTIRN pod modifications from standard USAF LANTIRN pods included addition of a GPS/INS for cueing of the FLIR 'soda straw' since the F-14A/B/D air-to-ground radar was not good enough to use for cueing nor was the F-14 INS since it drifted too much and was not GPS aided in those days. Also added were ballistics for GBU-16 1,000lb laser-guided bombs and laser-guided training rounds (LGTRs) as well as display signals paths to go to the F-14 RIO's PTID (which had to be used instead of the then-standard fishbowl TID) and the pilot's VDI instead of the TCS display. F-14 aircraft modifications included a dedicated 'hard wire' from the LANTIRN pod to a GPS antenna on the F-14 turtleback and 'hard wire' from the LANTIRN station to the cockpit displays.

There was no integration with the aircraft's weapon system, sensors or stores management system (SMS), which left the F-14 software untouched and prevented the costly and time-consuming code changes and tests needed when aircraft weapons system code is modified. The F-14 did not even 'know' the LANTIRN pod was on the airplane; GBU-16 and LGTR release was made manually by the pilot when the LANTIRN ballistics software displayed to the crew the countdown to release.

Prior to first flight, Rat soaked the F-15E pilots and WSO's who had LANTIRN experience for as much knowledge as he could and we got one F-15E simulator together to practice procedures even though the knobology and displays were different in the F-14. The initial F-14 flights that Rat and I did were medium altitude, round robin flights learning how to use the LANTIRN pod and practice simulated attack procedures (no weapons were aboard and eye safe laser mode was used). Several flights were then flown at Dare County bombing target with LGTRs… Shack! The final Dare County training runs were for two GBU-16 inert 1,000lb laser guided bombs… Shack again! Next was off to Puerto Rico to drop at Vieques.

We took the demo Tomcat, and a photo/safety chase Tomcat plus we had two F/A-18 Hornets from our Airwing join us from Cecil Field. They came with NITE Hawk FLIR pods and Laser Spot Trackers (LST). Since LANTIRN had no laser spot tracker, the Hornet's job was to fly a couple miles in trail to confirm our LANTIRN laser was over the intended aimpoint and that there was enough laser energy for the GBU-16 to guide on. We had good confidence based on experience at Dare County that Tomcat LANTIRN would continue to work well but Rat was concerned that if we flung a bomb off target, we might not know if there was a LANTIRN problem or if it was merely a malfunctioning GBU-16 guidance unit or a bad fin kit. Should a bomb get flung, we did not want to chase LANTIRN 'ghosts' if they did not really exist.

The first drops at Vieques were two more inert GBU-16s… Shack with video! Then followed four live GBU-16 drops, one of which failed to hit the aimpoint (but landed safely within the target range and planned hazard pattern). Postflight review of our LANTIRN tapes and the Hornet LST video quickly showed that the laser spot was on the intended aimpoint the whole time with plenty enough laser energy so we confidently attributed the failure to a bad GBU-16 and were able to get back at it for the final drops. Like Snotty, Rat was also visionary and clairvoyant with his plan incorporating our Hornet buddies! The other three live drops… Shack with video! It was great watching the on-target, high order explosions blowing up tanks! We were laughing like kids with new toys!

We got Capt 'Snort' Snodgrass, the FIGHTERWING Commander out on one of the drops with Rat as well as a LANTIRN Familiarization (FAM) for the VF-103 chase pilot, Lt Otto 'Lecter' Sieber. I took the chase RIO, Lt 'Lumpy' Larson out for a LANTIRN FAM too! The Hornet guys requested some side-by-side runs with ranges called out by voice on the tapes and qualitative descriptions by Tomcat and Hornet crew on when they could identify target features. We were a little concerned the info would get twisted but our Hornet buddies wanted to take the side-by-side video to the Hornet OAG as ammo to get something better for the Hornet than NITE Hawk. On the way home, I was able to give Lt Cdr Dana 'Devo' Dervay a LANTIRN FAM; he was our main FIGHTERWING coordinator and heavy lifter for LANTIRN.

Returning to Oceana in April 1995 with lots of great video and a demonstration successful beyond our earlier estimates, we flew a few more FAM flights locally with LGTRs and some without ordnance to give Snotty a chance to see LANTIRN for himself and got CVW-17 DCAG, CAPT Zortman out to see too. We were also able to get CAG 7, Capt Ron 'Farmer' McElraft and Capt Tom 'Chain' Zelibor out for FAMs too. Then we had to de-configure the airplane since the mods were not cleared for use at the boat and the only LANTIRN pod modified for Tomcat use had to go back to Martin Marietta. I thought it was an exceptional capability and real force multiplier for the Tomcat. I also figured it would take too long for the Navy to make a decision to buy, complete the development and then to field Tomcat LANTIRN, even building on the documented demonstration work we had completed. I never figured I would see it fielded in my remaining flying lifetime even with more than two years still ahead in my CO/XO tour. However, Snort went to work with the video we brought home and showed it to combatant commanders, Naval Aviation leadership and NAVAIR leadership.

A couple months later in June 1995, we got word that the Navy was going to buy LANTIRN for Tomcats. The Navy and Martin Marietta felt they could not have enough modified LANTIRN pods or Tomcats to support the next deployment planned in December 1995 but thought they could have six modified pods, nine modified airplanes and minimum essential further testing complete in about a year for a June 1996 deployment. Not only was that 'light speed' for the acquisition system in those days, but the Tomcat squadron deploying in June 1996 was us in VF-103! Now that's what I'm talking about! Lots of behind the scenes work began including required shake rattle and roll work of LANTIRN by NAVAIR and expanding the Tomcat release envelops for various precision air-to-ground loads and mixed air-to-air and air-to-ground loadouts.

In January/February, 1996 during COMPTUEX as we were leaving the Puerto Rican Operating Area, CAG Zortman and I were giving the embarked Flag, COMCARGRU FOUR a backfill on how the night vision goggle (NVG) training det at Roosevelt Roads went. VF-103 was also the first east coast Tomcat squadron to deploy with NVGs and six of the nine LANTIRN jets got modified with NVG compatible cockpits. Some of our crews got their initial NVG training during a small shore det because the moon cycle required flying later at night than the USS Enterprise cyclic ops times for COMPTUEX.

As we were wrapping up the update, we also mentioned to the admiral that during the final set of workups, JTFEX in April, VF-103 would have the first three of six LANTIRN pods we would use on deployment and the final three pods would arrive just prior to leaving. The admiral, a Tomcat RIO by background, mentioned as CAG and I were headed out the door that "we in the Tomcat community had not really embraced the air-to-ground mission and still had a way to go before NVGs and LANTIRN pods would make that much of a difference".

When we got into the passageway, CAG asked me what I thought about the admiral's parting comment. I told CAG that the admiral was quite mis-informed and I was not pleased with the use of 'we'... CAG said he figured I'd say as much. I confirmed with CAG that we were still scheduled to fly the admiral in a couple days as planned when we got near the Cherry Point Operating Area. I then cleared with CAG my 'on the spot' plan to schedule the admiral as wingman on a typical close air support (CAS) training mission with Lt Cdr 'Morty' Moradian as his pilot and a couple of JOs leading including Lt Mike 'Tung' Peterson as the briefer. On the day of the flight, I watched from the back of the ready room as a standard CAS scenario with a Forward Line of Troops, nine-line briefs, JMEMS weaponeering and air-to-ground deliveries were professionally covered as was typical. I watched the debrief too and afterwards asked the admiral if he still thought 'we in the Tomcat community still had not embraced the air-to-ground mission?' He replied that his eyes had been opened and commented he didn't realise that 'we' in the Tomcat community knew how to do what he just flew. I replied that 70% of the squadron was JOs who had come through the RAG since 1993 when Strike was added to the syllabus and they had never known a single-mission airplane. They were the same air-to-air killers the Tomcat community had always produced but they also were pros at air-to-ground including CAS by all crew and FAC(A) for four crews. The only thing they needed were the tools to do it well at night and with precision which is where NVGs and LANTIRN were going to make the difference. He promised to come fly with us again in JTFEX. I invited him to fly a LANTIRN flight and promised that it was user friendly enough to learn with an extended flight brief and a pilot already familiar. He accepted, saw the capability for himself during JTFEX and wrote a great P4 message to the world immediately afterward.

During POM in the month prior to deployment, VF-103 sent a jet and crew to China Lake to drop a GBU-24 Bunker Buster with Lt Cdr Pete 'Skids' Mathews as the RIO and a VX-9 det pilot up front. That way, if needed on deployment, we had an operational test-proven LANTIRN Tomcat bunker busting capability versus just an 'on paper' capability. VF-103 and CVW-17 also got in Skids, a RIO who had actual experience dropping a GBU-24, something few other aircrew in any community had done at that time.

The first ever Tomcat LANTIRN deployment and east coast Tomcats with NVGs went well and many others I have not mentioned were responsible especially the VF-103 Sailors who bore the brunt of the additional work required by the extensive aircraft modifications for NVG and LANTIRN. VF-103 crews formulated the baseline LANTIRN procedures and tactics that subsequent squadrons built on and further improved. NAVAIR continued to expand the envelope and the more flight clearances arrived shortly after deploying to include catapulting Tomcats with GBU-24s. Always thinking, the JOs found innovative ways to use LANTIRN that went beyond original intent.

Early in deployment, a division of Tomcats did a training event 600nm round-trip precision strike, fighting through air-to-air opposition and brought back hit assessment video on all four planned aimpoints... all within ten sec of planned time on target (GPS time on the recorded video display keeps everyone honest). Even more interesting was that all but the initial 50nm on ingress and final 50nm on egress were at 540kts... that's 500nm or almost an hour at 540kts on a normal night cycle with zero tanking! Some sabre rattling in Iraq brought us to the Persian Gulf on USS Enterprise sooner than planned and kept the USS Carl Vinson there longer.

The sabre rattling died down soon but both carriers operated together for a couple weeks. Cdr Dave 'Possum' Cully was CO of VF-31 on Vinson and we were able to arrange a swap of RIOs to get some VF-31 RIOs LANTIRN FAMs on training flights to Kuwait and VF-103 RIOs some F-14D FAMs with VF-31. No weapons were dropped or fired in anger on our 1996 deployment but with cross-decking of our LANTIRN pods to our VF-32 reliefs near the end of deployment, all subsequent Tomcat deployments came armed with LANTIRN. Numerous Tomcat crews have used LANTIRN very successfully in combat many times since and provided great support to our war fighting buds on the ground. It was fun to be among those involved on the ground floor of LANTIRN Tomcats and to see where it has led since. It also set the chinning bar higher for subsequent FLIRs used by the Navy and Marine Corps.

Capt Alex 'Yogi' Hnarakis, USN (ret) CO VF-103 Jan 1995 to Jul 1996

THIRD DECADE

In early 1990, prior to deploying aboard USS *Theodore Roosevelt* (CVN-71) VF-41 Black Aces carried this paint scheme. When they deployed for Operation Desert Shield, their paint schemes would be toned down to a full TPS scheme with dark grey over light grey markings. (Bob Lawson)

A rarely seen legacy formation between a F8F-2 Bearcat (121752), painted in VF-31 colours and a F-14A-130-GR Tomcat (161858) from VF-31 Tomcatters. This photo was taken in October 1990. (Lt Joe McKee via Tailhook Collection)

By 1990, the Tomcat was fully integrated into the Fleet with over 24 operational fleet squadrons and two fleet readiness squadrons supplying aircrews by 1987 and four reserve units operating Tomcats. The F-14A+ was now flying with VF-74 and VF-103, VF-24 and VF-211 as well as VF-142 and VF-143, allowing the Tomcat to fully realize the thrust it was intended to have. Even more promising was the advent of the F-14D which had been flown as a prototype since 1988 with first production deliveries due to the fleet in early 1990. By 1990, VF-74 and VF-103 had transitioned to the F-14+ and took them aboard USS Saratoga for their combat baptism, losing one to an SA-2 Guideline surface-to-air missile. VF-142 and VF-143 were embarked aboard USS Eisenhower with their F-14A+ Tomcats but left the theatre before combat ensued. The third Air Wing equipped with the F-14A+ was Carrier Air Wing 9 with VF-24 and VF-211.

SPEED IS LIFE

So many great memories of such a magnificent aircraft. My perspective is similar to others who have had the privilege of being trained as test pilots and have had the pleasure of testing various models and modifications of the mighty Tomcat. Having also had the opportunity to fly over 31 different types of military fixed and rotary wing aircraft during my 25-year career, I gained a unique appreciation for the awesome power and capability of the F-14. One particular event in my 3,000+ hour Tomcat career encapsulated this awesome combination of power and grace.

Having been privileged to flight test the F-14A+ (now designated F-14B) during my post-Test Pilot School tour at Patuxent River as a young lieutenant, I was given the opportunity following that tour to join the world famous Pukin' Dogs of VF-143 for the F-14A+'s maiden deployment as a department head. This was also scheduled to be among the first F-14 deployment in which the Tomcat would be cleared to drop air-to-ground ordnance.

During the CVW-7 turnaround training detachment to NAS Fallon, we engaged our F/A-18 sister squadron (VFA-136 Knighthawks, flying new F/A-18Cs) to develop mixed section and division air-to-ground strike tactics, as a way to test our new model's capabilities. During one particular 26-plane strike, I flew as alternate strike lead in a mixed section with an FA-18 strike lead, a fellow lieutenant commander and good friend of mine. Anxious to see what the new F-14A+ could do with its new, more powerful GE F110 engines, I made a deal with the strike lead that I would, in accordance with our philosophy of mutual support, stay with him from egress until we reached the supersonic corridor in Fallon's Dixie Valley range, at which time, I planned to 'light-'em up and see what this baby could do'. He agreed, interested himself in seeing what this new 'Turkey' could do against the 'future of the fleet'.

We ingressed at low altitude (this was pre-Desert Storm) and executed the 'Hornet Pop' from the deck to 27,000ft. Notably, on the way up, my F-14A+ remained in locked combat spread in military rated thrust (MRT), while the strike lead in his F-18C required full afterburner to make the climb to our 27,000ft high roll-in point. Following the roll-in and ordnance delivery, we egressed on the deck toward the supersonic corridor at 0.95 Mach, with my F/A-18 flight lead in full afterburner ('double bubble' tank configuration) and our A+ in and below military rated thrust, again locked in combat spread.

Upon reaching the edge of the supersonic corridor, I stroked full afterburner on the two GE F110 motors and was pressed back into my seat as if I were on a cat shot. In no time at all, we had reached 1.35 Mach and at the 'knock-it-off' shortly thereafter were better than three miles ahead of our

THIRD DECADE

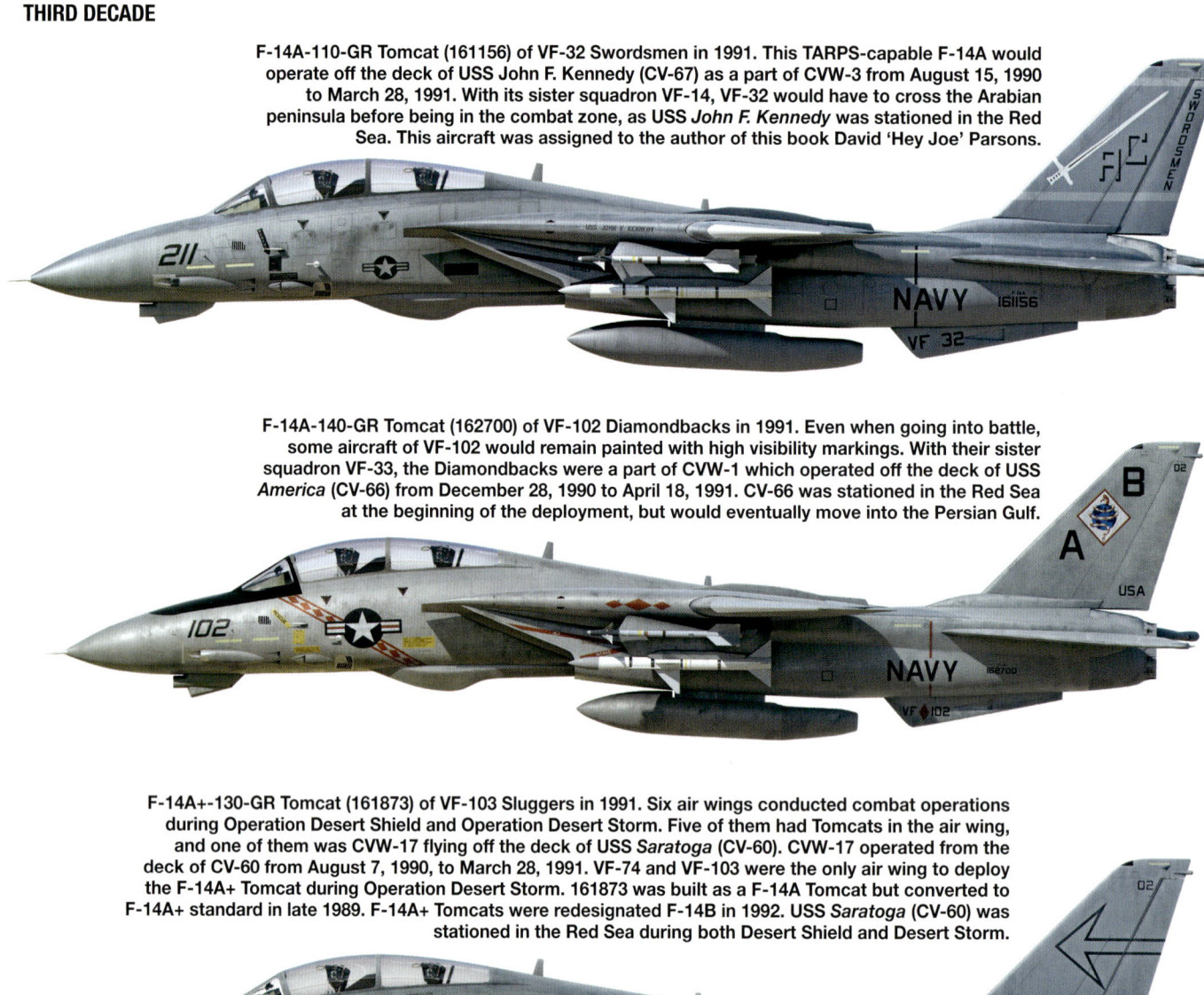

F-14A-110-GR Tomcat (161156) of VF-32 Swordsmen in 1991. This TARPS-capable F-14A would operate off the deck of USS John F. Kennedy (CV-67) as a part of CVW-3 from August 15, 1990 to March 28, 1991. With its sister squadron VF-14, VF-32 would have to cross the Arabian peninsula before being in the combat zone, as USS John F. Kennedy was stationed in the Red Sea. This aircraft was assigned to the author of this book David 'Hey Joe' Parsons.

F-14A-140-GR Tomcat (162700) of VF-102 Diamondbacks in 1991. Even when going into battle, some aircraft of VF-102 would remain painted with high visibility markings. With their sister squadron VF-33, the Diamondbacks were a part of CVW-1 which operated off the deck of USS America (CV-66) from December 28, 1990 to April 18, 1991. CV-66 was stationed in the Red Sea at the beginning of the deployment, but would eventually move into the Persian Gulf.

F-14A+-130-GR Tomcat (161873) of VF-103 Sluggers in 1991. Six air wings conducted combat operations during Operation Desert Shield and Operation Desert Storm. Five of them had Tomcats in the air wing, and one of them was CVW-17 flying off the deck of USS Saratoga (CV-60). CVW-17 operated from the deck of CV-60 from August 7, 1990, to March 28, 1991. VF-74 and VF-103 were the only air wing to deploy the F-14A+ Tomcat during Operation Desert Storm. 161873 was built as a F-14A Tomcat but converted to F-14A+ standard in late 1989. F-14A+ Tomcats were redesignated F-14B in 1992. USS Saratoga (CV-60) was stationed in the Red Sea during both Desert Shield and Desert Storm.

flight lead and still carrying more gas than he. As impressed as I was with this performance, the true measure of what this tactical capability brought to the Tomcat wasn't evident until the air wing debrief of the strike.

As luck would have it, both the strike lead and I were 'shot at' by two computer-generated SA-3 surface-to-air missiles, just as we reached the supersonic corridor. Watching the theatre-sized 'God's Eye' view of the debrief in real time, we could see the missile fly outs as each sped toward us. In an atmosphere of 'shock and awe', the assembled strike participants watched with mouths open as a 'coffin' appeared around the F/A-18 lead aircraft's airplane, signifying that the SA-3 had been 'bagged', while second SA-3 ran out of gas before catching our 'screaming cat'. When the computer generated missile display faded from the screen without reaching its intended target, there was a resounding cheer from the crowd, albeit a little louder from the assembled 'Turkey' drivers.

If, as the Israeli's say, 'speed is life', then flying the F-14 Tomcat was certainly part of a 'wonderful life'.

By 1990, Tomcats were deployed in Operation Desert Shield/Shield aboard five of the six carriers ultimately operating in both the Red Sea and Persian Gulf. The Tomcat had been developed in the Cold War to meet the formidable threat to Carrier Battle Groups by regimental-sized bomber raids equipped with a variety of air-to-surface missiles. As the Cold War appeared to ending in late 1991, the need for two Tomcat squadrons in each carrier air wing seemed superfluous. The Fleet Air Defense mission literally disappeared overnight. The Navy came out of Desert Storm convinced that air superiority was not a priority as much as improved air-to-ground weapons.

I joined the Be-Devilers of VF-74 with the likes of Gus, Cuds, Traps, Shaggy, Shaker, Biz, Potsie, Charlie Chan and Pep and embarked aboard USS Saratoga with our F-14A+ Tomcats. Saddam took the world by surprise and invaded Kuwait. Off we went on the mighty Sara. Suez canal transits numbered six, making it a 12-beer deployment (note: alcohol has not been allowed on Navy ships since prohibition. However, in the early 80s an exemption was allowed to permit ships underway without a port call for more than 90 days to issue two beers per individual usually during a flight deck 'steel beach' party on a no fly day, with beers carefully controlled and accounted for every step of the way).

We lost 21 sailors when an over-packed ferry boat capsized in the icy waters off of Haifa. We spent six months preparing for a showdown, flying endless mirror image strikes on a 'run for the border'. We wrote 'just in case' letters home to our wives and parents. We spent countless hours refining our strike plans and still were massaging them the night prior. Didn't matter cuz we couldn't sleep anyways. We became something so much bigger than ourselves as we zipped up our G-suits, stepped into our

HALF CENTURY, BABY! FIFTY YEARS OF THE GRUMMAN F-14 TOMCAT

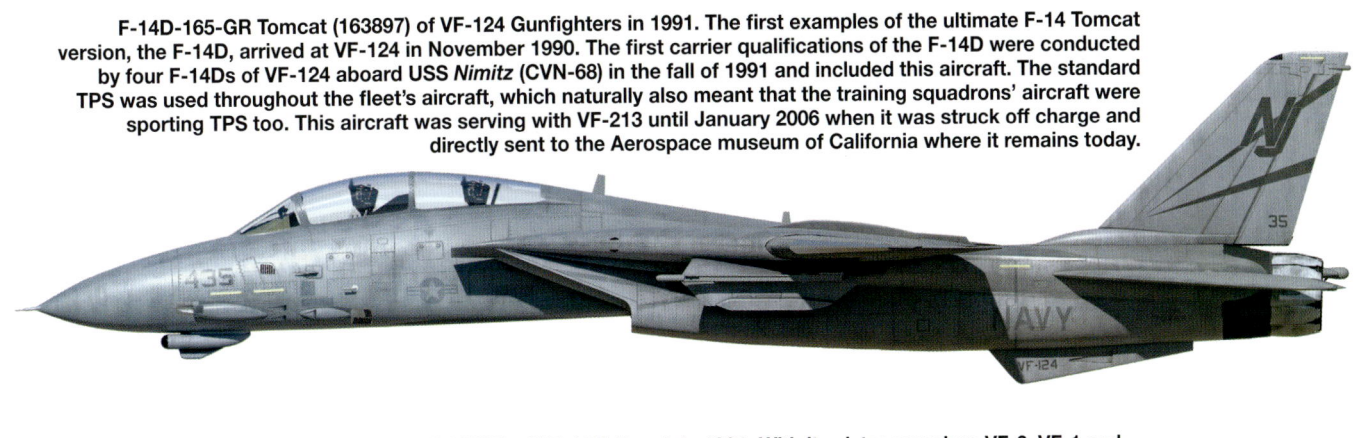

F-14D-165-GR Tomcat (163897) of VF-124 Gunfighters in 1991. The first examples of the ultimate F-14 Tomcat version, the F-14D, arrived at VF-124 in November 1990. The first carrier qualifications of the F-14D were conducted by four F-14Ds of VF-124 aboard USS *Nimitz* (CVN-68) in the fall of 1991 and included this aircraft. The standard TPS was used throughout the fleet's aircraft, which naturally also meant that the training squadrons' aircraft were sporting TPS too. This aircraft was serving with VF-213 until January 2006 when it was struck off charge and directly sent to the Aerospace museum of California where it remains today.

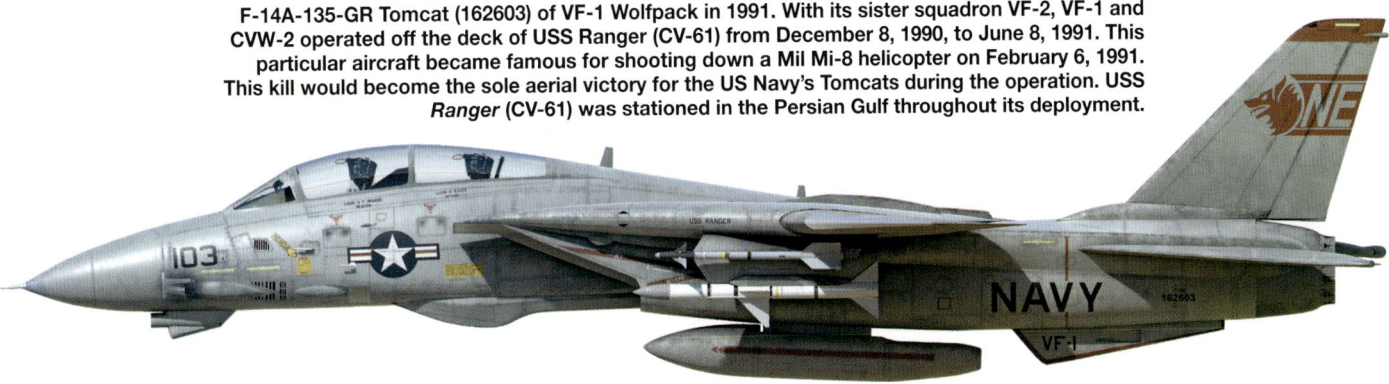

F-14A-135-GR Tomcat (162603) of VF-1 Wolfpack in 1991. With its sister squadron VF-2, VF-1 and CVW-2 operated off the deck of USS *Ranger* (CV-61) from December 8, 1990, to June 8, 1991. This particular aircraft became famous for shooting down a Mil Mi-8 helicopter on February 6, 1991. This kill would become the sole aerial victory for the US Navy's Tomcats during the operation. USS *Ranger* (CV-61) was stationed in the Persian Gulf throughout its deployment.

F-14A-110-GR Tomcat (161164) of VF-84 Jolly Rogers in 1991. CVW-8 aboard USS *Theodore Roosevelt* (CVN-71) conducted operations from the Persian Gulf with two Tomcat squadrons aboard: VF-41 and VF-84. As the war was drawing to a close CVN-71 relocated to the Red Sea but continuously launched aircraft on missions over Iraq. This is another example of a TARPS-capable aircraft, this one fitted with the ALQ-167 ECM pod. This deployment lasted from December 28, 1990, to June 28, 1991.

torso harnesses, slipped our .38s into our holsters and came together to strike in an opportunity of a lifetime. Steely-eyed, we were ready to release fury.

Somewhere in the arid, desolate desert of western Iraq, Scott Speicher disappeared in the darkness – two hours after Desert Storm began. The next day, Mongo and MRT shot down two MiG-21s in western Iraq. After landing, the high fives on the flight deck were a replay of those seen by millions in the movie Top Gun. We dodged SAMs and saw the ever-present streaks of AAA by night. We lost an A-6 and a Tomcat. As the realities of war erased the ecstatic high fives, we were comforted by the ubiquitous Father Lamonde who greeted and blessed us on the flight deck before each combat mission. We survived the gaggles and goat ropes on the tankers as we flew in and out of Iraq. We returned to a grateful nation and will never forget the Patriotic fervour of our Oceana fly-in with hundreds of proud Americans waving flags while dressed in red, white and blue.

As we shut down our trusty steeds we all wiped the tears from our eyes as we dismounted to reunite with our families, grateful to make it home.
Capt Scott 'Stewie' Stewart

UNFORGETTABLE
The Jolly Rogers during the Gulf War – here was an airplane that when you walked to man up, you expected to have a trouble free start. In fact, thanks to incredible maintainers, we had unsurpassed availability and full up systems. It was a pleasure to see the airplane mature over time, and provide what it was envisioned to be able to do – and after that, see it develop into the Bombcat.

While it took too long to reach its full potential, it did provide the fleet with some great service over the years. Yes memories, way too numerous to list here, remain. The F-14 was a joy to fly – none of us will forget.
Vice Admiral Marty 'Streak' Chanik, USN (ret)

GHOSTRIDER CALAMITY AND GRUMMAN IRON WORKS
A testament to the strength and resilience of the Tomcat as well as our aviators was the day Lt Cdr Joe 'Reb' Edwards and Lt Cdr Scott 'Grundy' Grundmeier launched in the Gulf on our first day of ops there in 1991. I was CO of the Goats as we rolled into the NAG immediately post war. We all launched on check flights that day as we had run from the Suez to the Gulf so a few machines needed profiles. We were up above the smoky gloom and turned in to bump heads after our Pro-Cs. After the merge I lost sight of Reb and Grundy as they unexpectedly descended into the haze.

After much chatter with ship, I found them on their final approach to the Ike (after a NORDO flyby and practice approaches the Boss knew they were in trouble). As I rendezvoused, I could see the nose of their jet was missing. They flew an OK (underlined) pass to a one wire. On landing we all learned that at turn in, the entire radome had separated

THIRD DECADE

A formation take-off from NAS Pt. Mugu of NF-14D-130-GR Tomcat (161867) and F-14D-160-GR Tomcat (163414) of VX-4 in October 1990. 161867 was one of the F-14D Tomcat testbeds. (Paul Minert Collection)

A very early F-14D-160-GR Tomcat (163414) of VX-4 Evaluators here seen at NAS Pt. Mugu in October 1990. (Paul Minert Collection)

A detail shot of the vertical stabilizer of F-14A-125-GR Tomcat (161603) in January 1991. At the time this aircraft was the squadron's CAG bird, sporting these very bright colours. (Paul Minert Collection)

smashing the canopy, spider webbing the bullet proof windscreen and both quarter panels in addition to punching a softball sized hole in the left quarter panel. Grundy suffered numerous cuts from the flying glass. Reb also suffered many cuts and had a broken left collar bone and a big chunk of Plexiglas imbedded in his left eye. So, with one good eye, a hole big enough to look out of (and a lot of wind blast), the ILS needles on the inside of the centre windscreen and Grundy's help with voiceless NAV, they made their way back to the Ike.

It was a piece of airmanship unlike any we had ever seen. CAG Jim 'Lord Jim' Sherlock called it the most incredible feat of flying he had ever heard of, including combat. They were both awarded the DFC. The jet recovered from its many injuries as did Reb and Grundy. Reb went on to be selected for the Astronaut Program and flew as the Shuttle pilot on STS-89.

Vice Admiral Dick 'Weasel' Gallagher, USN (ret)

SIX CRUISES

All I ever wanted to be was a lieutenant in a fighter squadron. First Tomcat flight was 40-degree dive-bombing with Mk82s at Pax River with Jim Piehl in 1975. My last Tomcat flight was day CQ on Ike with 'Mad Al' Myers... and the V1, V2 and V4 guys loved seeing the captain flying around as much as the XO and Gator in 1995.

In between I recall many memorable moments: blue water ops and several passes followed by a trap at 2.4 in the IO with 'Bullet Bob' Ellis – right into the rising sun with Oman scum all over the windscreen and canopy. Not a pretty sunrise that day. Ghostrider burner loop off a long bolter that sure looked like it was going to hit us parked inboard of El 2 (can't remember who ejected from it). Trap in zero-zero fog with Nestor Gantt in the North Atlantic – Mode II all the way! "I've got it now, God. And thanks."

Being met by CNAL and FAA after a JOT airwing flyoff at dawn without all the bother of coordination – "CAG's in the other jet!" Two Gypsies at 600 knots with corkscrew missile trails and a blanket of flak just east of Beirut airport on a TARPS run, then watching two towns disappear when USS New Jersey opened up. All ten Swordsman jets leaving Oceana for two weeks in Nellis – Vegas, including Tailhook, the day after taking command.

Flying with 'Mooch' Carroll – a lot! Including some beautiful sunset traps. Six cruises in Tomcats! Nothing comes close to the feeling you get flying the big Grumman 'Turkey'.

Rear Admiral Mark 'Vodka' Gemmill

UNRIVALLED IN COMBAT

Wanted to capture the midlife crisis/ transition the beast went through in the early 90s. As a relatively young guy, I was fortunate enough to experience both the Cold War fighter community and the larger than life Fighter Guy attitude that went along with it, as well as the

HALF CENTURY, BABY! FIFTY YEARS OF THE GRUMMAN F-14 TOMCAT

A F-14D-165-GR Tomcat (1638997) of VF-124 Gunfighters parked at NAS Miramar in March 1991. (Paul Minert Collection)

A F-14A+-150-GR Tomcat (163218) of VF-143 Pukin' Dogs in April 1991. The squadron would depart on a deployment aboard USS *Dwight D. Eisenhower* (CVN-69) from September 26, 1991, to April 2, 1992, as a part of CVW-7. (Paul Minert Collection)

VF-1 Wolfpack soldiered on through the 80s and in the 1990s. Their paint schemes had changed very little since they were formed in the early 70s. This aircraft (F-14A-135-GR Tomcat (162597) even carries the multi-coloured CAG band on the tail, indicating that the aircraft was assigned to the wing command. Time was running out for VF-1 when this photo was taken. The squadron would leave on a deployment aboard USS *Ranger* (CV-61) on August 1, 1992 and return on January 31, 1993. VF-1 was disestablished on October 1, 1993 (Paul Minert Collection)

transition that eventually lead the F-14 to being the airwing's bomber of choice. The two aspects I loved most about the Tomcat community were JO liberty calls and combat excellence. Two quick stories that epitomize both:

The first took place in the days when the squadron CO did 'sack tricks' at hail and farewells that didn't end until the lizard at the bottom of the tequila bottle was eaten in the process of doing handstand shots. During an Orange Air Detachment, Fuzzy, Elk, Speedy and I were invited back to the Sea Bee's private club at Roosevelt Roads to continue an evening of raging with some of the female Sea Bees. Although on base, this recreation facility had everything including an open bar, frozen daiquiri machines built into the wall, pool tables, and loud music to round out the atmosphere. Unfortunately, it also came with lots of other less inebriated Sea Bees that weren't 100% sold on our programme. What a raging time until Fuzzy knocked over one of the flaming shots we were pouring on the pool table. Being trained professionals in shipboard firefighting, Speedy and I expertly extinguished the blaze with a couple of beers that transformed a pristine pool table into a soggy charred mess. Outnumbered but realising the best defence is a good offence, Elk immediately broke the uncomfortable silence with: "This party stunk anyways, we're out of here!" The next morning CAG approached me to ask how our night was. His question was not a sudden interest in our social life, rather a way to inform us we would have to pay for the damages.

Fast forward to the post Tail Hook environment, during Operation Desert Fox. This was the first time since Desert Storm that the US bombed targets in Iraq, with the first day being an all Navy effort. On the first strike over the beach, the F-14 made it's combat debut as a self-lasing LGB-dropping machine, with a LANTIRN system that was virtually aircrew proof. After hours of target area study, Debo and I were convinced we could do better than the pod to funnel our way to our assigned target, a facility deep within an Iraqi city. At 20 miles, I located the river, counted five bridges north, went six blocks west away from the river to the expected target area, only to find my target was nowhere in the field of view. Repeating this process had equally unsuccessful results. Approaching the release point for our delivery and testing Debo's patience, I set my pride aside and resorted to slewing the GPS-equipped pod to the prestored target coordinates.

The target appeared instantly, was designated, and lazed with two seconds remaining until release. A far from pretty bombing run ended with two 2,000lb LGBs obliterating their target as well as the entire compound it was located in. This first successful LANTIRN debut in combat set the stage for one of the most successful three-day bombing campaigns in the history of strike warfare. On the last day of Desert Fox, nine out of

THIRD DECADE

A TARPS-capable F-14A-125-GR Tomcat (161604) being catapulted off the deck of USS *Theodore Roosevelt* (CVN-71) in 1993 during Operation Deny Flight. This was the last deployment VF-84 ever made. (Tailhook Collection)

ten Tomcats (many flown by first cruise nuggets on their first time over the beach) hit their assigned targets. The tenth missed because the target had already been destroyed seconds prior by bombs from the lead striker.

Despite huge changes in the post Tail Hook and post-Cold War environment, the Tomcat adapted and remained unrivalled in combat. I can only hope I make such an effective transition as I approach my mid-life crisis.
Capt John 'Snooze' Martins, USN (ret)

TIP OF THE SPEAR
Flying the F-14 was one of the most rewarding experiences of my life. To think that we were all on 'the tip of the spear' for that segment in our lives when we were young, thrill-seeking, and adventurous makes me proud to know that we were all part of something bigger than ourselves. I would never trade it for anything and would do it again if I had the chance to do everything all over. As the years linger by, I realise what a great cadre of people I had the pleasure of flying with and working with and as the wise old man once said: "In your youth you create memories that sustain you when you get older." We had many memories together, F-14s and bouncing at Fentress, the Diamondback six-man bunk room, night CAP, the Marshall stack, 30ft pitching decks in the North Atlantic, 'Chicken George' our favourite CAG LSO, the AWG-9 and Phoenix missile shoots, Reno, OCA vs DCA, 1v1, one circle, two circle, Desert Storm, many a fight during CAP in the Red Sea, and 'Dump it on Mudaysis' – the F-14 was and will always be the Queen Bee of aircraft.
Eugene 'Geno' Miller, Tomcat pilot

TOMCAT SAILORS
Every time I flew our great and wonderful fighter, surrounded by the world's best aviators, it always struck me with ample humility that for every short hour I spent aloft, some 50 sailors toiled for an hour themselves to enable my winged adventures. That in over 4,000 hours I never so much as fondled a D-ring with intent to utilise is testament to their skill and dedication. While I enjoyed relatively comfortable lodging, they had to worry about their sheets coming out of the ship's laundry with just a hint of dryness. This while stacked like corpses in 150-man berthing. They never enjoyed the luxury of 12-hour JO naps, nor decent liberty but they never let us down. Our sailors taught me far more than any of my winged contemporaries though association with the latter made me far more man than I could have anticipated. If I have earned the opportunity to salute anyone, I offer that sign of earnest respect to the sailors who made the Tomcat fly.
Capt Eric 'Sodbuster' Benson, USN (ret)

LOVE MY JET
Damn I LOVED working on that jet! It was such a challenge! But the rewards could bring tears of pride to my eyes. I've been shocked, stabbed, cut, bruised, pinched, burnt, smashed fingers, stood on my head for three hours in the cockpit to pull a heal rest, heck I've even fallen off of one once. I've said every cuss word known to man, and even made up a few and directed it to the jet, but the second someone other than a Tomcat sailor said something bad about MY jet, I would rip into them!
Brian Hegrat, Tomcat 'Line Rat'

FORTUNATE ONE
It was on a hot summer afternoon in 1975 that the dream took root. We were participating in an aviation indoctrination programme in Corpus Christi as part of our second class summer cruise; they had just shown us the movie, No Points for Second Place. From that moment on, I only wanted to fly one airplane – the Tomcat. Five years later, that dream came true. Twenty five years after that first flight, I could remember it as if it were yesterday. From that first flight with Nacho, to my first night trap with Pomp, to achieving 1,000 hours with Breeze, to my last flight aboard the boat with LTF and every one of them in between, with Ski, Taco, Squire, Spider, Killer, Charlie Woo-Woo and with the world-famous G-Man as my flight lead, I realise now how fortunate I was. Fortunate to fly one of history's greatest airplanes. Fortunate and proud to have served my country. And fortunate to have served with a great bunch of guys.
John 'Guido' Tartaglione, Tomcat pilot

The so-called 'peace dividend' that ensued in aftermath of Desert Storm resulted in a drastic cut to the Block 1 Strike funding by 1992 and cancellation of further F-14D production altogether. At that time, a total of 38 new production F-14A+ variants equipped with the higher thrust F110-GE-400 engines had been delivered along with 43 former F-14A aircraft upgraded to the F-14A+ configuration while awaiting the ultimate F-14D version which was first delivered in 1991. Thirty-seven new production F-14D aircraft were funded before the axe fell and 18 former F-14A models were funded for remanufacture to the D configuration.

The initial F-14D units were VF-11 and VF-31 which transferred coast to Miramar to undergo transition at VF-124. With only 55 F-14D aircraft completed by 1992 when the production line was closed down, only four squadrons were able to transition in addition to VF-124 and VX-4. VF-2 and VF-213 transitioned and ultimately, VF-11 transitioned to the F-14B from the D when aircraft availability after unfortunate losses resulted in not enough F-14D Tomcats to equip four fleet squadrons. Similarly, VF-211 had to transition back to A model Tomcats before their transition to the Super Hornet.

TURKEY DRIVER MEMORIES
Taking the runway on Fam-1, and thinking wow my first flight in a real fighter and I'm the only one with controls. First supersonic flight too!

Fam-2 takeoff, AFTERBURNER! Feeling each zone light off pushing you further into the seat. Now this is thrust.

Pulling the trigger for the first time with a live gun and feeling the cannon going to work. Almost made wearing a dry suit worthwhile.

Getting struck by lightning while trying to find the ship among the thunderstorms (our radar wasn't working) finally getting sight of her and coming into the break at 800ft only to find the clouds on the port side of the ship were more like a 600ft ceiling, during my RAG CQ and thinking 'so this is what the fleet is like'.

My first port call: New York City… what happened in NYC, stays there!

A four-day 'no notice' deployment while operating at Nellis AFB after Saddam invaded Kuwait. The only way to go on Cruise. We changed 14 Tomcat motors in two days, loaded aboard, bounced and were gone.

Six-hour flight on Christmas Day 1990 with 'Chain' Zelibor, most of which capping off the Iraqi border. Seeing the KC-135 boom operator in a Santa hat with his 'Happy Christmas' sign, several times, and 300 miles of cloud surfing in the late afternoon on the way home.

Two trips through the ditch, with light loaded F-14s in alert and Dusty Dogs flying gunship.

Green ink: Strikes, CAP, strike planning, alerts, and not much sleep. But lots of FMC jets, thanks Master Chief Hulbert!

Looking at all the AAA coming up on my first night strike and wondering if all that stuff was there yesterday in the daytime only harder to see.

Being 130 miles on the wrong side of the border with only one engine running. A week in Hurghada, scuba diving every day with all my 'dive qualified' squadron mates who had 'left' their dive cards at home with me as Divemaster! Stella beer.

'Mod' DLC. 1 bolter on my second cruise, a day Case III straight in MOVLAS pass, and they counted it.

Getting in trouble on my second cruise for doing all the things they taught me to do on my first one. Three years as a Gypsy. What a ride!
Capt C R 'Max' Dugan, USN (ret)

The peace dividend and reduced budgetary accounts drove OPNAV to consider a drastic cut to type/model/series aboard carriers. The A-12 debacle and savaging of both the F-14D and A-6F programmes led to other cuts such as the AAAM missile that was supposed to replace the AIM-54 Phoenix. OPNAV started comparing the A-6E Intruder with the F-14 Tomcat, and without precision strike capability the Tomcat looked to be a relic of the Cold War. However, enough tentative work had been done at Pax River to show the promise of the Tomcat in a precision strike role and the ultimate decision was to retire the A-6E Intruder altogether and neck down carrier air wings to single Tomcat squadrons. Furthermore, the Tomcat community would absorb the best of now orphaned A-6E aircrews providing subject matter expertise in dropping bombs to the Tomcat community. With one exception, the Tomcat squadrons to be disestablished were the non-TARPS units (with one rare exception: VF-84). VF-1 therefore did not survive the decade nor did VF-21, VF-24, VF-33, VF-74, VF-84, VF-51, VF-111 or VF-114. VF-84 was the one TARPS unit disestablished and its fabled heritage was adopted by VF-103 thus carrying on the Jolly Roger tradition. VF-124 also eventually stood down and all Tomcat squadrons shifted to single site operations out of NAS Oceana.

Meanwhile, the Tomcat had also reaped the benefit of a British digital flight control system (DFCS) developed by Marconi for the Harrier. Losses of Tomcats to out-of-control flight had plagued the community also from the start. An OSD Foreign Cooperative Test (FCT) funded a demo on the F-14A and D at Pax River resulting in favourable report of its feasibility to provide a digital flight control system (DFCS) for the Tomcat. DFCS first flew in summer of 1995 and installs proceeded rapidly once funding from OPNAV was allocated. The first fleet squadrons to get it in summer 1998 were VF-14 and VF-41.

THE A-6 COMMUNITY
I did my part to absorb the best of the A-6 community from a command tour on the West Coast, VF-24, partly by recruiting some of the best JOs from another great community, the Intruder. The Tomcat remains the most recognisable fighter in the world, and I could not be prouder to have been a part of its legacy.
Capt Jason 'Jazz' Leaver, USN (ret)

A-6 TRANSITION AND BOMBCAT
In the spring of 1994, I was class leader of the first A-6 transition group going through the RAG. We arrived at the same time that the Tomcat Community was getting LANTIRN, NVGs, Blue-Green lighting, and entering the precision strike arena. The aircraft was new to most of us but the strike mission wasn't. We'd spent a large part of our careers flying night missions 'alone and unafraid' into a target area and blowing stuff up, but other than a few passes through Indian Country we hadn't jousted in the varsity air-to-air arena mano a mano. After our first flight in the afterburning beauty we were hooked. And on top of the raw power of the Tomcat and its lethality in the A/A mission, the new schwacking toys (eye-watering LANTIRN video, GPS precision,

An F-14A-115-GR Tomcat (161293) of VF-111 Sundowners about to trap aboard USS *Kitty Hawk* (CV-63) on the squadron's final deployment, which lasted from June 24 to December 22, 1994. (Bob Lawson)

THIRD DECADE

For the VF-2 Bounty Hunters' 25th anniversary in 1996 this F-14D(R) Tomcat (159630) was painted in a retro colour scheme that resembled the squadron's earliest scheme.

and laser-guided bombs) arriving in the hands of F-14 crews would make any strike planner drool.

While a 'bug' going through the transition syllabus, one day I was called over to the wing commander's office where Commodore Snort gave me an assignment… Riddle: Why did the F-14 fleet crew bomb the Larne target near Vieques with live ordnance and nearly sink the tug towing it? Answer: Because no one told them they couldn't. Turns out the air-to-mud guys had a long list of similar incidents (bombing fisherman, ferry boats, spotting towers, camp fires, exotic wildlife, etc.) but never shared this folklore with the Strike Tomcats. In this case they were just lucky they didn't split the tug in two and end up as the sea story of sea stories. I'm sure there are other similar tales of woe and things that have happened since, but those are better debriefed at the club.

As the first A-6 transition XO/CO, I reported to VF-14 with Rookie at the helm of the mighty Tophatters and had the pleasure to fly with great sticks like Sly Fox, and Matt the Cat. My first fleet impression of the multi-mission Tomcat was on det out to 29 Palms, CA for a summer CAX (Marine speak for one hundred degrees of dry heat by zero eight hundred, all day long) to fly missions in support of our brothers in green, live in tents, eat MREs, and choke on dust with the grunts, all the while fighting everything from F-5s to AV-8s, F/A-18s, and a Cobra or two, and also dropping lots of live stuff in the Mojave desert. We adopted the motto, FBOTOTFP (Fused Bombs On Target On Time First Pass), and had a blast. For our due diligence in volunteering for this det to the desert garden spot we were rewarded with a Christmas det to Key West. Two hops a day, slick jets, ACM out the ying-yang, the Duvall crawl… life was sweet.

Later, while in command and with Bernie Parent as my XO, our deployment on JFK in '97 may have been the last of the good deal Med cruises that featured combat pay from Bosnia missions coupled with a maximus port visit calendar covering Palma de Majorca, Benidorm, Marseille, Cannes, Koper, Korfu, (need I go on?). Tres bieno.

A flashback to flying A-6s during Desert Storm, January 1991… one cold dark night in Iraq after bombing the #%$& out of a target deep in western Iraq the strike package was safely egressing towards the Saudi border to hit the KC-10s and then RTB to the Saratoga in the Red Sea. About 50nm from the border our fighter escorts accelerated ahead of us to get first in line for gas. A few minutes later we got a call from AWACS: "Raygun (our call sign), you have Cougars (MiG-29s) airborne heading your way at 800 knots." Yipes! With this older Grumman Iron Works product maxing out at 420 knots we knew we were toast. Only by diving for the deck and divine intervention did we make it back to the border and safety. Fast forward to Strike Tomcats and now, not only could we fight our way into the target, turn it into dust, hair, teeth, and eyeballs, but could then hose any fool that dared to meet us on egress. Anytime, Baby.

But when all is said and done, although the F-14 is an awesome flying machine, and there's nothing to compare to a Zone 5 catshot, it's the people that matter most. In previous airwings (during my 'subsonic days') I'd flown on strikes, shared a slider in the wardroom, or gone on liberty escapades with the likes of Traps, Stewie, Dirty Harry, Fozzie, Biff, Devo, Socks, Boots, Rat and Dollar, to name a few. And once inside Fighter Country my circle of warrior brothers expanded to include Lil Mac, Clem, Hey Joe, Snotty, Yogi, Rabes, BB, Nubs, Joey, Sodbuster, Cuds, Mean Jim, Kraut, Pink Floyd, Slapshot and many more. While the F-14 Tomcats are the hottest, sleekest, most lethal, and most powerful platforms on the flight deck, it's the people in the squadrons, the fighter crews, that remain extra special.
John 'Sneds' Snedeker, Tomcat RIO/Intruder B/N

THE MAJESTIC BEAST
My first introduction to the Navy, let alone the military, occurred during the summer of 1989 before my sophomore year in high school. I had recently moved to sunny Key West, FL and one of my stepfather's friends had flown into NAS Key West in a VF-101 Tomcat for a Tactics Det. Meeting Dave 'Hey Joe' Parsons (he was a brother-in-law to my new stepfather so I was actually meeting my new 'step-uncle') and his Tomcat buddies ignited a fire within me for the Navy and, more specifically, Naval Aviation. I will always remember the first time I set eyes on the 'Big Fighter' up close and personal when Hey Joe invited my family and me out to the ramp at Key West to see it. That moment changed my life forever. Ten years later at my winging I was selected to fly the mighty Tomcat (my first choice of course). As fate would

HALF CENTURY, BABY! FIFTY YEARS OF THE GRUMMAN F-14 TOMCAT

F-14A-125-GR Tomcat (161603) of VF-114 Aardvarks in 1991. The long serving VF-114's last deployment lasted from May 28 to November 25, 1991 when CVW-11 was operating in the Persian Gulf off the deck of USS *Abraham Lincoln* (CVN-72). However, this aircraft was not on the deployment; it had been transferred to VF-2 shortly beforehand. However, it would remain in the colours of VF-114 until well into June 1991. VF-114 would return to NAS Miramar and would be disestablished on April 30, 1993.

F-14A-85-GR Tomcat (159606) of VF-302 Stallions in 1991. CVWR-30 also had TARPS-capable aircraft, 159606 is an example of one such aircraft. It was written off on October 16, 1992 at NAS Key West. The reason for this is not known.

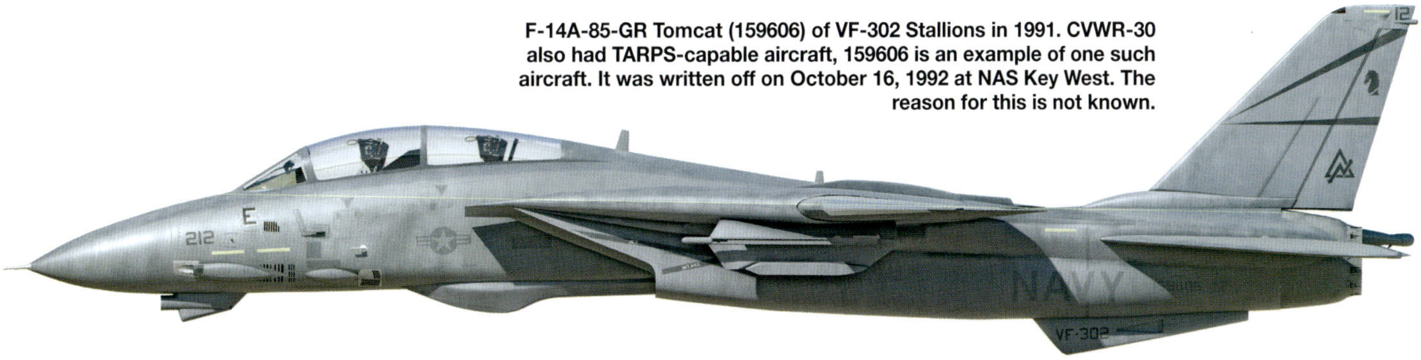

An F-14B-150-GR Tomcat (163217) of VF-143 Pukin' Dogs on display at Skrydstrup AB, Denmark, on June 16, 1996. CVW-9 was embarked aboard USS *George Washington* (CVN-73) in the Mediterranean at the moment of this photo. The wing sent three aircraft to the Danish air show in 1996 (along was an A-6E Intruder of VA-34 and an F/A-18C Hornet of VFA-136). This Tomcat was the first active duty Tomcat the author of this book ever saw. (Erik Holm via Michael Andersen)

THIRD DECADE

The same Tomcat here seen arriving at Skrydstrup AB on June 14, 1996. (Jan Nielsen via Michael Andersen)

have it, I was ultimately assigned to VF-32, the Swordsmen, which was Hey Joe's last fleet squadron. Needless to say, that coincidence has always meant a lot to both of us as we got to meet again in the 'Gypsy' ready room at Oceana and at the club later on.

Flying the Tomcat was a true pleasure. Sometimes it was a fair amount of work coaxing it to get airborne, but it was worth every minute. There's nothing like a day cat shot in the Tomcat, cloud surfing or raising a round of Turkey shots at the club afterwards with the best fighter pilots in the world. I clearly remember standing on the turtleback during a preflight while conducting operations off Souda Bay, Crete completely in awe that I actually got to land this plane on the carrier every single day and night. What an incredible and challenging plane! I believe that the Tomcat was a true icon of Naval Aviation. It defined an era and embodied the noble fighter spirit. I will truly miss the majestic beast, the Tomcat. I later transitioned to the F/A-18C Hornet. The weapons and systems coupled with its incredible handling capabilities make it a formidable platform and a treat to fly. I have truly been blessed with the opportunity to fly two fantastic planes, meet amazing people, and live such a great career.
Lt Jeff 'Baja' Hart, CVW-8 CAG LSO, previously IP at VFA-106, VF-32

MO OF THE RAG
My favourite memory was taking command of VF-32 during opposing supersonic flybys of Ike back in December '94. Favourite job: MO of the RAG. Hardest job: MO of the RAG. Craziest job: MO of the RAG. Most rewarding job: MO of the RAG. That was the tour that made me understand the sheer power of the heart and soul of Naval Aviation, the American sailor.
Cary 'Dollar' Silvers, Tomcat pilot

'MUTHA' TROPHY
Just thinking about 'the Mutha' brings a smile to my face. When BRAC shut down Miramar and VF-124 closed its doors, Mutha was suddenly without a sponsor since the CO of VF-124 acted as 'Mutha' and decided annually on the winner. So, the tradition made the trip to the east coast and passed to VF-101 where I was CO.

It took only an hour or so for my west coast instructors at 101 to educate and convince me that the camaraderie it brought along with it was worth the effort. Other than the statue was about as ugly a thing I've ever seen, squadrons would literally die in the attempt to win it and considered it to be more prestigious than any other traditional award.

As the competition heated up in the first year, one ranking squadron picked me up at my house in Va Bch in a painted up van to take me to play in the Fighter Fling golf tournament. Inside the van was a recliner, newspaper and Mac D's for breakfast. The funny thing about the story is that I ended up having to give the van a starter jump (battery was dead) because as I found out later the Rippers sabotaged it. Those were the days...
Rear Admiral Steve 'Coolie' Voestch, USN (ret)

SLUGGERS BECOME JOLLY ROGERS
In spring 1995, I was CO of the VF-103 Sluggers, Snort was the FITWING Commodore and 'Jay Bird' Johnson (who was my first department head as an Ensign in VF-142) was now CNO. The Sluggers were busy with the rapid prototype installation of the first LANTIRN pod in an F-14. Snort gave me a call one day and relayed that Jay Bird (former CO of VF-84 Jolly Rogers) had asked him to find an F-14 squadron willing to adopt the Jolly Rogers name and insignia to ensure the continuity of arguably the Navy's most recognised fighter squadron, (and to keep a F/A-18 squadron from potentially taking the name). VF-84 had fallen victim to the budgetary axe and had been scheduled to close its squadron doors for the very last time at the end of the fiscal year. This request was out of the blue, and certainly nothing I had ever given a thought to. I told Snort that I needed a few days and that I would get back to him.

I huddled first with my XO (Alex Hnarakis), department heads and CMC. There were some very strong opinions both for and against the proposed change. I discussed the proposal at an AOM, at a chiefs call, and then with all hands at quarters. We had decided to use the democratic process and put the proposal up to a vote. I personally started to warm to the idea, as did most others although there were still some rather vocal dissentions to the end.

While some argued that the mere mention of the name Sluggers, or just

HALF CENTURY, BABY! FIFTY YEARS OF THE GRUMMAN F-14 TOMCAT

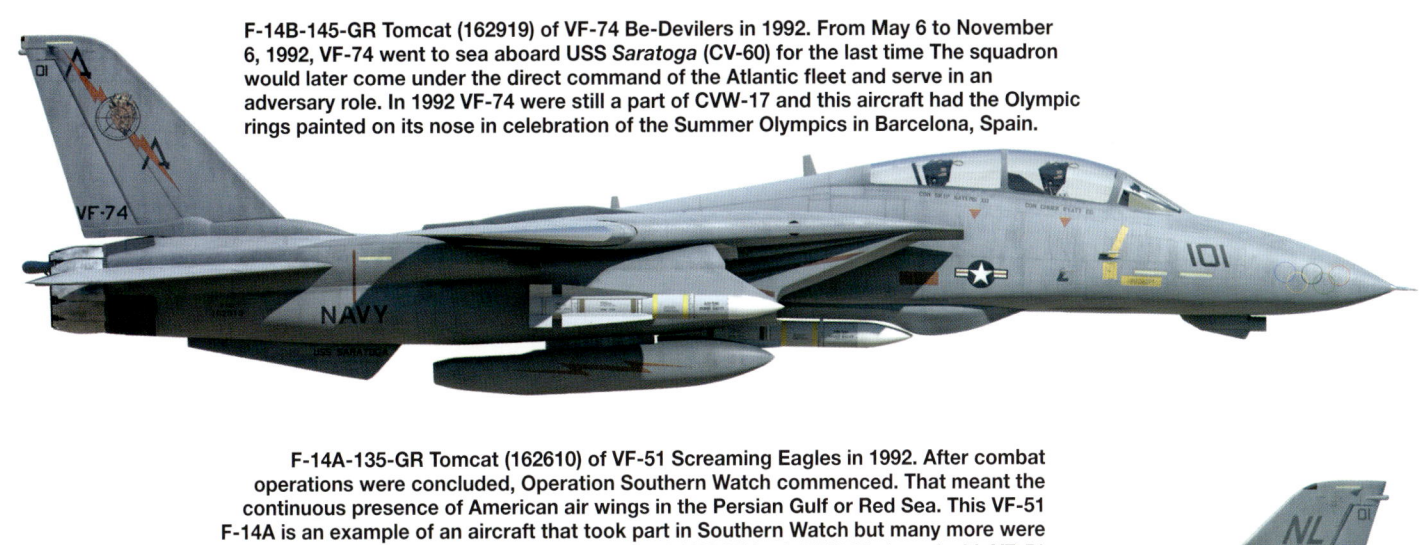

F-14B-145-GR Tomcat (162919) of VF-74 Be-Devilers in 1992. From May 6 to November 6, 1992, VF-74 went to sea aboard USS *Saratoga* (CV-60) for the last time The squadron would later come under the direct command of the Atlantic fleet and serve in an adversary role. In 1992 VF-74 were still a part of CVW-17 and this aircraft had the Olympic rings painted on its nose in celebration of the Summer Olympics in Barcelona, Spain.

F-14A-135-GR Tomcat (162610) of VF-51 Screaming Eagles in 1992. After combat operations were concluded, Operation Southern Watch commenced. That meant the continuous presence of American air wings in the Persian Gulf or Red Sea. This VF-51 F-14A is an example of an aircraft that took part in Southern Watch but many more were deployed between 1991 and 2003. USS *Kitty Hawk* (CV-63) had CVW-15 aboard with VF-51 and VF-111 for a deployment lasting from November 2, 1992 to May 3, 1993.

a quick glance at its ferocious insignia, would surely instil great fear in the mind of any God-fearing person and that there was no reason to change; the majority said B.S. to that and expressed that the squadron needed a name more "fitting for a fighter squadron" and a more "respectable" and "less ugly" insignia. While an important part of naval aviation history itself, the Sluggers' record just didn't stack up to the extensive combat experience and many victories achieved by past Jolly Rogers.

Most JOs and junior enlisted expressed that the skull and bones jets and insignia just looked "so cool", and they liked that the jets had been featured in a couple of movies, "everyone recognises a Jolly Roger". And who wanted a baseball bat in your squadron insignia when you could have a squadron T-shirt with the skull and crossbones? The Sluggers didn't really have a mascot, and besides, what mascot could compare with the actual bones of Ensign Jack Ernie (who reputedly died flying a Jolly Rogers aircraft in combat at Okinawa in the Second World War and was still carried on the squadron roster after saying over the radio: "Remember me to the Jolly Rogers!")? Well, a few days later the CMC and XO supervised a vote, and it overwhelmingly supported the change.

On September 29, 1995, in Hangar 23, Dan 'Traps' Cloyd disestablished VF-84 and transferred the great responsibility of 'keeper of the bones' to VF-103. The famous Jolly Rogers would live on and continue making carrier aviation history, and Ensign Ernie wouldn't have to transition to Hornet squadron... well, at least not for another ten years.
Capt Steve 'Snotty' Schlientz, USN (ret)

DESERT FOX
The ship arrived on station in the Persian Gulf in December 1998. The following day of arrival, CAG called a meeting with the CO/XOs. He handed me two strike folders to plan (nights two and four). I had not led more than two jets around in almost three years and he's making me the strike lead (what's he thinking??). Also remember I have no LANTIRN (FLIR pod) or night vision devices (NVD or goggles) training. Talk about not feeling up to speed. Thank God I inherited a great team of strike planners. We get our strike planned and I brief them to the admiral (Rear Admiral Dawson, black shoe and a great guy) and CAG. For you old Rippers, Capt Tony 'Eagle' Reade was the admiral's COS.

So there I am flying the first night, first strike. I'm sitting in the jet aft of the island, waiting to get the 11th hour 'abort' call like has happened to VF-103 on the Ike. When off the port side (left, for you AF guys) I see about ten TLAMS get launched from one of the small boys in our Battle Group. What a sight. The first night was all Navy, NO Air Force (not even their tankers) or Brits. It was designed for single cycle... surprise.

We're loaded with two GBU-16s (1,000lb-ers) and our target is within city limits of Baghdad. Tomcats were given most of the hard targets because of the LANTIRN. So ours has possibility of collateral damage (unacceptable, except to us who don't care). We find our targets and schwack 'em. Remember this is me flying night vision devices and LANTIRN for the first time. The learning curve was steep... at least for me; my RIO may think different. To watch these buildings go away was impressive. We meet AAA and ballistic launched SAMs.

On night two, first strike is mine. It's a double cycle with AF tanking and GR.1s from the UK. We're heading farther north to make the Republican Guards' life miserable. Targets are headquarters and barracks (as seen on CNN). I have three Tomcats carrying two GBU-10s (2,000lb-ers) each, eight Hornets with either GBU-16s or GBU-10s, HARM shooter and of course the Brits (who are always on their own programme it seems). Now this is my FAM 2 on NVD and LANTIRN. 2,000lb-ers are incredible to watch go off. My weapon of choice. There wasn't a building standing when we finished. Again, there was AAA and ballistic SAMs.

Night three was a two-strike night for me. My second hop landing at 0615 when the sun was rising (I still counted it as a night trap). On the first strike I was carrying two GBU-24s (2,000lb+ penetrators). First time the Navy has used these weapons in combat. Tomcats carried a lot of these. These are the bunker busters. Our target was hard but they crewed me with the best LANTIRN RIO in the squadron (again helping the weak link). He impressed the shit out of me. We came back and I briefed one hour later for the second strike. Both these

THIRD DECADE

An F-14D-165-GR Tomcat (163902) of VF-2 Bounty Hunters parked at NAS Oceana on March 7, 1997. (Don Linn)

An F-14B-145-GR Tomcat (162918) of VF-102 Diamondbacks in May 1997. The squadron would embark aboard USS *George Washington* (CVN-73) from October 3, 1997, to April 3, 1998, during a deployment to the Persian Gulf as a part of Operation Southern Watch. (Paul Minert Collection)

missions were over three hours. Second mission we're carrying the GBU-10s again. I love this bomb. It just makes shit go away. Let's just say I'm glad I'm not a Republican Guard. Oh yeah, FAM 3 and 4 for NVD and LANTIRN complete. I sleep for three hours and get up to put the finishing touches on my night four strike.

Night four was my second strike lead. I'm dragging butt, but I know the fun will stop soon. I have the LANTIRN God in my back seat again for more bunker busting with two GBU-24s. This strike again has three Tomcats, eight Hornets, four GR.1s from the UK, four F-16CGs and the HARM/SEAD package (Prowler and two Hornets). By night four the Iraqis were pissed off... go figure. Our targets are up north again and I can see the AAA just filling the skies on the ingress.

Some schmuck on CNN said they mounted a feeble opposition. Well he wasn't sitting where I was. Anyway, we're coming in and the AAA is going off above and beside me. For some reason, all I'm thinking about is my dad's story from Vietnam about how AAA at night looks like flying into a Christmas tree... he was right but it scares the crap out of you. I trap back onboard after three-plus hours for my third night trap and strike in under 24 hours (not recommended but fun). FAM 5 complete and I'm NVD/LANTIRN qualified. I'm exhausted, Desert Fox ends and I sleep until noon the next day.

I feel fortunate, my timing couldn't have been any better. The Tomcat is the machine when it comes to precision strike. The Hornets knew they couldn't touch us. The Swordsmen JOs rose to the occasion and impressed the shit out of me. We got everyone over the beach at least once. We dropped over 111,000lb of ordnance and had a 100% sortie completion rate (no spares launched).

The beer low light was on as we celebrated the New Year in the Red Sea heading back to the Med heading to Souda Bay, Crete for a port call to put out that light!
Capt Will 'Coondawg' Cooney, USN (ret)

WHEN IS A TOMCAT NOT A TOMCAT?
Kenny 'Pink' Floyd (VF-33), Luke 'Bernie' Parent (VF-102), and I (VF-33) were department heads during what was our combat cruise in 1991. We all cruised together in USS America for Operation Desert Storm, or as I like to call it, WWIraq – The Original. During that time, the Tomcat was a fighter and nothing but a fighter (except for TARPS missions). The only arguments we had in CAG-1 was whether or not we were ever going to be in a position with the ROE to use the

HALF CENTURY, BABY! FIFTY YEARS OF THE GRUMMAN F-14 TOMCAT

F-14A-115-GR Tomcat (161294) of VF-111 Sundowners in 1994. The iconic VF-111 sharkmouth and sundowner tail had long since become subdued in different shades of grey as the frontline Tomcat squadrons were painted in TPS. Throughout the 90s the number of fighter squadrons declined as they were disestablished due to the introduction of strike fighter squadrons and a general disarmament following the end of the cold war. The last deployment the Sundowners made was aboard USS *Kitty Hawk* (CV-63) from June 24 to December 22, 1994. The squadron would be disestablished on March 31, 1995.

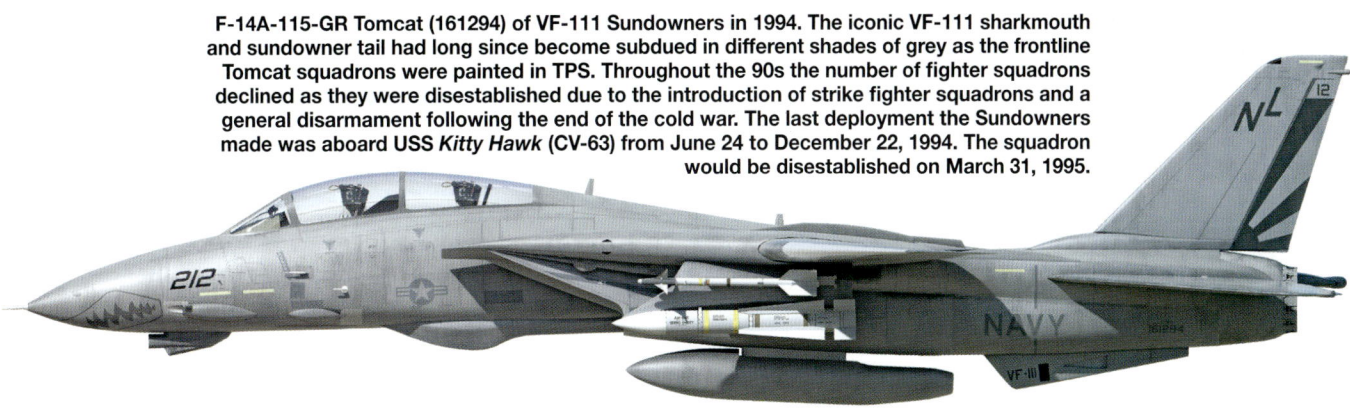

F-14A-90-GR Tomcat (159837) of VF-24 Fighting Renegades in 1995. A sports-themed paint scheme was applied to this VF-24 Tomcat. The San Diego Chargers were in the Superbowl on January 29, 1995, when they played the San Francisco 49ers. VF-24, being stationed at NAS Miramar just outside San Diego, showed support for the local team by adding a Chargers lightning bolt to the vertical stabilizer of this aircraft. Unfortunately it wasn't enough to secure the victory for the Chargers as they lost 26-49.

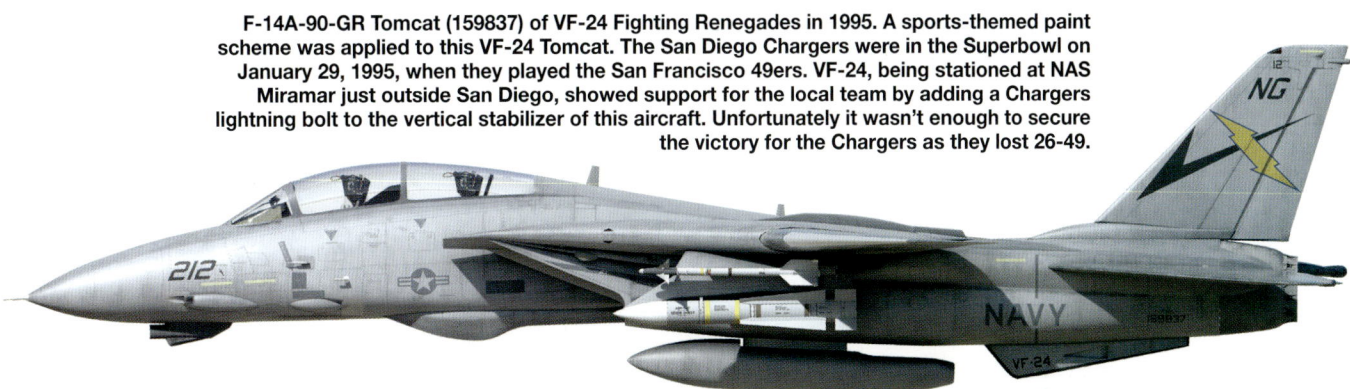

F-14B-145-GR Tomcat (162923) of VF-101 Grim Reapers in 1995. After September 30, 1994 VF-101 became the sole training squadron for Tomcat crews, but the tradition of colourful aircraft for the squadron COs and XOs remained. This aircraft was carrying some of the most unusual markings with its dark red antiglare panel. This aircraft would crash on March 2, 2002, as it launched from USS *John. F. Kennedy* (CV-67) while serving with VF-143. The nose gear collapsed and the crew were forced to eject. The incident claimed the life of pilot Lt Cdr Christopher M. Blaschum, which may have been due to the fact that the SAR helicopter was 10 miles from the ship at the time of the incident. The RIO, Lt Rafe Wysham, survived.

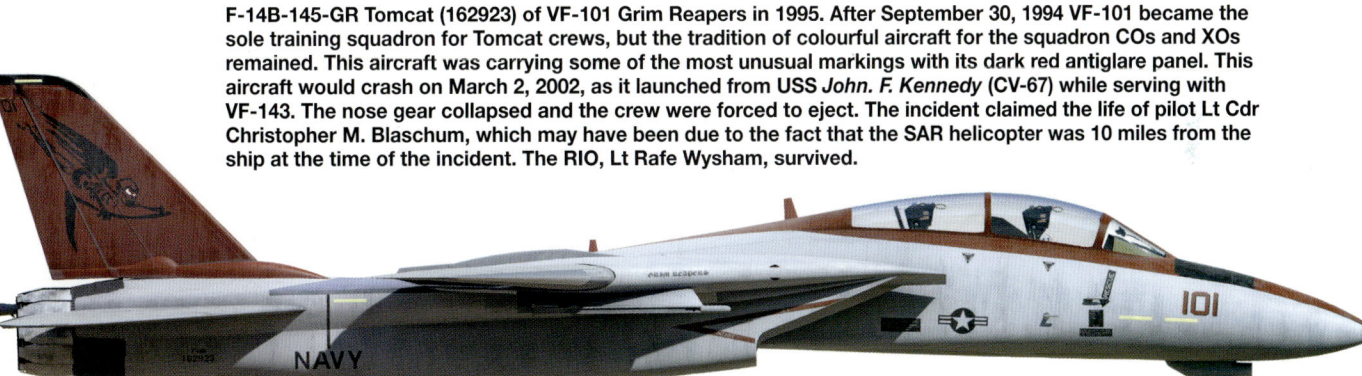

F-14D-165-GR Tomcat (163904) of VF-11 Red Rippers in 1996. The Red Rippers had a brief stint under Pacific fleet command from 1994 to 1996. They made three deployments aboard USS *Carl Vinson* (CVN-71), the last being from May 14 to November 14, 1996. Shortly thereafter they returned to the Atlantic fleet but had to trade their F-14D Tomcats for F-14Bs.

THIRD DECADE

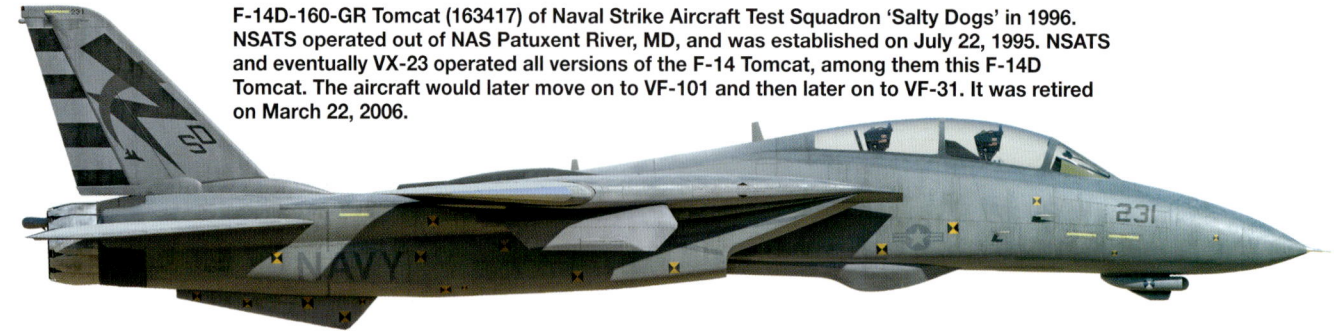

F-14D-160-GR Tomcat (163417) of Naval Strike Aircraft Test Squadron 'Salty Dogs' in 1996. NSATS operated out of NAS Patuxent River, MD, and was established on July 22, 1995. NSATS and eventually VX-23 operated all versions of the F-14 Tomcat, among them this F-14D Tomcat. The aircraft would later move on to VF-101 and then later on to VF-31. It was retired on March 22, 2006.

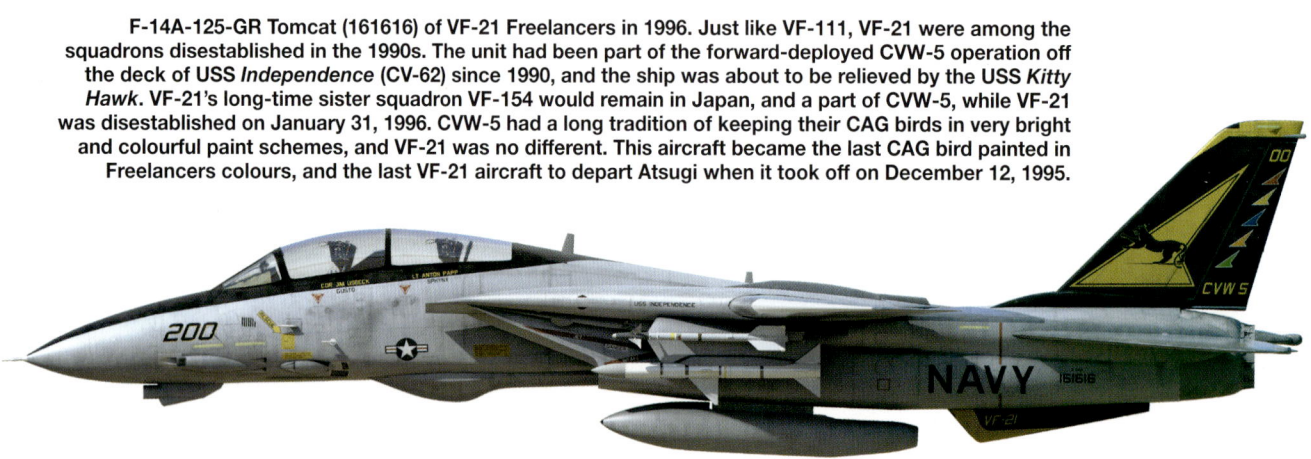

F-14A-125-GR Tomcat (161616) of VF-21 Freelancers in 1996. Just like VF-111, VF-21 were among the squadrons disestablished in the 1990s. The unit had been part of the forward-deployed CVW-5 operation off the deck of USS *Independence* (CV-62) since 1990, and the ship was about to be relieved by the USS *Kitty Hawk*. VF-21's long-time sister squadron VF-154 would remain in Japan, and a part of CVW-5, while VF-21 was disestablished on January 31, 1996. CVW-5 had a long tradition of keeping their CAG birds in very bright and colourful paint schemes, and VF-21 was no different. This aircraft became the last CAG bird painted in Freelancers colours, and the last VF-21 aircraft to depart Atsugi when it took off on December 12, 1995.

Phoenix or should we carry all Sparrows in the tunnel so we could be fast enough to run down anybody we would have to VID (visually identify). But nobody came up to play with us. So we CAPed. BARCAP, MIGCAP, HVUCAP, BONGCAP – you name it, we had a CAP for it.

Fast forward to the year 1997. Now Pink, Bernie and I are all skippers of Tomcat squadrons (Pink with VF-32, Bernie with VF-14, and me with VF-41). But this time our Tomcats are looking different. The wings, the canopy, the twin tails – they were all the same. The motors, too. Well, Pink had bigger motors than the ones Bernie and I had in our A models. But this time around the cockpits had changed colours, the weapons stations had other things hanging from them – it was not the same. We were now full-fledged strike-fighters, the very thing we had all heard was everything we did not want to be from our mentors back in the day – the Tomcat guys of an early day who said Tomcats were Fleet Air Defense (FAD) fighters and would not being going even over the beach! The Cold War threat back then warranted that perspective but with the dissolution of the Soviet Union, the FAD mission disappeared almost overnight. And with the new precision strike capability came the challenge of satisfying the leaders who now had access to new toys and wanted to play with them as much as possible.

We weren't the first guys to sail with Strike Tomcats in the Black Aces. 'Yogi' Hnarakis and his brethren in VF-103 had led the way bring the LANTIRN targeting pod into the fleet in 1996, and Pink had taken the Swordsmen to sea with LANTIRN, night vision capable cockpits, and the new-fangled digital TARPS capability. But now it was our turn in CAG-8. This time, Bernie and I had two Tomcat squadrons in the same air wing. We were to take 24 Tomcats to sea but the air wing was only going to have the time and kits to modify 12 F-14s with the new capability.

Of course both of us wanted to be able to play so we split the lot. Since I had the TARPS jets in 41, it seemed to make sense that VF-14 would take seven NVD/LANTIRN jets to sea and we would take five. Looked good on paper. Everyone gets training, everyone takes part in the action, everyone is happy. What I did not fully understand were the challenges of taking three different versions of the F-14A to sea, all with different capabilities and varying degrees of desirability in the eyes of operational leadership.

There were some fun nights prior to cruise as we made every effort possible to get our crews ready. Our jets were in varying stages of modification, there were a limited number of night vision instructors, there were a very limited number of LANTIRN pods available for training, and there were only so many nights when the moon allowed us to get goggle time in our various stages of night vision experience. It made for a challenging puzzle for the OPS officers and their schedulers. I remember one particular night when Lt Tom 'Virus' Baker and I were closing in on our total goggle hours needed to be designated as an NVD Instructor. We launched from Oceana on a 'marginal' night for NVDs. It was overcast over much of the east coast so our ability to see the ground and get some reasonable training was questionable. But we launched and we flew – slowly to get as many minutes out of our 20,000lb of fuel as we could. Over toward Tennessee we flew getting down to 3,000ft AGL for as long as we could stand it before the clouds made us turn around. We stopped and got gas at the Oceana hot pits and flew toward New York to see what the city looked like in the green blur of the Cat's Eyes (there is no commercial traffic to speak of around NYC at 0300, I can tell you). Come 0430 when we made a full stop landing at Oceana, our eyes were seeing everything in green and our bodies were screaming for a mattress. If I only knew then what I know now about fatigue and circadian rhythm. But we got our NVD hours.

The challenges really sprouted while deployed in John F Kennedy. With only being allowed six or maybe seven jets on the roof, with LANTIRN/NVD jets in high demand for training and demonstration, with TARPS still high on the list of needs, with maintenance demands of the mighty Tomcat growing with age, with limited numbers of aircrew qualified with NVD and LANTIRN, what is a CO to do? Bernie and I traded secrets and expertise between squadrons. We shared aircraft with each other (he sharing many more of his with me than vice versa as the fates played out). Tophatters flew in Fast Eagle

HALF CENTURY, BABY! FIFTY YEARS OF THE GRUMMAN F-14 TOMCAT

F-14B-140-GR Tomcat (162701) of VF-103 Jolly Rogers parked at NAS Oceana on December 17, 1997. (Craig Kaston via Paul Minert Collection)

jets and Black Aces flew in Camelot jets. Cats and dogs, living together – mass hysteria. We even mixed and matched aircrews a few times. But we trained and flew, all while seeing nine Med ports in the summer.

Oh, and there was the digital TARPS camera. It looked not unlike the security cameras one sees in a Farm Fresh supermarket. It was fixed looking straight down with a very narrow field of view. But we played with the 'cutting edge' technology, trying to find a way to send digital images via data link from over the horizon via the E-2 as would become the norm a couple years later. It made for some fascinating discussions of available technology for a system without an operator's manual to speak of and very limited tech support at sea.

All the changes in an airframe known for decades as the premier fighter of the Cold War, the king of the Outer Air Battle, the champion of the Chain Saw, were happening at once during a summer in the Med in 1997. The cruise was memorable on many levels. From trying to get the guys trained in the many new missions to convincing the flight deck that if they would only move those couple of jets a few feet we could get the wings swept forward to do fight control work. From working around intake cracks and limited time underway to get young pilots traps at sea. From the beaches of Spain to the mountains of Slovenia. It was an 'E' ticket ride in those early days of the post-cold war world – when the Tomcat changed its stripes.
Capt Ken 'Nubs' Neubauer, USN (ret)

THE LOVE OF A BEAUTIFUL WOMAN
When I got my wings, my first three choices were Tomcats East, Tomcats West, and Tomcats Anywhere. Since I was not the golden boy around the boat, Naval Aviation saw fit to put me in one of the less-sexy Grumman products at Oceana. One day Lieutenant, Junior Grade Guadagnini was driving along Oceana Blvd with his lovely bride, and said, while pointing at the Tomcats in the landing pattern, "Would you love me better if I was flying pretty airplanes like that?" To which the reply was made, "The Navy won't let you fly pretty airplanes!" I determined right then and there that I was going to figure out a way to fly the Big Fighter... so I could keep the love of a beautiful woman. Three years later as Deputy CAG, I started flying the F-14, a varsity sport that I would continue for the next 20 years, including combat flights in the skies over Afghanistan and Iraq. And wouldn't you know; that wonderful woman I married did indeed start loving me more – lending another scientific data point to the theory that fighter guys get the best chicks! At altitude, 'Guad'.
Rear Admiral Mark 'Guad' Guadagnini, USN (ret)

MEMORIES
RAG bird loop off the CAT with no one aboard (missed the ship by 100yds).

Mach 2.4 at 40k in a brand new jet with the XO in the back for an acceptance check.

Only aircraft launched that day to return to trap with the screws of the Big E out of the water and green water on deck.

AIM-54 direct hit on AQM at 54nm.

Single engine, no generators, fuel split, black night and 600nm bingo to Wake.

600kt burner break at the mast with an OK 3 and Hack to boot.

127 hits on the banner and one through the turnbuckle.

Red VDI filter in your face off the cat – blind and climbing.

Four vs unknown in Crow Valley – all F-14s deadly and surviving with six bandits out of action.

USAF F-5 in the break at sea as #4 – wave off and RTB without knowing his wing commander was in the tower.

Dark night on the bow with one nose tyre free-wheeling over the net...

630kts at 500ft through the hills north of LA on a TARPS run.

Twenty-three test hops to get jet's wings rigged – never did fly straight on-speed.

Four in the break from Santa Rita and looking up at the Cubi Club.

Division of Libyan MiGs in TWS at 18 miles, so close...

Three SA-6s in search of my section, 57mm at 19,500 with our division at 20,000, and escorting B-52s on their runs.

Losing family and wingman to flat spin and malfunctioning ejection seats.

Glorious sunrises and daunting sunsets.

Son and daughters on the platform during Tiger cruise for number 1,000, and 300kts accelerating 750kts at sea level in less than ten miles in a 'D' for the final flyby.

It just doesn't get any better than that...
Vice Admiral Tom 'Killer' Kilcline, USN (ret)

FLIGHT OF THE CATS
The Flight of the Cats was one of the most fun things to do as the VF-101 demo pilot. Tomcat, Tigercat, Bearcat, Hellcat and sometimes the Wildcat. Most of the time we were limited by the Wildcat with its speed, unless joined up on a B-17 for a picture or something when their speed was 180 kts or so. It would have been nice to fly the demo with DFCS, though I never got to do that, and it was sure a rudder dance with AFCS that slow with the wings back. It was an honour to fly with all these great airplanes of the past, I would have done it for free.
Vice Admiral Steve 'Web' Koehler, USN, former Commanding Officer VF and VFA-143

TOMCAT WARRIORS
My final Tomcat squadron was the Bounty Hunters of VF-2. Lil Mac and Stewie were reunited, this time as CO and XO respectively. By now the Tomcat had matured and we were lucky to be flying F-14Ds, equipped with digital avionics, powerful and reliable engines, APG-71 radars, IRSTs, NVGs and LANTIRNs. Alert intercepts, TARPS and attached TARCAPs were no longer en vogue – we were now self-escorting strike fighters more capable than anything in the Air Wing.

We 'Bullets' ruled the Air Wing both on and off duty. Flake shot a century banner – all by himself (Hoser would have been impressed!). Grumpy was the best tactical pilot I ever flew with (even if he didn't let his RIOs talk on the radios), nobody could fight – the jet or on liberty better than Burner, operationally Woody and Opie provided the game plan, and G-Man, Thumper, Purple, Crunchy, Sting, Weed, Rags, Jo-Jo, Stabs, Astro and Fun simply did the rest.

We were the finest group of warriors in the Air Wing and our tactical

THIRD DECADE

F-14A-95-GR Tomcat (160396) of VF-201 Hunters in 1998. As the 90s were drawing to a close, the reserve squadrons were either disestablished or redesignated to Strike Fighter Squadrons (VFA) with the arrival of the F/A-18 Hornet. On November 15, 1998 the last VF-201 Tomcat took flight. For the occasion the aircraft was named 'The Jimbob Express'. Notice the crew signatures applied before the last flight.

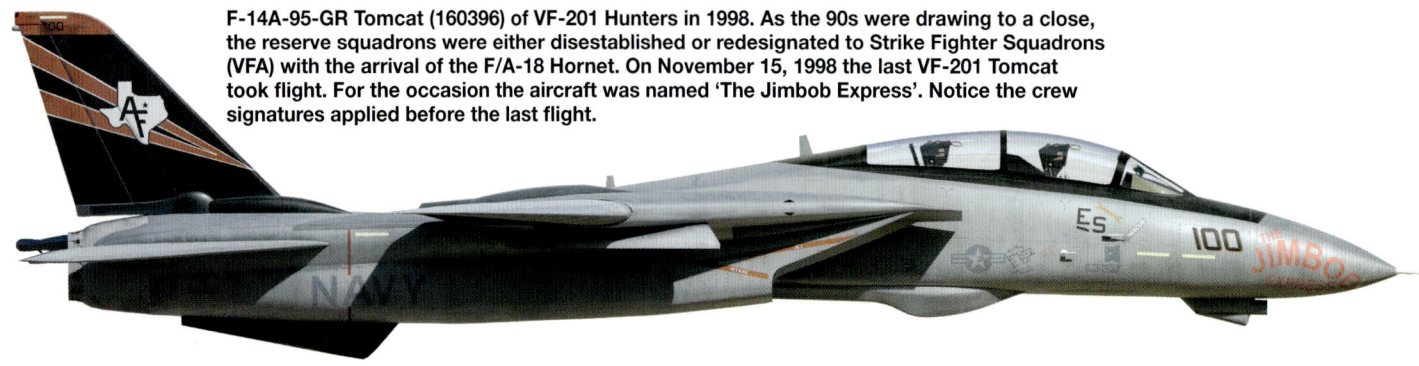

F-14A-130-GR Tomcat (161856) of VF-211 Fighting Checkmates in 1998. While VF-211's long time sister squadron, VF-24, had been disestablished by 1998, VF-211 would remain in service as a part of CVW-9. The squadron would deploy aboard USS *Kitty Hawk* (CV-63) on July 6, 1998, and sail to Hawaii, only to be deployed aboard USS *Independence* (CV-62) later in July 1998 to sail back to North Island. This aircraft was assigned to Cdr David 'Bio' Baranek who has contributed both photos and stories for this book.

F-14A-140-GR Tomcat (162698) of VF-14 Tophatters in 1999. Established in September 1919, the Tophatters have the longest continuous service period of any squadron in the US Navy. In 1999 the 80th anniversary was marked with this colourful paint scheme. VF-14 was part of CVW-8 operating off the deck of USS *Theodore Roosevelt* (CVN-71) from March 26 to September 22, 1999, as a part of Operation Southern Watch when 162698 was carrying these markings.

F-14A-115-GR Tomcat (161294) of VF-41 Black Aces in 1999. The effectiveness of a well-trained aircrew equipped with a LANTIRN (LTS) was demonstrated convincingly over Kosovo during daily missions into contested airspace defended by dense concentrations of surface-to-air missiles and Anti-Aircraft Artillery. During these missions, the Forward Air Controller Airborne known as FAC (A) came to the fore as Tomcat aircrews showed time and time again that they could prosecute the toughest targets effectively. Lt Cdr Brian Brurod and Cdr Joe Aucoin were awarded the Silver Star for their impressive performance during the difficult mission against Podgorica Airfield on May 2, 1999, in the midst of Kosovo operations.

A flight of an F/A-18C Hornet of VMFA-314 and an F-14A-130-GR Tomcat (161856) of VF-211 Fighting Checkmates during Operation Southern Watch on December 25, 1997. Both aircraft were part of CVW-9 flying off the deck of USS *Nimitz* (CVN-68). (David Baranek)

accomplishments and professional excellence spoke for itself. We filled the hit board daily; we called each other 'Jack Ass' and 'Fat Bastard'; we laughed at DCAG's attempts to land the Tomcat at night on auto throttles, we learned the 'fine art' of HAZREPs while enduring eight months of post cruise turnaround with hardly any jets to train with; we painted 'Bullets Rule' on the hangar roof in letters large enough to be read from the Space Shuttle; we bruised each other playing crud with the Snakes; we sunk the Belknap, won the Top Hook, Battle E, Safety S and Boola-Boola, and much to the JOs delight – the PXO shot down CAG at Air Wing Fallon! We worked hard and played hard as Bullets believed, 'if you are not having fun, you are not doing it right'. We sacrificed a rental car in Key West to the 'Liberty Gods' during a midnight run-in with a palm tree, and we knighted the 'Dubai Ten' following a night of buffoonery leading to HACQ. I never had a bad day of command.

Although my Tomcat flying days came to an abrupt end, ironically, the scourge of terrorism that we had witnessed first-hand on my virgin Tomcat cruise still needed to be eradicated from our world. Following September 11, we sat in humbled silence, America had been bloodied as it had never been before and the demons that had attacked us had no idea what kind of people they had taken on.

In the quiet moment before the whirlwind, Americans recovered, mourned and buried their dead, bandaged their wounds and then got down to business. President Bush warned our enemies, "The hour is coming when America will act," and confidently told our military, "You will make us proud". Certainly, in the years that followed, these were the Tomcat's finest hours. Tomcat warriors responded with renewed strength and decisiveness, performing magnificently in Operations Enduring and Iraqi Freedom. They made America proud.

We lost many shipmates, squadron mates and air wing mates along the way – in peacetime and in war. Our closest shipmates that gave the ultimate sacrifice were Griff, Belly, Bam Bam, Mark Lange, Spike, Biff, Flipper and Stench. At the countless memorial services we attended, we watched their wives and loved ones clutch a flag in place of their sacrificed sons and husbands as the Tomcat missing man formations flew overhead. Again we wiped the tears from our eyes.

Finally, we served with hundreds of enlisted Tomcat maintenance warriors, plane captains, troubleshooters and ordnance men – the youth of our nation who proudly and expertly maintained and prepped our Tomcats. Yellow shirts guided us, grapes refuelled us, catapult crews launched us, LSOs recovered us on pitching decks during blue water ops on the darkest of nights. These sailors spilled their blood upon the world's troubled waters and witnessed sunsets on a thousand distant and lonely lands. They reflected our diverse origins and were the embodiment of the American spirit of courage and dedication. Their forebears went by other names – Doughboys, Yanks, Buffalo Soldiers, Rough Riders and G.I.s. But during our cherished Tomcat careers, these 'Tomcat Warriors' were the surest guarantee of America's commitment. They answered the call to fight our nation's battles, flourished in the twilight struggles of the Cold War and showed what they were capable of in Desert Storm and the Global War on Terrorism. Each did their duty with pride and honour.

We will never forget our cherished and privileged times with the Tomcat. Hopefully in time, our children, grandchildren and future generations will honour the proud men, women and families of the Tomcat community who sacrificed and contributed so much to the defence of America's freedom.
Capt Scott 'Stewie' Stewart

LINGERING LOVE AFFAIR
After joining the first cadre at Miramar… six F-14 squadrons later I was fortunate to become the programme manager at NavAir (PMA-241) when we finally bested the attack mafia's naval aviation politics and created the F-14D, the fighter that the Tomcat was always supposed to be. Unfortunately, this time DOD and congressional politics got in the way of the new and remanufactured aircraft plan for the Tomcat fleet so we were unable to get the right Tomcat into the hands of so many deserving and faithful fighter pilots and RIOs. We did manage a few sleight of hand advances by quietly recreating the airplane's air-to-ground capability (which was always there). We also managed a new computer, digital flight control and CADC, all of which proved themselves in every one of the Tomcat models.

My last flight as a navy fighter pilot was in the cockpit of my true love. Life always passes too quickly, but my memories of this airplane and those who flew in it and supported it will never fade. It was a special fighter in a special time.
Rear Admiral Jack 'Gringo' Snyder, USN (ret)

TOPGUN AND THE TOMCAT

An F-14A-125-GR Tomcat (161616) of VF-213 Black Lions going vertical with a F-16N of NFWS, in December 1988. (Bob Lawson)

HALF CENTURY, BABY! FIFTY YEARS OF THE GRUMMAN F-14 TOMCAT

The origins of Dissimilar Air Combat Training (DACT), popularised in the movie Top Gun with its depiction of clashes between the F-14 Tomcat and the nimble A-4F Skyhawk, traces its origin back to the First World War and the famed ace of aces, Capt Eddie Rickenbacker, who rose to command the 94th Aero Squadron. Rickenbacker downed several aircraft that he was able to restore to flying condition and he then use to acquaint his pilots with their dissimilar performance characteristics. During the embryonic days of dogfighting, aircraft typically were either tight turning or fast enough to break away and reengage on their own terms. It was ill advised for a faster pursuit aircraft to try to turn with a more agile adversary. This lesson had to be relearned multiple times over the decades before the creation of the Navy Fighter Weapons School more popularly known as TOPGUN. TOPGUN institutionalized the use of adversary aircraft for DACT.

While Rickenbacker and his German foes were able to retrieve crashed or force-landed aircraft, restore them and continue to operate them due to their simple fabric, wood and wire construction, the advent of faster and more complex aircraft in the subsequent decades made this more problematic. During the Second World War, great effort was spent by all protagonists to capture and exploit the aircraft of their opponents. The Germans created a unit of Allied aircraft and took them on visits to frontline squadrons so that pilots could be exposed their characteristics. The British also formed an experimental unit to exploit captured aircraft and then visit Allied airfields to acquaint pilots with their adversaries.

The United States Navy found a crashed Japanese A6M Zero in a bog in the Aleutians and salvaged it. It became the first full-time 'adversary' asset in 1944 after being exploited extensively at North Island and NAS Anacostia. A dedicated exploitation unit was formed to retrieve aircraft found on various Japanese airfields and evaluate them in the air. The Japanese, for their part, were able to capture several US fighters and operate them, notably the plentiful P-40 Warhawks captured intact in their rapid conquests.

The jet age of fast high-powered dogfighting that manifested in the skies over Korea during the early 1950s made capturing aircraft problematic and it was not until a North Korean pilot defected to South Korea in his MiG-15 that one could be studied and exploited. The F-86 Sabre and MiG-15 were very similar in performance but there were still differences to be understood and exploited. The need for DACT became even more pronounced after the Korean War. The Navy had the Fleet Air Gunnery Unit (FAGU) and the Air Force created the Fighter Weapons School (FWS) at Nellis AFB. Both schoolhouses trained pilots to become instructors in their units and had a flightline full of dissimilar aircraft simply because of the wide variety of aircraft then in service. FAGU had the F9F Cougar, F4D Skyray, F-8 Crusader and FJ Fury available for students and instructors to fly whereas the FWS had the F-86 Sabre and F-100. Assigned to FWS, John Boyd had a standing challenge to best him in less than 60 seconds with him defensive. He usually took only 40 seconds of hard manoeuvring to win continuously. Tactics revolved around dogfighting with Boots Blesse coining the phrase 'no guts, no glory'.

The advent of IR-guided missiles like the AIM-9 Sidewinder, first used in combat against MiGs over Taiwan Straits in 1958, and the arrival of even more capable radar-guided missile-equipped fighters like the F-4 Phantom led many to believe the era of the dogfight was over.

When MiGs and US fighters clashed over North Vietnam in 1965, there was a rude awakening as MiG-17s scored the first victories over F-105s orbiting near their target with escorting F-100s unable to respond. The US had emphasized speed over manoeuvrability and had to relearn the lessons evident in DACT. The Air Force, Navy and Marines eventually all flew the F-4 Phantom which had Mach 2 performance but had no business trying to turn with the much nimbler MiG-17 Frescoes of the [North] Vietnam People's Air Force (VPAF). The Air Force had even deemphasized and prohibited 'hassling'

A true movie star! This F-14A-100-GR Tomcat (160681) was under the command of VF-111 Sundowners but here seen with the 'Fists of the Fleet' (VA-25) patch on the tail – and to make matters stranger it reads VFA-213! This aircraft was seen in these markings on August 18, 1985, for the filming of the movie Top Gun. (Craig Kaston via Paul Minert Collection)

TOP GUN AND THE TOMCAT

F-14A-90-GR Tomcat (159855) of NFWS in 1991. One of NFWS's missions was to better Tomcat crews for ACM. NFWS was based at NAS Miramar, CA, and had a number of different aircraft at its disposal. The aircraft selected would share the performance envelope with their Russian counterparts. The Tomcat and the Russian Su-27 Flanker shared many characteristics and thus NFWS used Tomcats to play the part of Su-27 adversaries. This Tomcat even was adorned in the same colours as Russian Su-27s complete with the red star on the tail, and the large red '31' beneath the cockpit. This aircraft became known as Red 31 or the Tomcatski, and served with NFWS in 1991 to early 1992 when it went back into fleet service with VF-2, before returning to NFWS in 1993. The aircraft was sent to storage at AMARC on March 23, 1998.

F-14A-130-GR Tomcat (161869) of NSAWC in 2000. Another adversary Tomcat from NSAWC at NAS Fallon, NV. Still the Tomcat played the part of the Flanker, only at this time the Flankers were mostly painted in a grey/blue splinter style camouflage scheme, which was imitated on a few of NSAWC Tomcats. Toward the 2000s the Tomcats were gradually being phased out of service, and this aircraft had a long service history behind it with frontline squadrons. The last few years of its active duty were spent at NAS Fallon, before it was sent to AMARC on January 15, 2002.

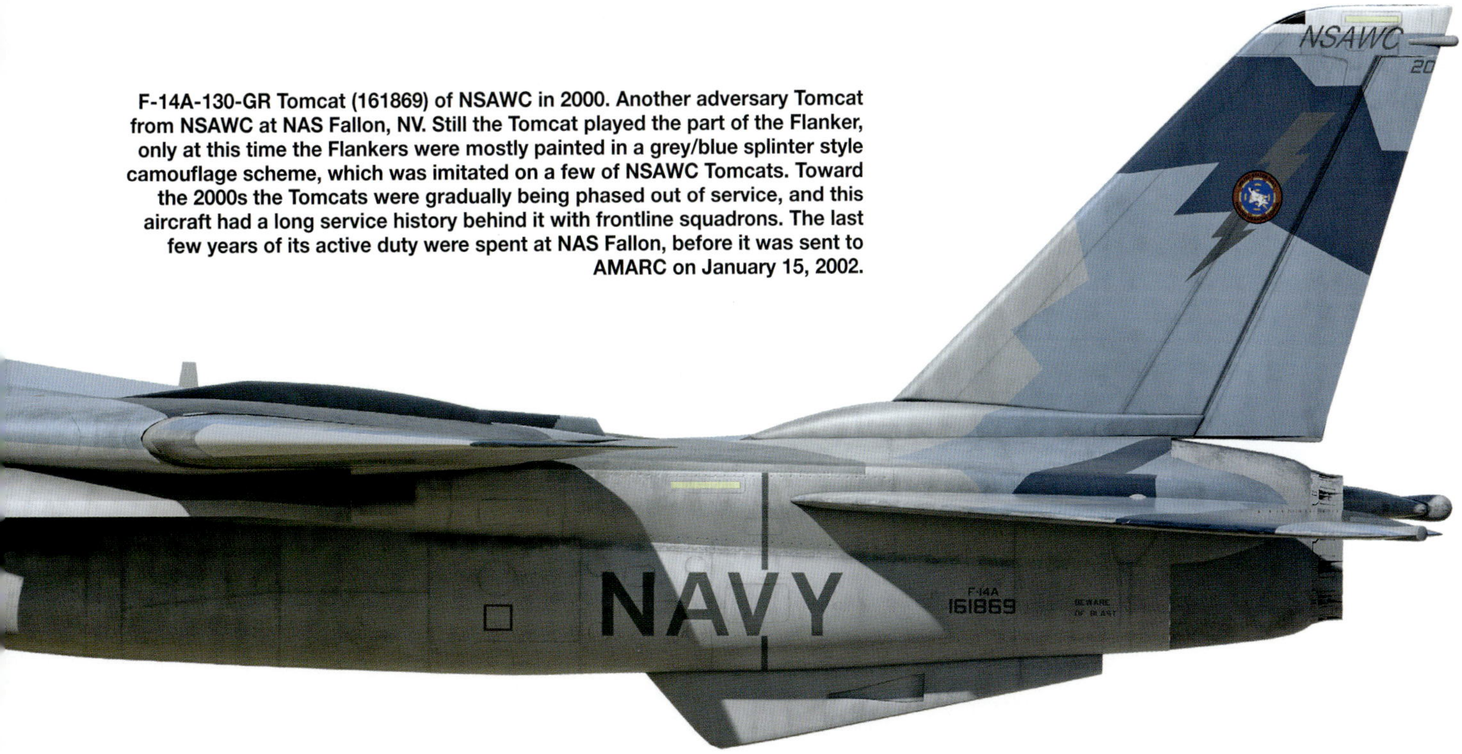

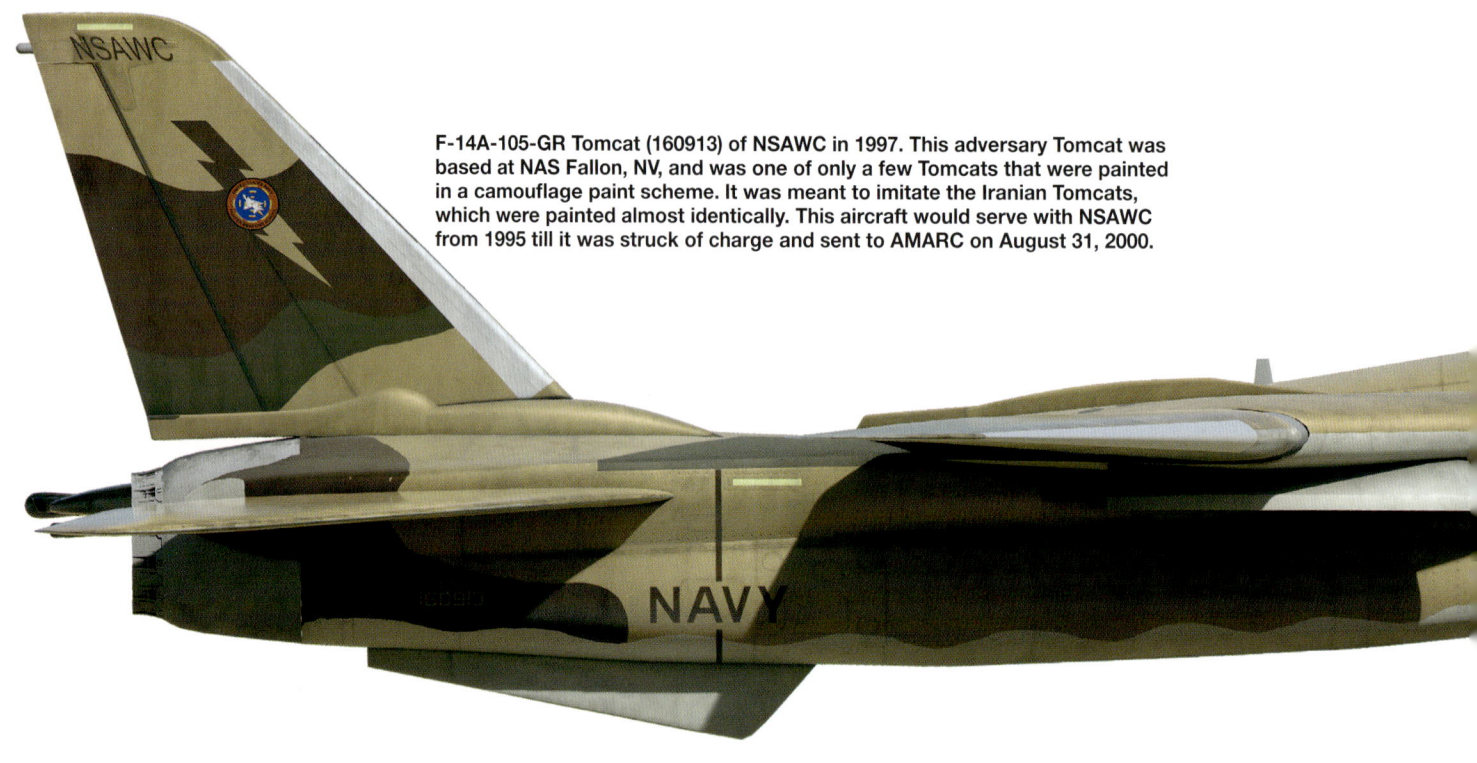

F-14A-105-GR Tomcat (160913) of NSAWC in 1997. This adversary Tomcat was based at NAS Fallon, NV, and was one of only a few Tomcats that were painted in a camouflage paint scheme. It was meant to imitate the Iranian Tomcats, which were painted almost identically. This aircraft would serve with NSAWC from 1995 till it was struck of charge and sent to AMARC on August 31, 2000.

The 'Tomcatski' or 'Red 31' – an F-14A-90-GR Tomcat (159855) painted in the colours of a Russian Flanker in December 1991. (Paul Minert Collection)

by 1965 due to mishaps. The Navy F-8 Crusader units had kept dogfighting of Air Combat Manoeuvring (ACM) alive as inheritors of the day fighter mission whereas the F-4 Phantom was the latest in interceptor technology, emphasizing dash speed and beyond visual range employment of radar missiles. However, ROE in Vietnam necessitated visual conformation of a bogey before firing so the Phantom's Sparrow missile advantage was negated by having to close to a visual arena in which the MiG's manoeuvrability gave it an edge. North Vietnam used GCI control of its fighters, so they looked for an encounter giving them the upper hand. The resultant exchange ratio was less then optimum or expected.

Aerial activity intensified after the initial encounter on June 17, 1965, and by September 17, 1968, there had been 360 hostile engagements with almost 600 air-to-air missiles expended, although there were occasional cases of 20mm cannon being used by the F-105 Thunderchiefs and the F-8 Crusaders. Missiles were the dominant weapon but there were far more misses than hits as evidenced by only one kill achieved on average for every ten firing attempts. Meanwhile, the Air Force had conducted an exhaustive study of the Air War called Project Red Baron with the initial report published in December 1966.

Project Red Baron continued to analyse air-to-air performance with Red Baron II and III published in 1973 and 1974. The Chief of Naval Operations (CNO) was also concerned and directed another review of air-to-air performance which was formally titled the Air-to-Air Missile System Capability Review but became known as the Ault Report after the head of the five man team responsible for it, Capt Frank Ault. Ault tackled his assignment with vigour from July-November 1968. A bombing halt had been instituted in March 1968 so the Navy had a chance to reflect on the three years of aerial combat.

Ault formally reported his findings and recommendations, which included reestablishment of a graduate level instructor course similar to FAGU under the auspices of VF-121, the F-4 Phantom FRS, at NAS Miramar. Lt Cdr Dan Pederson, a tactics Instructor at VF-121 was selected to lead the effort. He recruited Lt Jim Ruliffson as the second Instructor (Ruliffson would later command TOPGUN after attending Test Pilot School. TOPGUN formally became the Navy Fighter Waepons School in March 1969. DACT was an important part of the flying syllabus using A-4E Skyhawks that were readily available in the Instrument RAG at Miramar, VF-126. The A-4 was perfect to replicate the tight-turning MiG-17 that gave so much trouble to the Phantom aircrews over Vietnam.

Even as Project Red Baron and the Ault Report were digging into the encounters over North Vietnam, the United States received an important gift from Israel that helped in understanding the threat. Israeli agents had convinced an Iraqi pilot to defect with a MiG-21 in August 1966. After exploitation in Israel lasting 12 months and involving over 100 hours of flights, the aircraft was obtained by the Defense Intelligence Agency on a loan in exchange for the US providing Israel with the latest F-4E Phantom. The MiG was sent to Area 51 and evaluated by Air Force and Navy pilots under the codename Have Doughnut, a three-month intensive exploitation and evaluation effort before returning it to Israel. The following year, Israel sent two MiG-17s to the United States also to Area 51, thus becoming Have Drill. These two Syrian MiG-17s had inadvertently landed at an Israeli airfield, mistaking it for a friendly Lebanese base. Much like the exploitation of 'Koga's Zero' in 1942-3, The US now had actual adversaries to evaluate and use in familiarizing US pilots. These were prized assets so the Air Force Weapons School and Navy Fighter Weapons Schools looked for surrogates. The F-5 and T-38 were similar in size and performance to the MiG-21 as evidenced by the E-M diagrams comparing the two aircraft. The MiG-17 was faster than the A-4 Skyhawk but its turning performance was similar and the roll rate much slower which was exploited in tactics developed to counter it. Both Have Doughnut and Have Drill provided important and crucially relevant info to the instructors at both Fighter Weapons Schools.

By the time of the first flight of the Tomcat, TOPGUN was churning out F-4 Phantom aircrews and eager to incorporate the Tomcat. 'Rookie' Robb became the first Tomcat pilot to fly against the MiG-17 and was astounded by the turning performance.

'Hoot' Gibson was part of the first cadre of senior F-4 Phantom aircrew

TOP GUN AND THE TOMCAT

sent to form VF-1 and made the first deployment on USS *Enterprise*.

OUTFIGHTING A PHANTOM
I had just 30 hours in the F-14 when I went up against a 1,000 hour F-4 guy. We called 'Fight's on!' and 30 seconds later I was sitting in his six. We ran the engagement three times. The results were always the same. An F-14 with a nugget (me) at the stick could outmanoeuvre, outturn, and outfight a Phantom flown by an old hand.
Capt Bob 'Hoot' Gibson

AIM/ACEVAL
One particular event (of many) makes me smile. It was back in 1975. I was on the staff at TOPGUN and Hoser was at AIM/ACE up at Nellis. We had arranged to meet over the desert at Chocolate Mt. and do an ACM performance comparison between the F-5E and the F-14A. By then I had a fair amount of time in the F-5 and it felt sort of like a second skin to me. I could do some really neat stuff with it and I figured I could at least give Hoser (with Bill 'Hill Billy' Hill as his back seater) a respectable fight. So we got together over the blazing desert below (with Clint Eastwood staring up at us, no doubt), took a two mile lateral separation and the fight was on. In no time we were beak to beak and for me the fight went downhill from there. I tried all my slickest moves, but in fairly short order I was looking back across my vertical stab at two huge intakes camped out at my six with 'guns' coming into my headset.

Well, this went on for several more set-ups with the same end result. Finally Hoser said we'd start with me behind him at 1,500ft. Ooohhh yeeahhh! I said to myself. He for damn sure can't shake me off his dead six. Wrong again. He proceeds to go hard nose up and do one of his famous 'Vorboschka' manoeuvres (stick full forward and in one corner, rudder full opposite) and now I'm watching this huge F-14 planform basically stopping in mid-air, pitching nose over as I slide out in front of him, and then recovering nose low behind me and rolling back to a perfect guns tracking solution at my six. I had no more questions. I spent the rest of the day looking for my 'appendage' which had been so thoroughly knocked in the dirt.

The bottom line though is that not only was the Tomcat an awesome airplane, but in the hands of one of the few fighter pilots of Hoser's league, it was absolutely eye-watering. Dale 'Snort' Snodgrass was another one of those gifted sticks that the rest of us can only admire and envy. I was lucky to get to fly it. My admiration and thanks go to the Grumman Tank & Iron Works for a FINE fighting machine.
Alex 'Rattler' Rucker, Tomcat pilot CO, VF-14 Tophatters

THE 'FRISBEE' REALLY COULD FIGHT
As a young naval aviator there was nothing more I wanted to do (after they decom'd the last F-8 Gunfighter squadron) than to 'git-in' the Tomcat. I had a long and circuitous road getting there. As a consequence I had a lot of time in the 'Scooter'. Lordy, lordy, I love that 'sports car'. My first aerodynamic sweetheart.

Then, after a 'trip in the penalty box' I finally got the chance – orders to the West Coast Tomcat RAG. Rubbin' elbows with guys like Rat, Mac, Sobes, Shooter, Black, etc. and then, suddenly I was there on the back of a Tomcat doing the walkaround. First impression... holy smokes, this thing is HUGE! Followed by the realisation that the 'Aluminum Overcast' was always going to be fight centre, and you had a thrust-to-weight ratio around .68 to 1 (F-14A). Fighter? Yeah right. Maybe a great interceptor...

That was kinda my attitude for a significant period of time (including as a student at Fighter Weapons School) until I met, and got to fly wing with a guy named Bunkie (Dave Berke). Dave was an original ACE/AIMVAL guy who competed with Hoser for best kill ratio... a real fighter pilot's fighter pilot. That first flight on his wing was unbelievable. Bunkie and Cowboy, and Loco and Shooter proceeded to go 2v6 with a group of Reserve F-4S Phantoms.

To make a long (but quick) story short, I was 'prosecuting' my second Phantom when Bunkie slid in front of me (after downing four himself), at which time I transmitted: "Bunkie, if you don't get out of the way, I'm gonna shoot you first." His nonchalant answer was "okie dokey" at which time I finished the 'fight'. I had never seen someone fly the 'Cat like that.

More than any other single engagement in my career, that one with Bunkie in the Tomcat was my 'awakening', and I realised the true meaning of the old saying 'it's a poor craftsman who blames his tools'. I was never the 'ace of the base' but from that time forward in the Tomcat, Hornet, Scooter, Tiger, etc. I always strove to ensure that I was doing my damnedest to fight to MY best ability.

In retrospect I often wonder what she (the Tomcat) could have been with the proper 'care and feeding'... power plants and upgrades... I only flew As and chased Bs and Ds... but I often wonder... especially when I look at the latest versions of the Flanker. In my heart of hearts I'll always wonder what could have been.
Capt Chip 'Loco' McNees, USN (ret)

HALF CENTURY, BABY! FIFTY YEARS OF THE GRUMMAN F-14 TOMCAT

While some of NFWS's F-14 Tomcats were painted in elaborate camo schemes, this F-14A-70-GR Tomcat (158997) was carrying the standard TPS, as seen at NAS Miramar in March 1992. (Paul Minert Collection)

F-14A-100-GR Tomcat (160667) of VF-51 Screaming Eagles in 1986. 160667 is arguably the most famous Tomcat there ever was, after it was painted in a fictitious livery for the movie Top Gun. Notice the names of the two main characters from the film Lt Pete 'Maverick' Mitchell and Lt(jg) Nick 'Goose' Bradshaw on the canopy rail. The Tomcats used for the film were from VF-51 and VF-111 (the two fighter squadrons from CVW-15), which wasn't deployed at the time. Rumour has it that the fictitious livery was added so no actual fighter squadron would become more famous than the others. The squadron patch of this aircraft was in fact the patch of VAW-110 'Firebirds', who were flying E-2C Hawkeyes out of NAS Miramar, and the other Tomcat painted for the movie had a VA-25 'Fists of the Fleet' patch on the tail.

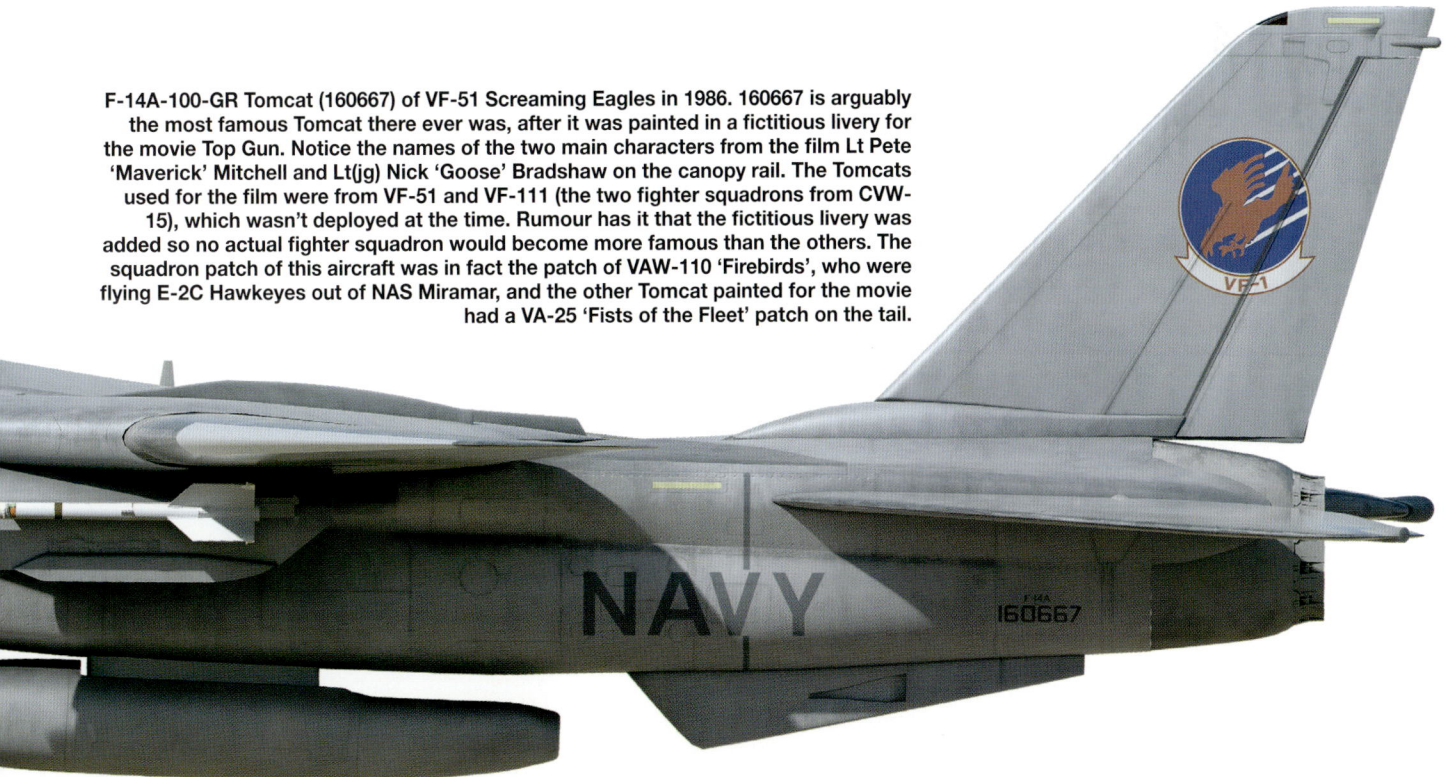

As VF-74 Be-Devilers took on the role of adversary squadron, this unique camo scheme was applied to their jets. This F-14A-120-GR Tomcat (161432) was seen parked at NAS Oceana on May 26, 1994. The AA tailcode was retained despite the squadron being under direct command of the Atlantic Fleet. (Paul Minert Collection)

HALF CENTURY, BABY! FIFTY YEARS OF THE GRUMMAN F-14 TOMCAT

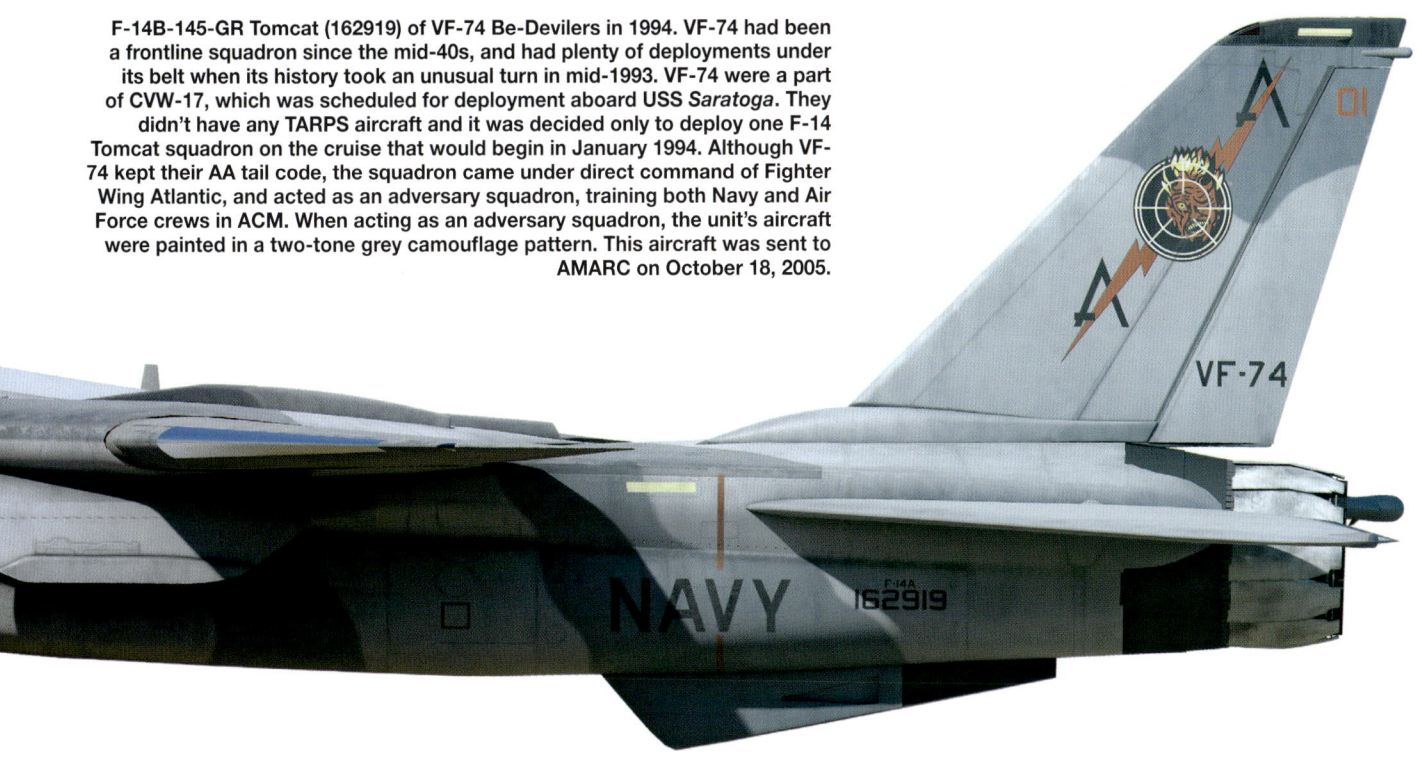

F-14B-145-GR Tomcat (162919) of VF-74 Be-Devilers in 1994. VF-74 had been a frontline squadron since the mid-40s, and had plenty of deployments under its belt when its history took an unusual turn in mid-1993. VF-74 were a part of CVW-17, which was scheduled for deployment aboard USS Saratoga. They didn't have any TARPS aircraft and it was decided only to deploy one F-14 Tomcat squadron on the cruise that would begin in January 1994. Although VF-74 kept their AA tail code, the squadron came under direct command of Fighter Wing Atlantic, and acted as an adversary squadron, training both Navy and Air Force crews in ACM. When acting as an adversary squadron, the unit's aircraft were painted in a two-tone grey camouflage pattern. This aircraft was sent to AMARC on October 18, 2005.

SIR BUCKETHEAD REMEMBERS

Hardest cat shot I ever had was with Chain, in a VF-11 Ripper Tomcat, 215 knots end speed... well beyond the LBA of the F-14... broke my neck, broke my Tomcat... I didn't fly until 18 months later, but my Turkey flew the next day, so did Chain. When next we met, it was abeam with me in a Super Fox (A-4F) with some poor Cat 1 in his FRS 'A' model Tomcat... got to fight Snort on his last 1v1 in Tomcats, with Mean Jim in his trunk, flying a slicked to the bones, VF-103 'B', me in a slick lot six F/A-18A... 300ft overcast at Oceana... solid to 15k in the TACTS range... 20k hard deck... 1.5nm abeam, 500kts, triple Immelmans into the forties then canopy-to-canopy all the way back down...

Nothing you can fight gives you such a large and dynamic picture inside the phone booth. For size, looks, power and grace the Tomcat is a gorgeous slow fight – but that's fighter aviation, one day cold callous, impartial, the next makes you want to stay a fighter pilot forever.

My whole career it's been here – a fixture on the flight line, on the range and in the break – nothing else with a pointy nose has been as much fun to fly and to fight... the last pure fighter the Navy will ever see... all the rest will be strike fighters. A Cold War relic that remade itself after Desert Storm One to become the preferred deliverer of PGMs. I feel honoured to have flown and fought this plane... never thought my career would outlive it. Semper... Sir Buckethead.
Capt John 'Sir Buckethead' Cole

THE LAST GUNFIGHTER TACTICS DET

After deployments with VF-32, I later flew F-5s in the adversary role giving me the opportunity to go to Key West and participate in the last VF-101 Key West Tactics detachment. It was an opportunity which I did not want to miss, as I have many fond memories of Key West tactics dets, both my own when I went through VF-101 as a Cat 1 RP, and several flown on the Red side over the years. To me, perhaps the best part of the det is just having the opportunity to once again fly in formation with the 'Big Fighter'. There is something special about the Tomcat, it has that magical presence that few aircraft have ever had, and I loved flying to and from the working areas with an F-14 on my wing, just to watch it making its way through the sky.

As adversary pilots we also looked forward to Tomcat dets because we knew we would never lose sight. For pilots used to keeping track of two or three F-5s in an engagement, being a single F-5 keeping track of two F-14s in an engagement made life just a little bit easier. This combined with the fact that the Tom was a more difficult airplane for the student to learn how to fight his (or her) plane (than a Hornet) meant more BFM for us.

Hornet pilots would just get some separation, then put both boots up on the dash and pull for all they were worth, followed by Fox-3 (AMRAAM). With Toms we had higher odds of having engagements go several turns at a minimum. While there were some significant differences to be found fighting the different Tomcat models, much of this was masked for RPs as they worked their way through fighting the airplane and expanding their understanding of BFM. When fighting F-14As, we might spend a little more time watching them in areas of the envelope where they might be more compressor stall prone or once they were pretty slow, especially if the slow was compounded with low altitude.

You can pretty much group F-14Bs and Ds together and their higher thrust brought them a capability to go vertical almost anytime. The liability of that thrust was that when left to mostly its own devices (pilots hanging off the tails) it could quickly become an arcing machine. Of course, As were more than capable of this too. I remember my own trip to Key West as an RP, and during a 1v1 with an F-5, finding myself somehow just about on my gameplan in a relatively planar two-circle fight where I should have been winning the rate war, but wasn't seeing much change. I told this to my RIO Kevin 'Hanus' Haney and he promptly replied that perhaps our 525 knot airspeed might have something to do with it. So as a good student I promptly went to 6.5gs, patiently waited as the F-5 marched towards our nose rather quickly now, followed by 'Fox'. This was a lesson not soon forgotten and one which I try to always keep in mind as an adversary driver.

My job is to instruct, and some days that is facilitated by me fighting my best fight in the F-5, and others maybe

An F-14A-90-GR Tomcat (159855) from NSAWC here seen sporting a two-tone blue and grey camo scheme in May 1996. (Paul Minert Collection)

throttling back to Mil, arcing around waiting for the student to figure things out and hopefully end up with a sight picture that will be remembered. Being significantly outclassed in thrust to weight, our big advantage with a Tom is rolling, so we would usually look to try and keep our energy up, or look to jump deep into the phone booth and keep everyone nearby. One of the great things about doing adversary work is that if the Blue side is doing well and we get whacked, we feel good because the training is going well, particularly in BFM where sometimes you can almost see the light bulb coming on across the circle.

For those days when things aren't going so well on the Blue side, well we probably found some enjoyment in being on the weapons delivery side or maybe just tying the fighters for a good long time, and if we've done our job well we will have some good material for the debrief. All in all it was another great Key West Tactics Det, some good times, some boring times. Lots of enjoyment just flying with and around the 'Big Fighter' one more time, but a somewhat melancholy end watching the Toms and thinking that it might be the last time we ever get to watch that big beautiful beast with her wings back rolling into the break.
Capt C.R. 'Max' Dugan, USN (ret)

TOMCATS AS ADVERSARIES

Unlike the USAF Fighter Weapons School which had luxury of latest aircraft for instructors to fly, the Navy Fighter Weapons School (TOPGUN) started with borrowed and castoff A-4 and T-38 aircraft for use as adversaries. The end of Vietnam brought a handful of brand-new F-5E Tigers originally intended for the South Vietnamese Air Force which gave them a supersonic adversary albeit in few numbers. Prayers were answered when the dedicated F-16N arrived but its tenure was relatively short lived as the brutal ACM sorties took their toll resulting in early retirement. TOPGUN had always wanted its own F-14 Tomcats to keep its RIO instructors current and provide an adversary replicating the Iranian threat. Nothing better than the actual aircraft you may potentially face to practice against. TOPGUN eventually got a few Tomcats of its own that were painted in Iranian and FSU markings (replicating a Su-27).

The USAF Fighter Weapons School also desired to use friendly Tomcats and 'hired' Navy Tomcat Squadrons to participate in its syllabus flights. By the summer of 1990, Carrier Air Wing 3 was looking for things to do after the anticipated deployment aboard USS *John F Kennedy* was cancelled. Port Calls for Fleet Week in New York and Boston with Air Wing embarked were nice distractions, but it also meant the OPTAR (fuel) for training was suddenly scarce and critical parts priority was at a low level. Lt John Olligies had a friend at USAF Fighter Weapons School looking for Tomcats to challenge the F-15C Weapons Instructor Course as surrogates for Iranian Tomcats.

Our executive officer (XO) Bob Davis was a former TOPGUN Instructor and knew the WIC Director of Operations (Gazer) and had flown with Air Force as a Red Eagle out of Nellis. He had arranged with Gazer to send Roger Budd and me to Nellis in a VF-32 Tomcat in 1989 to fly with the Eagle WIC course to prep us for our upcoming participation in TOPGUN. We spent a couple of weeks with the Fighter Weapons School (FWS) flying in a variety of roles. I became aware that both the FWS and 422d TES at Nellis were always in need of RED Air support. Note: At that time the original F-5E aggressors had been struggling with structural problems and the USAF was borrowing F-16As but did not have sufficient assets to meet need.

So in 1990, I reached out to him about the possibility of bringing VF-32 to Nellis. It was a great time playing 'let's make a deal' with the USAF WIC (Weapons Instructor Course) getting them to pay for our fuel, lodging and per diem

including vehicles. They wanted us to be configured as the Iranian Tomcats (no external tanks) and to be inventive with counter Eagle tactics.
Jon 'Ollie' Olligies, Tomcat pilot

WILY BOGIES
One of the F-15C Fighter Weapons School students had to do a 're-fly' after tangling with us so I would call that one a win for the 'wily bogies' they asked us to be.
Gene 'Casper' Edwards, VF-32 Tomcat RIO

BANDITS!
In 1993, mid-tour in command of Fighter Squadron 74, we received the bad news that the Be-Devilers were to be disestablished to feed F-14Bs into the product improvement modification pipeline. To say this was a blow to squadron morale is an understatement.

The squadron was blessed with an exceptional cadre of department heads and enlisted leaders, cruise-seasoned aircrew and an outstanding maintenance department. Fighter Wing ONE further directed VF-74 to turn over four of our ten jets, some aircrew and key maintenance personnel to our sister squadron. Fortunately, we were funded to continue flying and maintaining our six remaining Tomcats for the next 14 months.

I gathered my XO, Cdr 'JJ' Morrow, the department heads, CMC and the maintenance master chief to discuss our situation and to brainstorm a way ahead. We reached consensus that our principal responsibility would be to prepare our squadron mates for 'life after the disestablishment', so it was important to take advantage of every training opportunity we could identify, both for our aircrew and maintenance personnel. That said, our ops boss, Lt Cdr 'Mary' Hartman, contacted the Nellis Range Complex to explore training opportunities.

We were surprised to find that the USAF would pay Per Diem and OPTAR for USN squadrons to support Red Flag training at Nellis, AFB. The icing on the cake was the participating squadrons could use the Nellis weapons complex to conduct live ordnance training to support their respective T&R (Training & Readiness) matrix goals. So, with Fighter Wing ONE's blessing, the Be-Devilers decided to take the training show on the road to prepare our aircrew and maintenance personnel for their follow-on assignment.

In preparation for our first detachment, I conducted a CO's call with the troops to explain the plan. The vision I proposed was well received and one of the young fellows in the corrosion control shop suggested that we consider painting our aircraft like an adversary, similar to VF-43. This idea took a little getting used to, but painting the aircraft truly motivated and united the maintenance department toward a common goal... playing the part of an adversary. So the Ops and Maintenance officers did some research on aircraft paint schemes and we began the process of converting from 'haze grey' to 'tactical blue'. In all, the Be-Devilers safely conducted four detachments to Nellis, enjoyed an unprecedented FMC rate, enabled each aircrew to actually complete the CNAL T&R Matrix, qualified our ordnance handling teams and in the process had the best time of our lives in an outstanding liberty port... Las Vegas.
Capt Skip 'Skipdawg' Sayers, USN (ret)

TOPGUN TOMCAT
The jet most special to me is BuNo 159615 which was the one 'Boog' and I flew in October 1994 when I was CO of TOPGUN. We were on a class det to Fallon and had to make an aft wingsweep landing (~55 degrees) after a combined side hydraulics failure and a few other problems. We weren't sure how the 210kt approach speed was going to do there on a warm day with no brakes... NWS, etc. Only ground down a bit of the hook before the wire. I was happy to buy the crash crew beer that day.
Vice Admiral Dick 'Weasel' Gallagher, USN (ret)

Painted in the colours of the IRIAF Tomcats, this F-14A-105-GR Tomcat (160913) served as an adversary aircraft under the command of NSAWC in April 1998. (Paul Minert Collection)

FOURTH DECADE

The Diamondbacks flew F-14B Tomcats on their last deployment before being redesignated to VFA-102. This photo was taken on December 19, 2001, when CVW-1 were aboard USS *Theodore Roosevelt* (CVN-71) in support of Operation Enduring Freedom. (US Navy)

THE LAST DECADE

HALF CENTURY, BABY! FIFTY YEARS OF THE GRUMMAN F-14 TOMCAT

I have been associated with the Grumman Iron Works aircraft my entire 28-year career, flying the A-6 Intruder through my command tour and then the EA-6B and venerable F-14 Tomcat as Commander Carrier Air Wing 3. The Tomcat was agile yet rugged and strong. I truly loved how LANTIRN worked for LGBs and then updated tapes arrived for JDAM, which in conjunction with the AWG-9 radar gave it awesome lethality in both the air-to-air and air-to-ground mission with great range. It was a great honour and pleasure to fly even if for one fleeting tour.
Rear Admiral Joe 'Killer' Kilkenny, Commander Carrier Strike Group Ten

THEY WERE ALL BIG GUYS
Some observations from my time as a SEAL JTAC working Close Air Support (CAS), and instructing at NSAWC on Naval Special Warfare (NSW) and JTAC (Joint Terminal Attack Controller) COI.

One early spring, I was working with students from the JTAC course during an Air Wing det. On one CAS event, Capt Dave 'Roy' Rogers, then NAS Fallon CO and former N5 at NSAWC, asked to bring some visitors out to the range to observe the CAS Event. When he arrived, I briefed the visitors on range safety and the schedule of events. Shortly thereafter a division of F-14s arrived on station armed with live Mk82 and 83 bombs and GBU-16s. The F-14 squadron was hammering everything in sight. All bombs were on the correct target array with TOTs under ten seconds. Capt Rogers (a former A-6 Pilot) was standing next to me. I commented on how accurate the F-14s were with timing and bombing accuracy. His comment back to me was: "For an organization that was designed solely for fleet air defence, and air-to-air, they have wrapped their arms around the CAS mission and mastered it." Compared to the Navy F/A-18, The F-14s were the most reliable for showing up for CAS in questionable weather. The only exception to this was the USMC F/A-18s Marine Air lives for CAS.

While briefing of the CAS events during CVW training, the standard or acceptable error for the TOTs was plus or minus ten seconds. I would challenge the aircrews to a plus or minus five seconds on the first pass of each section. The bet was a six-pack of beer or first round at the club. I spent a lot of money paying off bets to the F-14 crews.

Navy F-14 FAC (A)* aircrews were a welcome boon to special operations. A LANTIRN-equipped F-14 with a FAC (A) trained aircrew was a major force multiplier for small special operations forces. They could do it all from controlling fixed and rotary wing air support to calling in sea and shore based artillery. The only other FAC (A) aircrews that could do that were the USMC F/A-18Ds. However, the shortfall for them was having to use the NITE Hawk pod. I would always tell the Army Special Forces and SEAL operators to always request a Navy FAC (A) for support on combat operations.

One thing I always observed with the F-14 crews was that they were all big guys usually over 5ft 11in. Most looked like they played football for the Naval Academy. F/A-18 crews were generally 5ft 9in and under. The F-14s and the crews that flew them were the Dick Butkus of the strike fighters... big guys and big powerful planes ready to crush anything that came into their zone. They just looked scary when they were coming at you down low, and most F-14 flight crews looked like they could handle a good bar brawl. The F/A-18 were more of a stiletto of the aircraft and acted like they should be wearing dockers and polo shirts with a cardigan sweater tied around their neck. The USMC F/A-18 aircrews are a different story and not to be confused.
Andy 'Senior' Nelson, SEAL JTAC(I)

FOURTH DECADE

F-14A-135-GR Tomcat (162604) of VF-14 Tophatters in 2001. CVW-8 was aboard USS *Enterprise* (CVN-65) from April 25 to November 10, 2001 on a deployment to the Persian Gulf as a part of Operation Enduring Freedom. Shortly after the deployment (on December 1, 2001) the squadron was redesignated to VFA-14 in preparation for the arrival of F/A-18E Super Hornets. This aircraft was sent to AMARC on February 2, 2002.

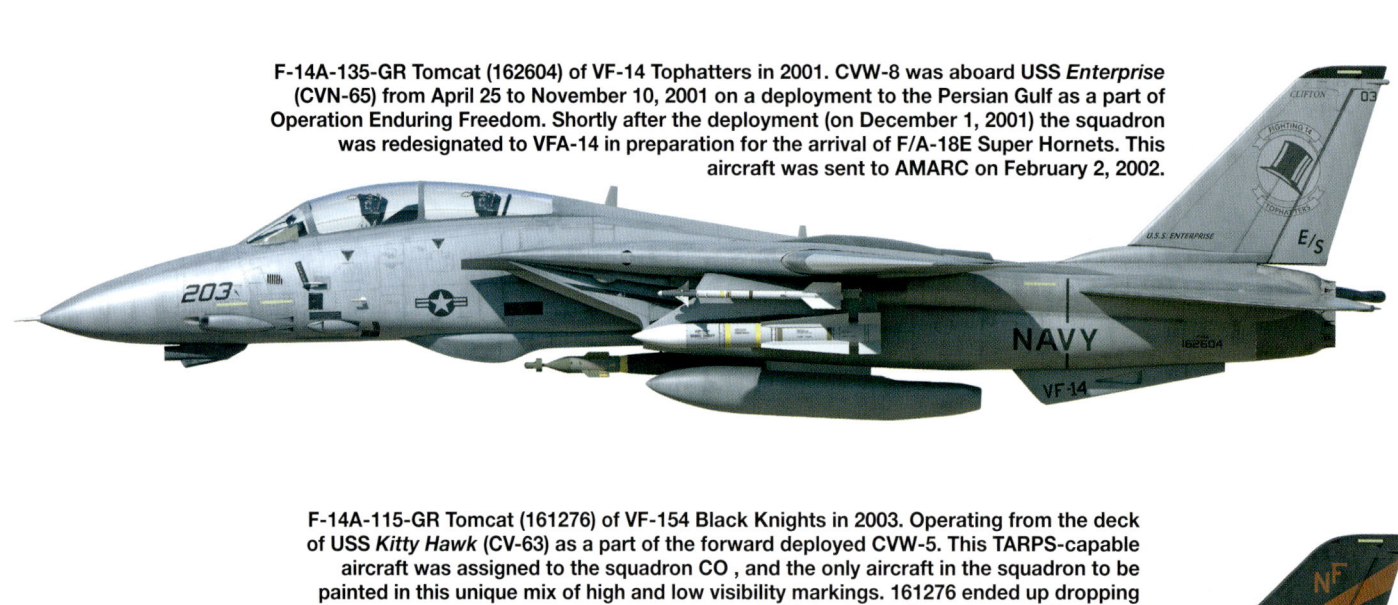

F-14A-115-GR Tomcat (161276) of VF-154 Black Knights in 2003. Operating from the deck of USS *Kitty Hawk* (CV-63) as a part of the forward deployed CVW-5. This TARPS-capable aircraft was assigned to the squadron CO , and the only aircraft in the squadron to be painted in this unique mix of high and low visibility markings. 161276 ended up dropping 45 LGBs during Operation Iraqi Freedom.

F-14B-145-GR Tomcat (162925) of VF-11 Red Rippers in 2002. CVW-7 was aboard USS *John F. Kennedy* (CV-67) from February 7 to August 17, 2002. USS *John F. Kennedy* was in the North Arabian Sea and the embarked air wing was conducting missions as a part of Operation Enduring Freedom. The Red Rippers Tomcats would be sent on one more deployment before transitioning to the F/A-18F Super Hornet. 162925 would remain in the service of VF-11 until it was sent to AMARC on April 5, 2005.

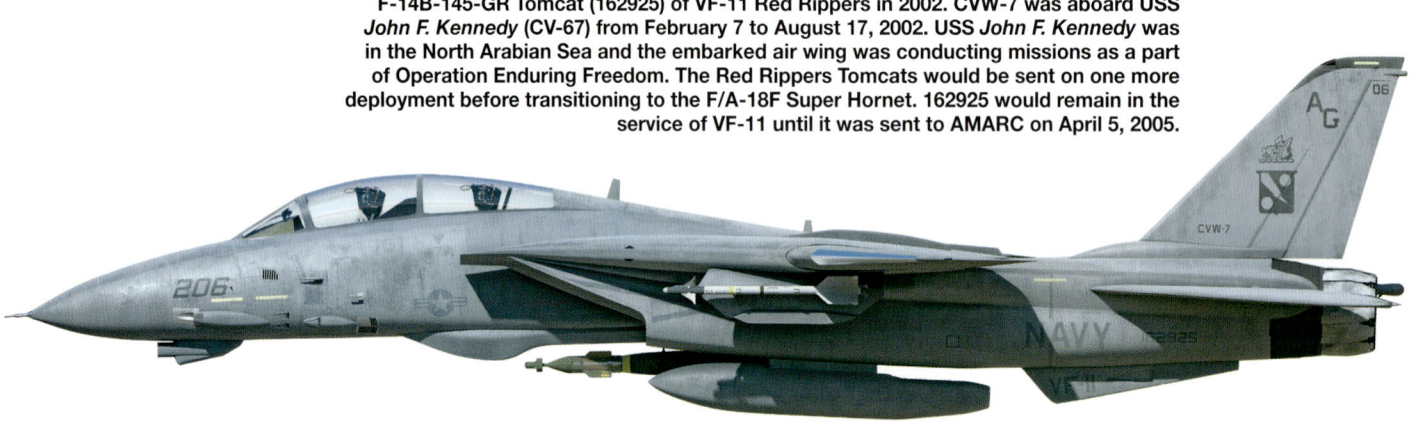

F-14B-120-GR Tomcat (161437) of VF-11 Red Rippers in 2005. VF-11 were awaiting the arrival of their new aircraft the F/A-18F Super Hornet in the first half of 2005. The squadron decorated several of their jets in special markings, including this St Patrick's Day themed example. On April 1, 2005, the squadron were redesignated to VFA-11, and the Tomcats were retired.

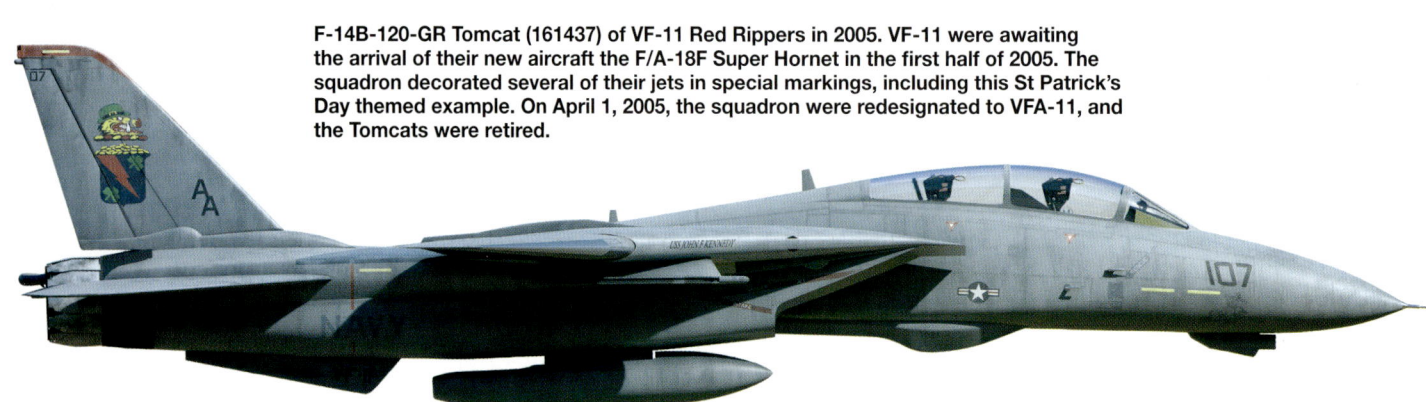

An F-14A Tomcat of VF-211 Fighting Checkmates seconds before being catapulted off the deck of USS *John C. Stennis* (CVN-74) on January 1, 2002, during Operation Enduring Freedom. VF-211 was part of CVW-9 on the deployment that lasted from November 12, 2001, to May 28, 2002. (US Navy)

An F-14B-145-GR Tomcat (162912) of VF-11 Red Rippers about to launch from USS *John F. Kennedy* (CV-67). CVW-7 was deployed in the North Arabian Sea from February 7 to August 17, 2002, for Operation Enduring Freedom. (US Navy)

FOURTH DECADE

F-14B-145-GR Tomcat (162926) of VF-143 Pukin' Dogs in 2005. This last CAG bird sports modex number 143. VF-143 were stationed at NAS Oceana, awaiting their replacement F/A-18E Super Hornets. On March 1, 2005, the squadron was redesignated to VFA-143, thereby marking the end of the Tomcat era with the Pukin' Dogs.

HALF CENTURY, BABY! FIFTY YEARS OF THE GRUMMAN F-14 TOMCAT

F-14B-150-GR Tomcat (163217) of VF-103 Jolly Rogers in 2004. The last deployment for the Jolly Rogers with the Tomcat lasted from June 7 to December 13, 2004. The deployment took CVW-17 aboard USS *John F. Kennedy* (CV-67) to the Persian Gulf in support of Operation Iraqi freedom. Notice the four mission markings below the canopy on this very sharp looking CAG bird. This was the last deployment aboard a conventional powered aircraft carrier, as CV-67 was retired soon after the deployment ended.

F-14B-140-GR Tomcat (162699) of VX-9 Vampires in 2001. VX-9 was in some ways a conglomerate of VX-5 and VX-4. The lineage of VX-9 stems from VX-5 but with VX-4's disestablishment being imminent, personnel and aircraft from VX-4 were transferred from VX-4 to VX-9 in June 1993. The squadron would operate out of NAS Pt. Mugu, CA, and NAS China Lake, CA. 162699 was originally a F-14A but was converted to F-14B standard in the mid-1990s. It would end its service life with VX-9.

FOURTH DECADE

A formation of three aircraft from CVW-17 (F/A-18C Hornet of VFA-83, S-3B Viking of VS-30) flying above the Caribbean as a part of a training exercise in preparation for an upcoming deployment to the North Arabian Sea. The F-14B-145-GR Tomcat (162918) of VF-103 Jolly Rogers closest to the camera is here seen equipped with the LANTIRN pod. (US Navy)

An F-14A-125-GR Tomcat (161612) of VF-211 Fighting Checkmates performs a high-speed pass of USS *John C. Stennis* (CVN-74) on May 5, 2002, while deployed in the North Arabian Sea. (US Navy)

BOMBCAT OVER AFGHANISTAN

While on deployment with VF-11 and CVW-7 in March 2002 aboard the USS John F Kennedy (CV 67) in support of Operation Enduring Freedom, I was flying a Red Ripper F-14B (Upgrade) Tomcat with Cdr Chris 'Lung' Aquilino who was the Red Ripper CO at the time. We became the first Tomcat aircrew to expend a JDAM (a 2,000lb GBU-31) in combat. Our target was a cave housing Taliban personnel and weapons south of Gardez, Afghanistan on elevated terrain commonly referred to as the 'Whale Back'. The Whale Back was hotly contested ground in Operation Anaconda, which was essentially a sweeping push by US Army SOF, US Navy Seals, USAF SOF and other international forces to funnel Taliban fighters into valleys east of the Whale Back and capture or kill them. The weapon release was successful, with good effects on target.

Navy fighters provided critical support to ground forces during Anaconda and were credited with killing many Taliban fighters and destroying many enemy vehicles and weapons caches and undoubtedly saved the lives of many US military personnel.
Kevin 'Sparky' Protzman, Tomcat RIO

WE WILL NOT FAIL

The clouds of scepticism were swept away over the skies of Kosovo, Afghanistan and Iraq, where these specially trained Tomcat crews plied their trade with skill and professionalism.

I hope those with a knowledge of the Tomcat's glorious and storied history will indulge me when I assert that perhaps the Tomcat's finest hours were spent with the Marines of B/1/2 (Tanks) over 'RPG Alley' in Nasiriyah, or the Army's 101st Aviation Regiment Apaches on their daring raid through the Karbala Gap, or the Screaming Eagles of the historic 101st Airborne Division in their street fight with the Republican Guard in Hillah. I know that mine were. In fact, I would even like to think that the mighty Tomcat helped us put to rest the ghosts of Guadalcanal with an unspoken pledge: 'We're here, brothers, and we ain't leaving. Together we will not fail.'
J J 'Troll' Patterson VI, VF-41, SWATSLANT, VF-11, VF-31, NSWDG

A RESOLUTE WARRIOR

There's so much to say about the last of the cats from Grumman Iron Works: follow on to the failed attempt by McNamara to force the F-111 common platform down the services' throat; Cold War Fleet Air Defender from the Russian Bear; star of one of the most successful aviation movies ever; undefeated aerial combat veteran; badass airshow performer; and pickup tactical recce asset. But for me, the crowning moment in the history of the Tomcat came at the end: the decision to turn it into the Bombcat. The Navy leadership and programme managers learned a lesson the Air Force never did from Desert Storm: aerial fighters with no bomb delivery capability were virtually worthless after the first few days of modern air combat. Used sporadically in the Bosnia/Kosovo air campaigns, the Bombcat came into its own when this nation was attacked by terrorists using caves in Afghanistan as their hiding place. F-14s equipped with LANTIRN were soon delivering death and destruction onto those enemies of America. Then later, the F-14 was further re-rolled as a land-based special operations forces direct support aircraft earning respect from those operators. Whether as an interceptor, aerial fighter, recce platform, or tactical bomber, the F-14 was a resolute warrior and important national asset. It will be missed by all real flyers.
**Col Ed 'Otto' Pernotto, USAF (ret)
JSOC Naval Liaison during OIF**

An F-14D-170-GR Tomcat (164601) of VF-31 Tomcatters takes off from USS Abraham Lincoln (CVN-72) on December 21, 2002. VF-31 were a part of CVW-14 which was deployed aboard CVN-72 from July 20, 2002 to May 6, 2003. (US Navy)

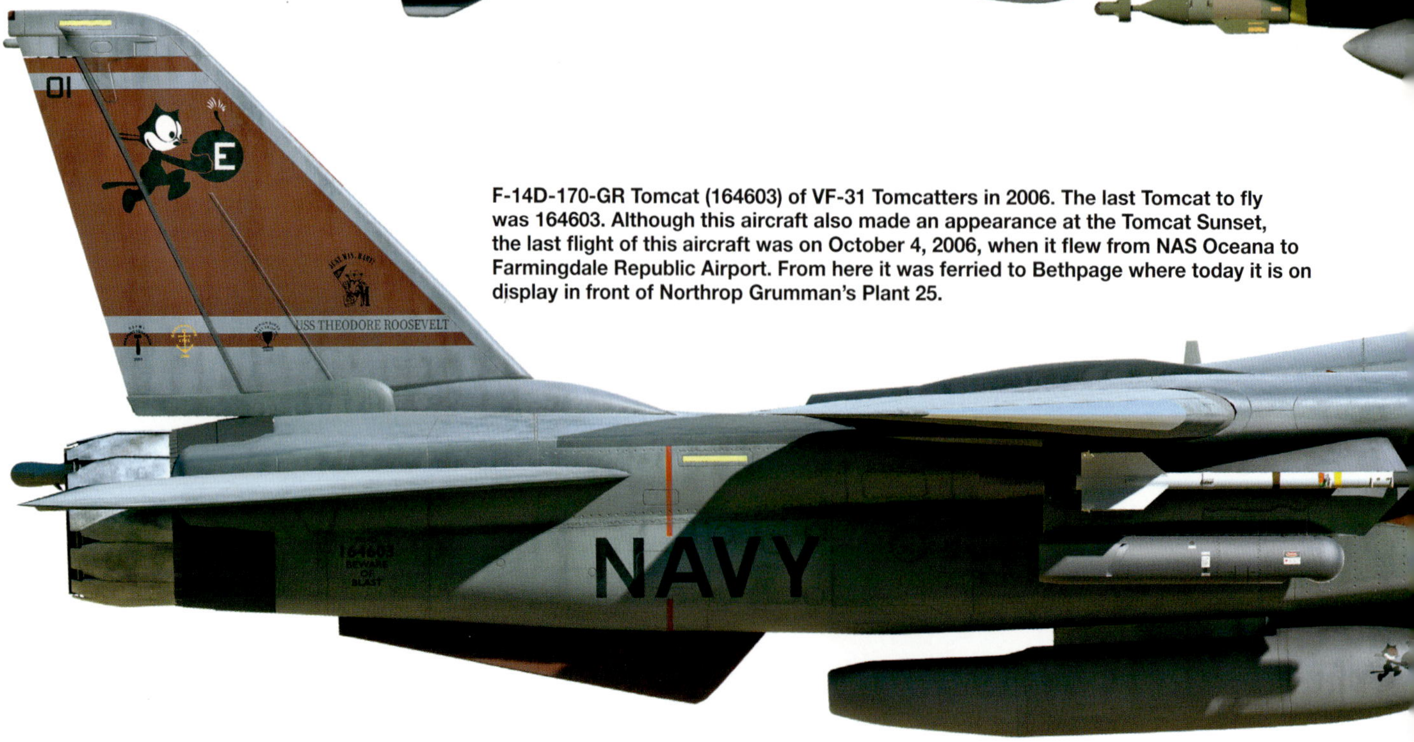

FOURTH DECADE

F-14D-170-GR Tomcat (164603) of VF-31 Tomcatters in 2006. The last Tomcat to fly was 164603. Although this aircraft also made an appearance at the Tomcat Sunset, the last flight of this aircraft was on October 4, 2006, when it flew from NAS Oceana to Farmingdale Republic Airport. From here it was ferried to Bethpage where today it is on display in front of Northrop Grumman's Plant 25.

HALF CENTURY, BABY! FIFTY YEARS OF THE GRUMMAN F-14 TOMCAT

F-14D-165-GR Tomcat (163894) of VF-2 Bounty Hunters in 2003. The Bounty Hunters' last Tomcat CAG bird had a very busy last deployment. VF-2 were deployed aboard USS *Constellation* (CV-46) from October 17, 2002, to June 2, 2003, to take part in Operation Iraqi Freedom from the Persian Gulf. With no fewer than 49 LGB drops and 10 JDAM drops this aircraft did earn its retirement. VF-2 became VFA-2 on July 1, 2003, when it traded its F-14Ds for F/A-18F Super Hornets.

F-14D-170-GR Tomcat (163898) of VF-31 Tomcatters in 2003. CVW-14 was deployed aboard USS *Abraham Lincoln* (CVN-72) from July 20, 2002, to May 6, 2003, on a very eventful deployment where missions were flown both in support of Operation Enduring Freedom and Operation Iraqi Freedom. This F-14D displays a number of mission markings as evidence that the Tomcats were used to their full capability even if their retirement was drawing very near. The aircraft was written off on USS *John C. Stennis* (CVN-74) on March 29, 2004, for unknown reasons.

FOURTH DECADE

The VF-2 Bounty Hunters CAG bird preparing to take off from USS *Constellation* (CV-64) on January 3, 2003, for another mission as a part of Operation Iraqi Freedom. (US Navy)

Preparing for a night launch on March 22, 2003 from USS *Theodore Roosevelt* (CVN-71) this F-14D Tomcat of VF-213 Black Lions is armed with AIM-9L Sidewinders and what appears to be a JDAM bomb, as it will conduct another mission as a part of Operation Iraqi Freedom. (US Navy)

Armed with AIM-9L Sidewinders and AIM-54C Phoenix missiles this F-14A-115-GR Tomcat (161276) blasts off from USS *Kitty Hawk* (CV-63) on March 14, 2003, as CVW-5 takes part in Operation Iraqi Freedom. (US Navy)

The Tomcat Farewell held at NAS Pt. Mugu on July 23, 2004. (Craig Kaston)

FOURTH DECADE

F-14D-170-GR Tomcat (164350) of VF-31 Tomcatters in 2006. This aircraft took part in the Tomcat Sunset ceremony at NAS Oceana commemorating the Tomcat's long service and retirement. The ceremony lasted from September 20-23, 2006. This aircraft in on display at the Palmdale Heritage Air Park, Palmdale, CA.

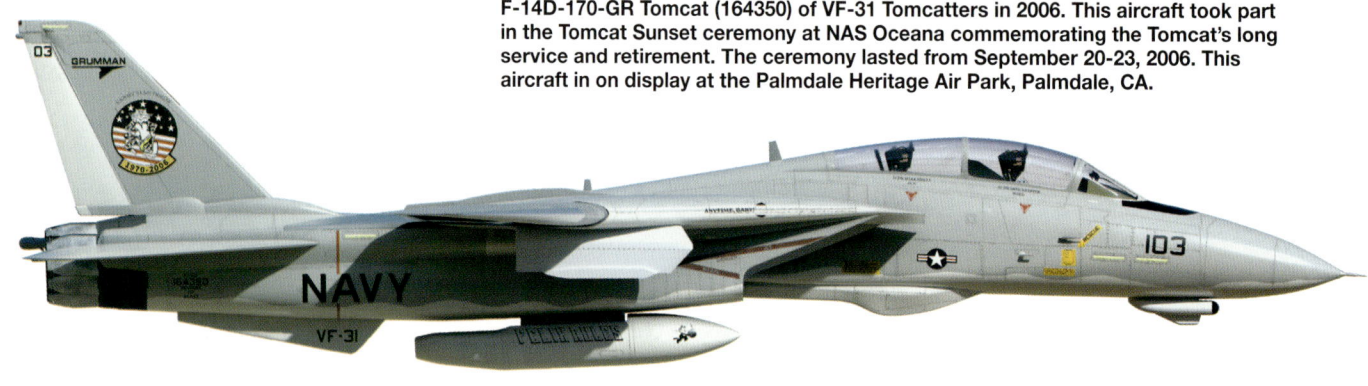

F-14D-170-GR Tomcat (164342) of VF-31 Tomcatters in 2006. The last CAG bird of VF-31 also made an appearance at the Tomcat Sunset in late September 2006. Today this aircraft is on display at the Wings over Miami Museum, Miami, FL.

F-14D-170-GR Tomcat (164601) of VF-101 Grim Reapers in 2005. The last display ever performed by a VF-101 Tomcat was made by this aircraft on April 20, 2005. Painted in this retro paint scheme, 164601 would remain with VF-101 until the very end (almost), as the Grim Reapers were decommissioned on September 30, 2005. The aircraft was delivered to Castle Air Museum, Atwater, CA, on September 20, 2005 (10 days before the squadron was decommissioned).

F-14D-170-GR Tomcat (164602) of VF-213 Black Lions in 2005. The very last Black Lions CAG bird was painted in this very colourful paint scheme on their last deployment. The deployment took CVW-8 to the Persian Gulf and lasted from September 1, 2005 to March 11, 2006. The aircraft was sent to AMARC on March 28, 2006.

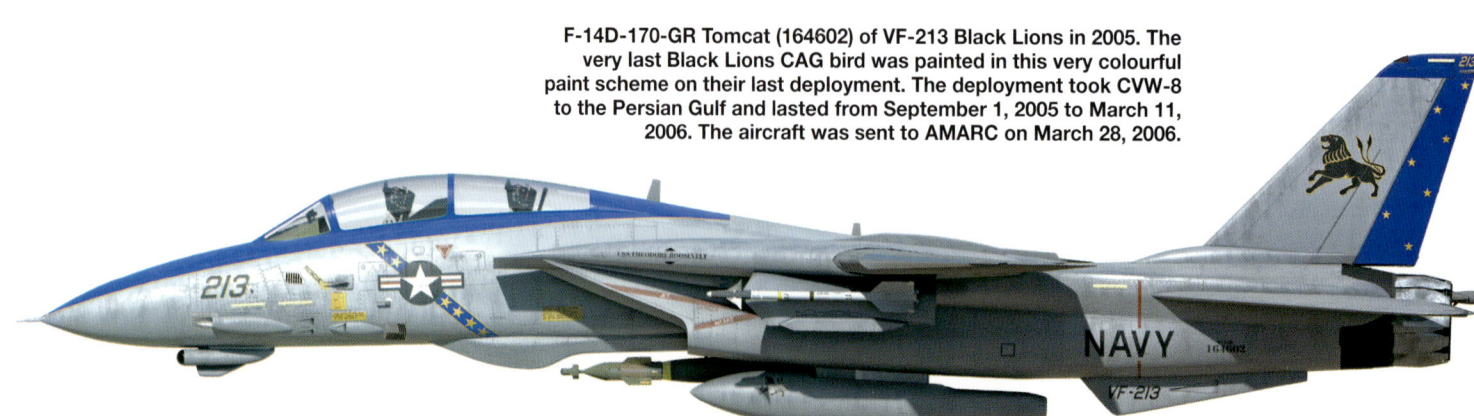

HALF CENTURY, BABY! FIFTY YEARS OF THE GRUMMAN F-14 TOMCAT

F-14D-110-GR Tomcat (161159) of VF-213 Black Lions in 2006. The last ever combat trap was made by this jet on February 8, 2006. CVW-8 was deployed aboard USS *Theodore Roosevelt* (CVN-71) from September 1, 2005, to March 11, 2006. The trap took place in the Persian Gulf. This aircraft is on display at the National Museum of Naval Aviation, Pensacola, FL.

The last departure of a F-14 Tomcat from NAS Pt. Mugu. This F-14D-160-GR Tomcat (163416) of VX-30 Bloodhounds departed on July 23, 2004. (Craig Kaston)

'Last Ride'. Vandy 1's last departure from NAS Pt. Mugu on June 25, 2004. (Craig Kaston)

BETTER THAN THE MOVIE
After five fighter tours, I have lots to be thankful for.

Many memories of: the Phase Leaders Office in the RAG; Key West Tactics Dets; O-Club debriefs; winter Med deployments; summer Gulf deployments; opposing supersonic fly-by squadron COC as outgoing CO (last flight?); to flying off Kitty Hawk as CO. Never any regrets... wouldn't have it any other way. It was better than the movie and I wouldn't have wanted to live during any other era...
Vice Admiral 'Mad Al' Myers, USN (ret)

THE HOTTEST CHICK
Flying Tomcats was like dating the hottest chick in school. I reported to VF-101 in 1981. We were all young, strong and fast – and so was our fighter. We were also a little arrogant, irreverent, daring – and so was our fighter. Then Capt Dave 'Frostie' Frost, CO of VF-101 and retired vice admiral, used to say: "The only

FOURTH DECADE

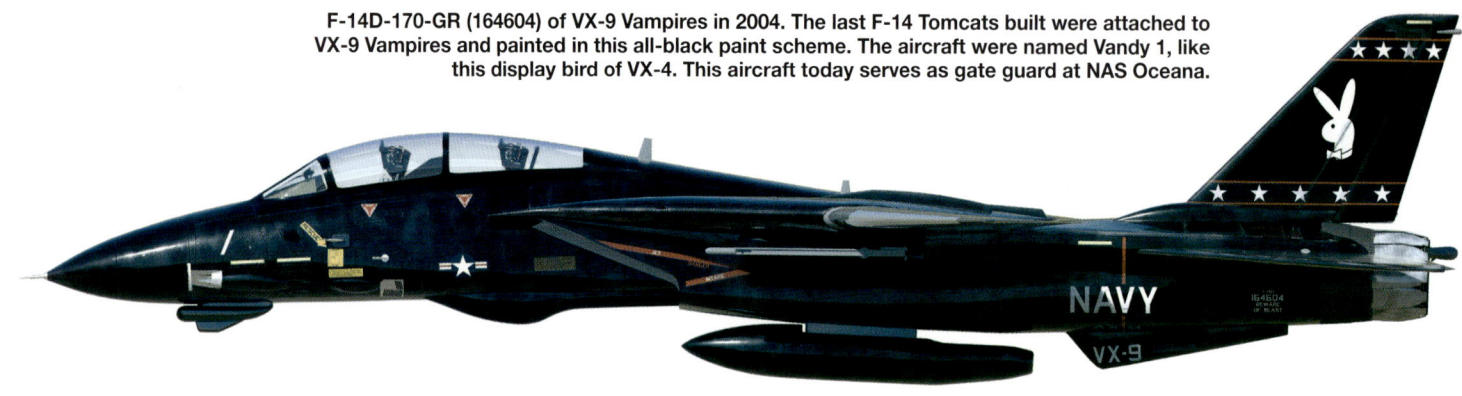

F-14D-170-GR (164604) of VX-9 Vampires in 2004. The last F-14 Tomcats built were attached to VX-9 Vampires and painted in this all-black paint scheme. The aircraft were named Vandy 1, like this display bird of VX-4. This aircraft today serves as gate guard at NAS Oceana.

people impressed by fighter pilots were little boys... and other fighter pilots." We laughed hard, and deep, and often... but no one laughed at the babe we dragged around town – that Grumman Iron Works afterburner crackling muscle backed beauty. So we fell in love. Puppy love at first, but after close to 4,000 hours and 1,000 trips home from work, I think it's the real deal. We spent our youth and middle age together. Then… all of a sudden, it's over? It hurts, it truly hurts. They say that everybody loves their airplane, just like every mother loves her child. But not everybody got to date, then marry the hottest chick in school... I did.

Capt Mark 'Clem' Clemente, USN (ret), former Commander Fighter Wing One

DEEDS OF DERRING-DO

In July 1982, as Ensign Kervahn, I reported to VF-101 for initial F-14 training. In September 2004, as Captain Kervahn, I turned out the lights as the last FITWING commodore. In retrospect, those 20 plus years were spent at Mach. I cannot capture my experiences in any single defining moment; however, my time with the Tomcat was punctuated with countless deeds of derring-do in the air or on liberty in five Tomcat squadrons. Much too many to recount. Meeting and working with the famous and infamous personages of fighter aviation who passed through my career. Watching the unsung heroes of Naval Aviation, the maintainers, perform miracles akin to open heart surgery so America's fighter would make the mission. Growing up with the muscle car of fighters has been nothing less than humbling. As I look in the mirror, I can still see that cocky young ensign who owes so much to the people and the centrepiece of the Tomcat community, the F-14. Those years of devotion to the Tomcat have passed as quickly as the big fighter going through the number. This, now as an older captain to paraphrase John F Kennedy, can say; "what did I do to make my life worthwhile, I can respond with a great deal of pride and satisfaction: I flew the Tomcat!"

Capt Will 'Wilbur' Kervahn USN (ret)

FINAL FLIGHT FOR VF-101

I first flew the last F-14D (BuNo 164601) to depart the Grim Reaper fold while at VF-124 at NAS Miramar on June 14, 1994, and flew it five more times at that command undergoing refresher training for my fleet department head tour. I flew her again in 1997-1999 as a staff instructor at VF-101, then again on loan from VF-31 as I prepared to go to VF-31 as Executive Officer, carrier qualifying on board USS Eisenhower (CVN 69) in February 2001. She brought me and my RIO back safely on May 10, 2001 after the worst airborne engine fire I have ever experienced, returning for a field arrestment.

It took some months to repair the damaged caused by the fire, and she came up in time for work ups and the subsequent deployment. As Felix 100 in CAG markings, she flew several successful combat missions for me and my aircrew in VF-31 during Operations Enduring Freedom, Southern Watch and Iraqi Freedom on the longest F-14 deployment in history. This includes three remarkable close air support missions in Baghdad where the crews in this jet had to conduct low-altitude strafing runs – extremely dangerous over a hostile, urban area – once to stop Fedayeen trucks attempting to conduct suicide attacks into Coalition convoys, which were headed north to take control of the Baghdad International Airport.

Felix 100 was painted with symbols for each successful weapon delivery and target destroyed, and symbols for the three missions involving strafing runs on this deployment. Returning to VF-101 as Gunfighter 160 and a new coat of paint to reflect the original F-14 colour scheme used at VF-101 when the squadron first received Tomcats in 1976, it was a workhorse in the command. It also flew the last F-14 TACDEMO Airshow ever, on Sunday, September 18, 2005, performing flawlessly, which was also the last operational flight for VF-101--and it was quite a sight. It's been a little tough to adjust to life without airplanes.

We know she's in good hands with the Castle Museum staff. There have been three squadrons whose colours have flown on that aircraft: VF-124, VF-31, and VF-101. VF-101 owned her for the largest part her lifespan and she was preserved in those markings.

The journey to Castle was a proud but somewhat sombre moment for the Grim Reapers. The last jet, Gunfighter 160 BuNo 164601, was the fourth-to-last Tomcat ever built, one of only 55 F-14Ds ever manufactured (there were 712 total US F-14s, and 80 made for Iranian, one of which was never delivered).

It flew absolutely perfectly, with no discrepancies during the whole flight across the country. We took off Monday morning at approximately 12:00 EST, stopped at NSA Millington, TN and Kirtland AFB in Albuquerque, NM, before spending the night in NAS North Island, San Diego--which used to be NAS San Diego, the same base where VF-10 stood up all those years ago. On Tuesday, September 20, at approximately 11:45 PST, we launched from NAS North Island on Runway 18 for the final journey. The cliffs of Point Loma dropped off the right wing as we climbed to altitude and turned north. It was a short trip to Castle, where the weather was beautiful. We entered the landing pattern via a left break, and performed four touch and go landings to burn down fuel before the final landing at 12:55 PST. The jet needed to keep turning until it ran out of fuel. At 13:26:40 seconds, the right engine quit; at 13:26:46, the left flamed out (though chugged and fought hard to keep running), and VF-101 was officially out of the business of flying and operating aircraft.

The Museum folks and the crowd at Castle were superb. It was tough to leave Gunfighter 160, she was a great jet. Her career highlights from the maintenance logs and records:

March 31, 1992: Flew its first functional check flight (FCF).

March 1993: Accepted by the US Navy after completing retrofit mods.

April 1993: Accepted by VF-124.

December 1994: Transferred responsibility to VF-101 Det Miramar.

January 2001: Accepted by VF-31 after completing SDLM.

March 11, 2005: Transferred to VF-101.

September 18, 2005: Last F-14 Tomcat Tactical Demonstration Flight at NAS Oceana Air Show.

The crew of 164604 'Vandy 1' is preparing for the final flight in the F-14 Tomcat. (Craig Kaston)

FOURTH DECADE

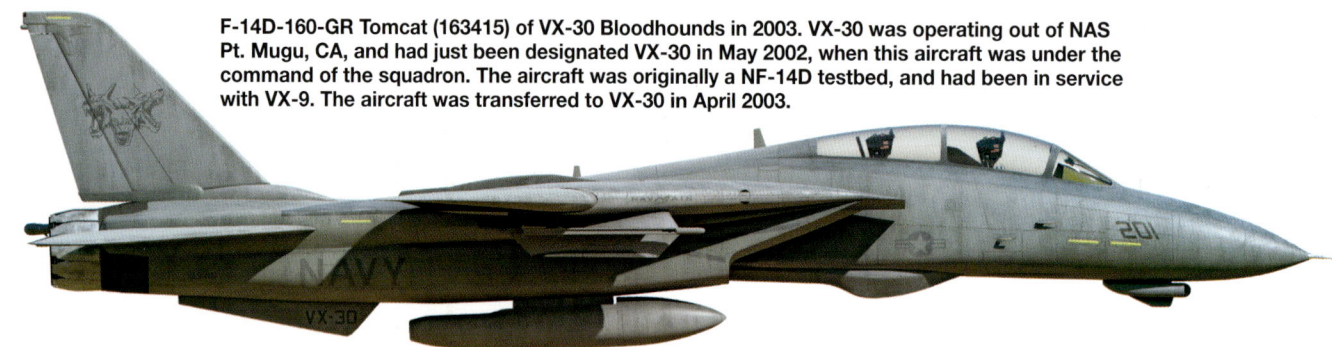

F-14D-160-GR Tomcat (163415) of VX-30 Bloodhounds in 2003. VX-30 was operating out of NAS Pt. Mugu, CA, and had just been designated VX-30 in May 2002, when this aircraft was under the command of the squadron. The aircraft was originally a NF-14D testbed, and had been in service with VX-9. The aircraft was transferred to VX-30 in April 2003.

Vandy 1 takes a final bow before taxiing out on the runway for the final departure. (Craig Kaston)

...and off to take off on the last ride. (Craig Kaston)

September 19, 2005 (12:04 EST): Departed Line 7, spot 1 for the last Grim Reaper flight, takeoff from NAS Oceana.
September 20, 2005 (12:55 PST): final landing at Castle AFB; final flameout at 13:26:46 PST.
Capt Paul 'Butkus' Haas, USN (ret)

LAST TOMCAT CRUISE
Felix and the Black Lions performed brilliantly on the last Tomcat cruise. They didn't miss a sortie, carried and delivered the latest air-to-ground ordnance with deadly accuracy and were as lethal in combat as ever! The Tomcat is definitely going out at the top of its game! Fighter Spirit is was alive and well and it was a honour and privilege to be the last Tomcat CAG!
All the best!
Rear Admiral Bill 'Size' Sizemore USN (ret), Commander, Air Wing Eight for final Tomcat Deployment in 2005

ALL GOOD THINGS...
Now, decades years later, after commanding an F-14 squadron and then getting to serve as the NAVAIR programme manager on top of that, I feel truly blessed with having been a member of such an interesting and vibrant community. I'm sure that most naval aircrew believe their community is the best, but my parochial observation is that there was something about the Tomcat community that set it apart from the rest. This was due in part to the fact that we flew an aircraft that was not only pleasing to the eye, but one that we knew would go down in history as one of the great fighter aircraft, joining the ranks of the Spitfire, Mustang, and other greats. Many of us likened it to the 'muscle cars' of the 60s and 70s – its looks exuded the raw power that it possessed, and it was not something to be flown by the faint of heart.

We were also well aware that this was an aircraft that had captured the American people's imagination and had become somewhat of a national icon (obvious examples are the movie Top Gun and TV series JAG). The other element of the community was the people – there were so many Type A personalities that I lived, flew, and partied with, and I again feel blessed that I was given this opportunity. My life would have been much poorer had I not known the likes of Sox, Zobes, Okie, Snort, Santa, Hoser, Moon, Moons, Half-Moon, Python, Wrecker, Mules, Rocky, Wizard, Fitzmo, Dirt, Vegas, Irish, Stinger, Flash, and many, many others.

As with an Irish wake, we celebrated the Tomcat's life as it entered its final year of service. We can think back to the Desert Storm days, when the F-14 was relegated to flying CAP missions and recce sorties here and there while Intruders, Hornets, and even S-3s were happily dropping bombs on the bad guys. Fast forward to Bosnia, OEF and OIF – and the Tomcat was the battle group commander's platform of choice when a high level of strike accuracy was required (and when Hornets could not drop a PGM unless it was being designated by a Tomcat) – and you get a clearer vision of the metamorphosis of this great aircraft. When you couple its new capability with the fact that it is still one of the most elegant and versatile aerodynamic designs, there can be little doubt that the Tomcat would be flying for years to come if we still faced a credible air-to-air threat. As is often said, all good things must come to an end – if I could go back and relive any part of my life, it would most definitely be the time that I spent in the F-14 community – but since the end cannot be forestalled, we can treasure both the experience, and the contribution that the Tomcat has made to our Navy and our country.
Rear Admiral Pete 'Caps' Williams, USN (ret)